The Greatness of Humility

The Greatness of Humility

St Augustine on Moral Excellence

Joseph J. McInerney

Foreword by C. C. Pecknold

Ⓒ

James Clarke & Co

James Clarke & Co
P.O. Box 60
Cambridge
CB1 2NT
United Kingdom

www.jamesclarke.co
publishing@jamesclarke.co

ISBN: 978 0 227 17600 9

British Library Cataloguing in Publication Data
A record is available from the British Library

First published by James Clarke & Co, 2017

Copyright © Joseph J. McInerney, 2016

Published by arrangement
with Pickwick Publications

Front cover: vector designed by Freepik

Contents

Foreword

by C. C. Pecknold

SAINT AUGUSTINE BEGINS HIS most extensive, detailed argument with ancient Roman culture by confessing that he knows "how great is the effort needed to convince the proud of the power and excellence of humility, an excellence which makes it soar above all the summits of this world, which sway in their temporal instability, overtopping them all with an eminence not arrogated by human pride, but granted by divine grace." (*City of God* I.Preface)

It is not that humility is unknown to Romans. It is that it is not really admired. To Roman ears, humility is weakness and pride is strength. To suggest that humility is an "excellence," a *virtus*, a virtue which raises up the human person is indeed an arduous task. But it is a task Augustine alone rises to accomplish in the *City of God*. By his own acquired skills of argumentation, and also by an act of faith, trusting that God's own descent into the economy of the flesh—the Word of God taking on the "form of a servant" even unto the point of death on a Roman cross—Augustine demonstrates that the best argument of all is the person of Jesus Christ, whose descent into a humiliating death brings about resurrection and glorious ascent to the right hand of the Father. (Phil 2:5–11)

Elsewhere, Saint Augustine says that humility is the first rung on the ladder of perfection, and in his argument with pagan moral philosophy, demonstrates why humility, not pride, leads to happiness. Following Augustine, a whole host of thinkers in the West will follow this argument with methodological variation. Saint Benedict has twelve degrees of humility, and Saint Anselm has seven. Medieval universities often had gates of humility through which all matriculating students passed. Humility is at the heart of the whole idea of apprenticeship to masters, of communal formation, of *manuduction*, of obedience to an extrinsic, transcendent end, and it becomes crucial for a Christian understanding of friendship (raising up Aristotle's view of friendship). Humility is not the form of all the virtues—that is reserved for *caritas*—but *humilitas* is necessary to receive all the theological virtues, to be receptive to the divine action which can heal and elevate the human person. It is the virtue required for Christian formation – as Chesterton once wrote, humility makes firm the feet which may grip the ground like trees.

Augustine's method can be seen simply in the preface to the *City of God* already referenced. It is a method of finding analogical footholds in those sources that Rome does admire, and showing why it is not unreasonable to think differently about humility than they do. For example, he cites a line from Virgil's *Aeneid*, "To spare the conquered, and beat down the proud," because he finds in it a faint echo of what has been revealed to Christians: "God resists the proud, but he gives grace to the humble." (James 4.6) If so great a Roman poet as Virgil could recognize that "pride goeth before a fall" in terms of battle, then Augustine saw they had at least a shadowy resemblance in their own literature which could help them to understand why pride might be more problematic than they think, and humility more worthy of praise.

Joseph McInerney has followed a similar method throughout *The Greatness of Humility*—but he has significantly extended its reach into the modern era. In the first half of this book, McInerney presents one of the most concise and elegant overviews of why the virtue of humility should be understood as central to the entire Augustinian corpus. He begins with the same classical sources that Augustine responds to in order to teach us the nature of his task, and then he shows us precisely why humility is the royal road, not only to the good life, but to eternal glory, to being made partakers of God. Yet in a stunning second movement, McInerney turns to our own cultured despisers of humility—those thinkers who, once again, find it difficult to believe that humility is a virtue at all.

David Hume famously derided humility as one of the "monkish virtues." He loathed celibacy, fasting, penance, mortification, self-denial, silence, solitude, and the chief virtue required for them all: humility. All of these were meaningless pursuits, and the virtue required of them all could not be considered a virtue because it did not lead a person to fortune, or to social prestige, or proper employment. Humility is bad for the profit motive. Hume never once considers that mastery of the world might not be the chief end of "dependent rational animals" (to borrow a phrase from Alasdair MacIntyre, whose influence on the present work is noteworthy and admirable). Hume never pauses to reflect on the humility required to learn from others, a form of dependence that Hume himself must have experienced, but did not properly acknowledge. To be fair, Hume did think modesty – allied with the virtue of temperance –might be a way of evoking sympathy in others, and thus serve some "social function." But isn't this the kind of "sentimental humility" we might rightly distrust as weak, ineffectual, and that usually irks us as disingenuous?

Nietzsche is more consistent, and his rejection of humility more total. For him, humility is just at the heart of "slave morality." The compassion of Christianity makes people into slaves of the powerful. Nietzsche thinks this slave morality is unnatural. Such "monkish virtues" undermine the raw, natural power of our will to dominate. It is precisely the *libido dominandi* that Augustine wants us to reject that Nietzsche thinks we should embrace. Humility is a pathetic tactic of the weak, whose resentment of the strong has led them to a "re-valuation of all values." In Nietzsche's view, Christian humility has led us astray from what is truly alive and good: our noble powers of mastery. Nietzsche advocates the overthrow of humility precisely to restore things to their natural order, wherein masters are considered good and noble, and slaves weak and sickly. In the line which runs from Hume to Nietzsche, we can see that humility is not always considered a virtue anymore – indeed, it has been considered a vice. Nietzsche understood that humility was ordered to compassion and divine charity, neither of which he thought were natural. At least we can commend Nietzsche for knowing that in rejecting Christianity, he was rejecting charity itself.

Based on these atheistic treatments of humility, one might wonder if Augustine's path has been unraveling in the West. How will it turn out? McInerney follows Augustine's path anew, however, to show us the greatness of humility once again. He finds many new analogical footholds in today's cultured despisers, and admirably accomplishes a similar task of convincing the proud of the greatness of humility. It is still an arduous task, but McInerney shows us that it is a task which remains situated in the heart of Western civilization – the virtue of humility contains the essential seeds for the renewal of the mind and conformation of the soul to the image of Christ.

Feast of Saints Perpetua and Felicitas, 2015
Washington, D.C.

Abbreviations

Abbreviations for the Works of St. Augustine

Abbreviations referring to St. Augustine's writings follow the format detailed in *Augustine Through the Ages: An Encyclopedia*, edited by Allan D. Fitzgerald. Grand Rapids, MI: Wm. B. Eerdmans, 1999, pp. xxxv-xlii.

B. Vita	*De Beata Vita* (On the Happy Life)
C. Adim.	*Contra Adimantum Manichei Discipulum* (Answer to Adimantus, A Disciple of Mani)
C. Fel.	*Contra Felicem Manicheum* (Answer to Felix, A Manichean)
Cat. Rud.	*De Catechizandis Rudibus* (On the Instruction of Beginners)
Civ. Dei	*De Civitate Dei* (The City of God)
Conf.	*Confessiones* (Confessions)
Div. Qu.	*De Diversis Quaestionibus Octoginta Tribus* (Eighty-Three Different Questions)
Doc. Chr.	*De Doctrina Christiana* (On Christian Doctrine)
Duab. An.	*De Duabus Animabus* (On the Two Souls)
En. Ps.	*Enarrationes in Psalmos* (Expositions of the Psalms)
Ench.	*Enchiridion ad Laurentium de Fide Spe et Caritate* (A Handbook on Faith, Hope, and Love)
Ep.	*Epistulae* (Letters)

Ep. Jo.   *In Epistulam Joannis ad Parthos Tractatus* (Tractates on the First Letter of John)

Ex. Gal.   *Expositio Epistulae ad Galatas* (Commentary on the Letter to the Galatians)

Gn. Adv. Man.   *De Genesi Adversus Manicheos* (On Genesis, Against the Manichees)

Gr. et Lib. Arb.   *De Gratia et Libero Arbitrio* (On Grace and Free Will)

Jo. Ev. Tr.   *In Johannis Evangelium Tractatus* (Tractates on the Gospel of John)

Lib. Arb.   *De Libero Arbitrio* (On Free Will)

Mor.   *De Moribus Ecclesiae Catholicae et De Moribus Manicheorum* (The Catholic Way of Life and the Manichean Way of Life)

Nat. B.   *De Natura Boni* (On the Nature of the Good)

Nat. et Gr.   *De Natura et Gratia* (On Nature and Grace)

S.   *Sermones* (Sermons)

Sol.   *Soliloquia* (The Soliloquies)

Trin.   *De Trinitate* (The Trinity)

Abbreviations for the Works of Plotinus

Enn.   *Ennead I, Ennead V, Ennead VII*

Note Regarding the use of English Texts of Augustine's Works

Readers will note the wide variety of English translations referenced in this study. The method for selecting the various translations was to choose English texts that were as faithful as possible to Augustine's Latin texts, offered the best insights of modern scholarship into the context and meaning of Augustine's writings, and also provided a translation that was readable for contemporary students of Augustine's thought. Fortunately there is no shortage of outstanding English translations available for Augustine's writing. For some of the less prominent works of Augustine I made significant use of two multi-volume translations of Augustine's works, which were *The Works of St. Augustine: A Translation for the 21st Century* and *The Fathers of the Church: A New Translation*. Both series offer highly readable translations produced by some of the most prominent Augustine scholars working in the English language. Although I used the *Works of St. Augustine* translation of *The Trinity* as my primary reference for that work, I did not limit myself to that series or the *Fathers of the Church* series for some of Augustine's other influential works, such as *The Confessions, The City of God*, and *On Christian Doctrine*. For these works I chose translations (Chadwick for *The Confessions*, Dyson for *The City of God*, and Shaw for *On Christian Doctrine*) that I felt were best suited to address the topic of humility and its relationship to moral excellence.

English Translations of Augustine's Work

Answer to Adimantus, A Disciple of Mani. Translated by Roland Teske. In *The Manichean Debate*, 176–226. The Works of St. Augustine: A Translation for the 21st Century, edited by Boniface Ramsey, I.19. Hyde Park, NY: New City, 2006.

Answer to Felix, a Manichean. Translated by Roland Teske. In *The Manichean Debate*, 271–98. The Works of St. Augustine: A Translation for the 21st Century, edited by Boniface Ramsey, I.19. Hyde Park, NY: New City, 2006.

The Catholic Way of Life and The Manichean Way of Life. Translated by Roland Teske. In *The Manichean Debate*, 17–106. The Works of St. Augustine: A Translation for the 21st Century, edited by Boniface Ramsey, I.19. Hyde Park, NY: New City, 2006.

On Christian Doctrine. Translated by J. F. Shaw. Mineola, NY: Dover, 2009.

The City of God. Translated by R. W. Dyson. Cambridge: Cambridge University Press, 1998.

Commentary on the Letter to the Galatians. Translated by Eric Plumer. Oxford: Oxford University Press, 2003.

Confessions. Translated by Henry Chadwick. Oxford: Oxford University Press, 1991.

Eighty-Three Different Questions. Translated by David L. Mosher. The Fathers of the Church: A New Translation 70. Washington D.C.: The Catholic University of America Press, 1982.

Expositions of the Psalms. Translated by Maria Boulding. The Works of St. Augustine: A Translation for the 21st Century, edited by John E. Rotelle, III.15–20. Hyde Park, NY: New City, 2001.

A Handbook on Faith, Hope and Love. Translated by Bernard M. Peebles. New York: Cima Publishing, 1947.

The First Catechetical Instruction (On the Instruction of Beginners). Translated by Joseph P. Christopher. Baltimore: J. H. Furst Company, 1946.

On Free Will. Translated Anna S. Benjamin and L. H. Hackstaff. New York: Macmillan, 1964.

On Genesis, Against the Manichees. Translated by Roland J. Teske. The Fathers of the Church: A New Translation 6. Washington D.C.: The Catholic University of America Press, 1991.

On Grace and Free Will. Translated by Robert P. Russell. The Fathers of the Church: A New Translation 59. Washington D.C.: The Catholic University of America Press, 1968.

On the Happy Life. Translated by Ludwig Schopp. Writings of St. Augustine, 5. New York: Cima, 1948.

Letters. Translated by Wilfrid Parsons. The Fathers of the Church: A New Translation 18. New York: Fathers of the Church, 1953.

On the Nature of the Good. Translated by Roland Teske. The Works of Saint Augustine: A Translation for the 21st Century, edited by Boniface Ramsey, I.19. Hyde Park, NY: New City, 2006.

On Nature and Grace. Translated by Peter Holmes and Robert Ernest Wallis. In *Augustine: Anti-Pelagian Writings*, The Nicene and Post-Nicene Fathers, edited by Philip Schaff, 5. Peabody, MA: Hendrickson, 1994.

Sermons. Translated by Edmund Hill. The Works of St. Augustine: A Translation for the 21st Century, edited by John E. Rotelle, III.1–11. Brooklyn, NY: New City, 1990.

Soliloquies. Translated by Thomas F. Gilligan. The Fathers of the Church: A New Translation 1. New York: Cima, 1948.

Tractates on the First Letter of John. Translated by Boniface Ramsey. The Works of St. Augustine: A Translation for the 21st Century, edited by Boniface Ramsey, III.14. Hyde Park, NY: New City, 2008.

Tractates on the Gospel of John. Translated by John W. Rettig. The Fathers of the Church: A New Translation 78–79. Washington DC: Catholic University of America Press, 1988.

The Trinity. Translated by Edmund Hill. The Works of Saint Augustine: A Translation for the 21st Century, edited by John E. Rotelle, I.5. Hyde Park, NY: New City, 1991.

On the Two Souls. Translated by Roland Teske. The Works of St. Augustine: A Translation for the 21st Century, edited by Boniface Ramsey, I.19. Hyde Park, NY: New City, 2006.

Abbreviations for Multi-Volume Translations of the Works of St. Augustine

WSA   *The Works of St. Augustine, A Translation for the 21st Century*
The WSA abbreviation is followed by part number, volume number and page number.

FCNT   *The Fathers of the Church: A New Translation*
The FCNT abbreviation is followed by volume number and page number.

Introduction

The Question of Moral Excellence

THE INTELLECTUAL LEGACY BEQUEATHED by Augustine of Hippo (b. 354 AD) to the Catholic Church and the Western philosophical tradition has indeed been great. As one of the most influential figures in the history of Western thought, there are few fields related to theology or philosophy that have been unaffected by his work. A prolific author, Augustine is perhaps best known for the theological, philosophical, and moral insights of his *Confessions* and the comprehensive theology of history he presents in *The City of God*. Despite the importance of these two works, stopping at them without examining any of Augustine's remaining thought would truly be to remain at the summit of an enormous iceberg. In addition to his responsibilities as bishop, Augustine not only engaged in the intellectual debates of his day, controversies with Manichees, Donatists, and Pelagians being primary examples, but also engaged intellectual aspects of his faith that transcended the time and place of his ministry. Whether writing his commentaries on Scripture or engaging in the speculative examination of the Christian God in *The Trinity*, Augustine invariably produced writings of such insight and originality that he has held the attention of Christian and non-Christian readers during his day and throughout the sixteen hundred years separating him from the present.

The subject of my study, an issue on which Augustine spent significant time and effort, is the paradoxical view he formulated concerning the relation between humility and moral excellence. For Augustine, only the humble person can truly achieve greatness.[1] In a sermon delivered sometime after the year 420 AD he asserts,

1. For the purpose of my study I will use the terms greatness and excellence as

> We are striving for great things; let us lay hold of little things, and we shall be great. Do you wish to lay hold of the loftiness of God? First catch hold of God's lowliness. Deign to be lowly, to be humble, because God has deigned to be lowly and humble on the same account, yours not his own. So catch hold of Christ's humility, learn to be humble, don't be proud. Confess your infirmity, lie there patiently in the presence of the doctor. When you have caught hold of his humility, you start rising up with him.[2]

It will become evident over the course of this study that the given text is not an exception from Augustine's typical view of humility and greatness. He repeatedly and emphatically asserts that human excellence comes by way of humility.

Despite Augustine's emphasis and his repute as one of history's great thinkers, it is quite legitimate to ask, "How is this the case?" or maybe better, "Does the idea that humility leads to greatness make any sense at all?" To answer these questions, one could turn to other Christian thinkers to see if there is a consensus on the issue. The Christian tradition, although not completely unanimous on the subject, certainly provides much support for Augustine's position.[3] Given Augustine's influence over that tradition, however, it seems better to look at other traditions and non-Christian thinkers to find a source less affected by Augustine's thought through which to evaluate his stand on humility and greatness. Turning to Aristotle (b. 384 BCE), another of history's most influential thinkers, we see a position quite literally opposed to that of Augustine. For Aristotle, the greatest person is the person of magnanimity. Magnanimity is the crown of all the other virtues and as such receives significant attention from Aristotle. One of

---

roughly equivalent. Although greatness implies a public aspect—i.e., the praise that others offer to a person of excellence that is lacking in the word excellence—we will see that both terms are apt descriptions of the virtue ascribed to a person of merit. In instances where the social or public implications of excellence are discussed, I will use the term greatness. In discussions where the public aspect is not central, I will use greatness and excellence interchangeably.

2. Augustine, S. 117:17 (WSA III/4:220), *Sermons*, in *The Works of St. Augustine: A Translation for the 21st Century*, ed. John E. Rotelle. Hereafter cited as WSA followed by part, then volume, then page.

3. Benedict of Nursia, Bernard of Clairvaux, and Thomas Aquinas are just three examples of eminent Christian thinkers who support and propose a view of humility and greatness similar to that of Augustine's. Cf. Thomas Aquinas, *Summa Theologica* 2.2.161.5: "Humility holds the first place, inasmuch as it expels pride . . . and makes man . . . open to receive the influx of divine grace . . . . In this sense humility is said to be the foundation of the spiritual edifice."

magnanimity's salient features, in Aristotle's view, is its disinterest in small matters. The magnanimous person does few things, but the few things he or she does undertake are grand in scope and value.[4] Aristotle's position seems to be in direct contradiction to that of Augustine.

While it is by no means sufficient to deduce a fundamental disagreement between thinkers on the basis of two isolated texts, these statements do represent a substantive and significant difference that runs throughout the course of Western thought, from its roots in classical antiquity through modernity and even to the recent focus on the place of virtue within ethical discourse. To thoroughly examine the differences that lay behind the positions these citations represent, it is necessary to explore the philosophical, theological, anthropological, and moral principles supporting each view.

Virtue is one concept that holds particular importance for the topic. Fortunately the idea of virtue and the individual virtues themselves have become key topics in contemporary philosophical and theological literature.[5] Current research in philosophy and theology has produced some positive appraisals for the virtue of humility,[6] while contemporary feminist theology has generally questioned its value.[7] In a recent exchange between philosophers, Larry Arnhart lays the lack of magnanimous statesmen in the twentieth century at the doorstep of Christian humility.[8] In response, Carson Holloway asserts that Christian humility does not prevent the development of magnanimous statesmen and goes on to argue that the closely related Christian principle of charity is the only sure means to inspire a magnanimous person to undertake the burdens of statesmanship.[9] The contemporary outlook on the value of humility is quite varied, depending in large part upon the moral and anthropological presuppositions an author brings to its examination.

---

4. Aristotle, *Nicomachean Ethics* 1124b25.

5. Alasdair Macintyre's *After Virtue*, Peter Berkowitz's *Virtue and the Making of Modern Liberalism*, and Romanus Cessario's *The Moral Virtues and Theological Ethics* are just three recent samples of philosophical, political, and theological approaches to the study of virtue.

6. Cf. Fullam, *Virtue of Humility*, Ruddy, "Christological Approach to Virtue, and Bobb, "Competing Crowns" for three recent studies on the importance of humility.

7. See Ruddy, "Christological Approach to Virtue," 33–47 for a summary of contemporary feminist thought regarding humility.

8. Arnhart, "Statesmanship as Magnanimity," 263–83.

9. Holloway, "Christianity, Magnanimity, and Statesmanship," 581–604.

Despite the competing views in the contemporary dialogue concerning humility, one need only look to the philosophers of modernity to find a more unified and frankly hostile approach to the idea. The most passionate critiques of humility flow from the pens of many of the most prominent thinkers in the modern period. David Hume, Karl Marx, and Friedrich Nietzsche unabashedly criticize the role of humility in civil society. For Hume (b. 1711), an authentic humility that goes beyond the façade of external modesty is valued by no one.[10] Marx (b. 1818) likewise disparages humility, which he saw as a drain to the revolutionary drive he sought to inspire in the proletariat. He saw Christian humility as an impediment to the courage and pride through which the working class could assert its independence.[11] Nietzsche (b. 1844), whose work criticizes both Jewish and Christian thought, is no less sparing in his criticism of humility. He views humility as a sham virtue, foisted upon humanity by the lying rhetoric of a slave mentality.[12] Yet despite the vigor of modern attacks, the Christianity of the same period continued to uphold the traditional value of humility.[13]

The prize at stake in the controversy regarding humility is nothing less than the meaning of human excellence. The debate seeks to answer what it means to be a great human person. To put it in the Aristotelian terms of Alasdair MacIntyre, it pursues a response to the question, "What sort of person am I to become?"[14] Or, from the perspective of Ciceronian terminology, it seeks to articulate a vision of that in which the glory of the human person consists.

The thesis of my study is the idea that the height of human greatness includes and is dependent upon humility. In recognizing the importance of humility to greatness one can see in Augustine's counterintuitive argument for an intrinsic relation between humility and greatness an accurate and authentic description of moral excellence that exceeds notions of human greatness that either neglect or repudiate humility. Humility is an indispensable attribute for the development of human excellence, and few can match Augustine's understanding and advocacy for that position.

---

10. Hume, *Treatise of Human Nature* 3.3.2

11. Marx and Engels, "Excerpt From The Communism of the Paper Rheinischer Beobachter," 268–69.

12. Nietzsche, *On the Genealogy of Morality*, 1.13.

13. One example of the continuing Christian tradition regarding humility in the modern period is Pope Leo XIII's treatise *The Practice of Humility*.

14. MacIntyre, *After Virtue*, 118.

In contrast to Augustine, I will use the thought of David Hume and Friedrich Nietzsche as the two authors best suited to represent understandings of excellence that reject humility as an integral element of human greatness. The rationale for my focus on Hume and Nietzsche is twofold. First, both Hume and Nietzsche provide explicit and well-formulated treatments of the relation between humility and greatness. Their quality of thought and cogency of expression on the issue have few equals and thus provide an important and influential counter to the thought of Augustine. A second, related reason stems from the historical influence of each thinker. Alasdair MacIntyre describes Hume's influence on the Scottish Enlightenment and the subsequent development of modern moral philosophy in pointed terms. "He (Hume) was identified, and rightly so, as the antagonist *par excellence,* the philosopher whose views had to be defeated in open philosophical debate. He became the one thinker in opposition to whom decade after continuing decade Scottish philosophers had to frame their enquiries."[15] MacIntyre also champions the importance of Nietzsche's influence, asserting that Nietzsche is the moral philosopher without peer in relation to what MacIntyre calls the Enlightenment project to discover the rational foundations of an objective morality. This is the case from MacIntyre's perspective because Nietzsche was the first philosopher to understand "not only that what purported to be appeals to objectivity were in fact expressions of subjective will, but also the nature of the problems that this posed for moral philosophy."[16] Although, as a prominent contemporary philosopher there are many who argue against MacIntyre's controversial positions,[17] there are few who would raise objections concerning his emphasis on the importance of Hume and Nietzsche to modern and contemporary philosophical discourse.

Ancient and Modern Approaches to Human Greatness

Any philosophical argument for a particular conception of human greatness is an embodiment of the philosopher's view concerning the nature, purpose, and goodness of the human person. Perhaps the one (and possibly only) element in common to the thinkers I will examine to support the argument of my study is the fact that they approach the idea of human

15. MacIntyre, *Whose Justice?*, 322.

16. MacIntyre, *After Virtue*, 113–14.

17. Cf. Keating's, "Ethical Project of Alasdair MacIntyre," 101–16 for an overview of the reception of MacIntyre's thought.

excellence through moral principles. In the case of Aristotle, the goodness of the human person is seen to lie in a person's ability to conform his or her moral activity to right reason. Excellent habits or virtues, in his view, empower a person to achieve such conformity. A person's development of virtue is the result of repeatedly making good moral choices. For Aristotle, then, the greatest people are those who have developed the habits of excellence.[18] The epitome of excellence in Stoic thought is the sage. Although the Stoics placed significant emphasis on the knowledge of a sage, a true sage was not only knowledgeable but was also able to live a life of virtue in accordance with nature that is in conformity to the reason that guides the fate of the cosmos.[19]

A modern example of the approach to human greatness through morality can be seen in the thought of David Hume. Although clearly at odds with the moral philosophy of classical antiquity, Hume still proposes his understanding of human greatness within the context of his moral thought. For Hume, the excellence of the human person is derived from the feelings of approbation elicited by the moral choices of a particular person.[20] From the view of the Western philosophical tradition, both ancient and modern, moral greatness is fundamental to human greatness.

Despite this one shared aspect, however, there is a significant divide between the ancient authors of my study and the modern regarding their approach to human excellence. Rationality and intelligibility lay at the center of ancient moral analysis. We will see that Aristotle, Stoics, Neo-Platonists, and the Christian philosophy of Augustine all propose an intrinsic link between intellect and morality. Fundamental to the eudaemonistic moral vision of these ancient thinkers is the integration of reason into the behavior and character of the human person. Although each of the ancient schools has different views of virtue, common to each of them is the idea that the character of a person must be integrated with reason for a person to achieve virtue. We will see that the link between virtue and reason is crucial to each school's understanding of human excellence, despite the differences in their approach to virtue. Such is not the case, however, for the selected modern authors, Hume and Nietzsche. Both, for different reasons,

18. Cf. Aristotle, *Nicomachean Ethics* 1098a7–18 for an initial summary on the good of the human person. This is a topic I will develop later in my study.

19. Diogenes, *Lives of Eminent Philosophers* 7.87–89. Cf. Sharples, *Stoics, Epicureans, and Sceptics*, 101.

20. Hume, *Treatise of Human Nature* 3.1.2.

reject reason as integral to the moral life. For Hume, reason is an inactive principle that of its nature only educates and cannot inspire the choices that constitute moral activity.[21] Emotion and feeling rather than reason are the principles, according to Hume, that drive moral choice and therefore serve as the guiding principles of his ethics. Nietzsche, on the other hand, sees the expression of power as the principle governing morality, going so far as to assert a view in which the virtues are seen as irrational rather than rational.[22] "An earthly virtue is it which I love: little prudence is therein and the least every day wisdom."[23] The lack of reason in Nietzsche's moral theory is one of the most significant elements separating his thought from that of his eudaemonistic predecessors.

Given the relationship established between human greatness and moral theory by ancient and modern philosophers, my methodology will be to examine the moral principles that constitute human greatness in their view. By means of this examination I will demonstrate how those principles yield a particular understanding of the relation between humility and greatness. I will also demonstrate why these eminent authors offer such profoundly different accounts of the issue.

Method and Structure

The central focus of my study will be the moral thought of Augustine as it relates to his understanding of humility and greatness. Before addressing that thought, however, I will cover three ancient philosophers pertinent to the topic. I have chosen the ancient thinkers to be investigated in the study on the basis of two criteria: (1) the relevance of an author's thought to the topic of humility and greatness and (2) the effect of an author's thought on the views of Augustine. I will begin my discussion in chapter 1 with the thought of Aristotle, articulating the moral and anthropological principles that formed his view of the magnanimous person, who occupies the height of Aristotelian moral virtue. Despite the relatively indirect exposure of Augustine to Aristotle's moral theory (it is likely that the only work of Aristotle's read by Augustine was *The Categories*),[24] it is important to include Aristotle's thought in the study for two reasons. First, although not a direct influence

21. Hume, *Treatise of Human Nature* 3.1.1.

22. Hunt, *Nietzsche and the Origin of Virtue*, 81.

23. Nietzsche, *Thus Spake Zarathustra* 1.5.

24. Augustine reports his study of the categories in *Conf.* 4.16.28.

on Augustine's intellectual development, Aristotle's thought was to grow in stature as the centuries passed,[25] becoming one of the primary sources for the elaboration of medieval philosophy, and in many ways, a primary foil in the development of modern thought. For example, Aristotle's rational understanding of the virtues provides a significant contrast to the feelings-based approach of Hume and the will to power Nietzsche associates with virtue. As a consequence, the Aristotelian tradition is of great importance to the study's comparison of modern views of humility and greatness with those of Augustine. Second, given the merit and importance of Aristotle's moral thought, any philosophical analysis of the relation between humility and greatness must account for the treatment of magnanimity and its related vices provided by Aristotle in the *Nicomachean Ethics*.

Following my discussion of Aristotle's moral principles I will consider the Stoic moral thought communicated through the pen of Cicero (b. 106 BCE). The philosophical influence of Cicero on Augustine can hardly be overstated. It was the *Hortensius* of Cicero (read by Augustine at the age of nineteen) that would prove instrumental in changing Augustine's course from a career as a professional rhetorician to that of a seeker of wisdom.[26] Although Cicero considered himself a skeptic, he is one of the most important sources for Stoic moral thought, as his *De Finibus Bonorum et Malorum* is one of only three primary treatises concerning the Stoic ethical system in use by scholars today.[27] Part of the influence Cicero exerts upon Augustine stems from his role as a transmitter of Stoic moral doctrine. Augustine's moral theory has been characterized as Stoic appropriations of Platonic thought, where the Stoic equation of virtue to happiness is combined with a Neo-Platonic understanding of happiness as the mind being possessed by transcendent truth. Augustine's combination of the two yields

25. The importance of Aristotle's thought is manifest in such later works as the *Summa Theologica* of Thomas Aquinas. Even where Aristotle's arguments are rejected, his influence is still significant. Cf. Gerson, "Plotinus and the Rejection of Aristotelian Metaphysics," 3–21 for a discussion in which Aristotle's primary argument on a topic is rejected, but his terminology and central presuppositions are adopted.

26. Augustine, *Conf.* 3.4.7. Cf. Hagendahl, *Augustine and the Latin Classics*, 486–95 for a discussion concerning the influence of the *Hortensius* on the thought of Augustine. Hagendahl characterizes that influence as sparking Augustine's interest in philosophy rather than causing him to lay aside secular ambition or embracing Christianity, both of which would come later in Augustine's life. Cf. Testard, *St. Augustin et Ciceron*, 18–49 for further discussion regarding the importance of Cicero and the *Hortensius* to Augustine's intellectual development.

27. Thorsteinsson, *Roman Christianity and Roman Stoicism*, 5.

an understanding of happiness in which virtue becomes beatitude once a person has appropriated wisdom, whose source is the Logos of God.[28] In addition to his influence on Augustine, Cicero's noteworthy reflections concerning the glory of the human person are directly relevant to the study of humility and greatness, and thus also merit examination in my study.

A second school of philosophy that had significant impact on Augustine's intellectual development was that of third century Platonism, labeled neo-Platonism by modern scholars. The philosopher Plotinus (b. 205 AD) was arguably the most significant exponent of neo-Platonism and will therefore be the focus of my treatment regarding the relation between Platonism and the thought of Augustine.[29] Although modern scholarship is unsure if Augustine actually read the work of Plotinus[30] (Augustine uses only the general label of Platonists in his mention of their books in the *Confessions*),[31] many similarities with neo-Platonism as articulated by Plotinus can be seen in Augustine's work, and many of these similarities have particular bearing on his understanding of morality and human excellence. Neo-Platonic metaphysics provided a new context in which Augustine could understand the problem of evil, which separated him from the teachings of the Manichaeans and, more importantly for my study, provided a significant context for his understanding of moral evil.[32] Although not generally remembered for his moral thought, Plotinus's understanding of *tolma* as the reason for the soul's fall into matter[33] and his emphasis on the purifying aspect of virtue[34] would find significant parallels in Augustine's understanding of morality. In addition, Plotinus's portrayal of the human person's highest destiny as

---

28. Wetzel, *Augustine and the Limits of Virtue*, 68.

29. Cf. Armstrong, *St. Augustine and Christian Platonism* for a description of the primary links and differences between the pagan Platonism of Plotinus and the Christian Platonism of Augustine. Cf. Brown, *Augustine of Hippo*, 86 for a characterization of neo-Platonic influence on Augustine. Cf. pages 79–107 for a general discussion of the importance of neo-Platonism and philosophy to Augustine's thought. Cf. Rist, *Augustine*, 3 for a description of the Platonic texts to which Augustine was likely exposed.

30. Cf. Crouse, "*Paucis Mutatis Verbis*," 37–50 for a brief overview of the debate regarding the nature of Augustine's exposure to the Platonic sources that influenced his thought.

31. Augustine, *Conf.* 7.9.13.

32. Brown, *Augustine*, 90–91.

33. Torchia, "St. Augustine's Treatment of Superbia," 67.

34. Plotinus, *Ennead* I.2.3. Cf. Gerson, *Plotinus*, 199.

intellectual union with intellect and the One[35] is perhaps the closest classical view to Augustine's position in which the human person reaches the greatest height through the intellectual possession of God.

In chapter 2 I will continue to address the intellectual foundations upon which Augustine built his understanding of humility and greatness. The views of the Stoic and neo-Platonic philosophers covered in the first chapter are certainly significant to that foundation, but are eclipsed in their significance for Augustine by the influence of Christian Scripture. The role of Scripture in Augustine's thought became increasingly important as that thought matured. In his early years, Augustine had been alienated from Scripture by its style and his own pride of learning.[36] In the years following his conversion to Christianity, however, Augustine would turn to Scripture as the primary source and inspiration for his vast literary corpus. His dependence on sacred Scripture is manifest not only in his constant reference to it throughout all of his writings, but also in the series of scriptural commentaries he penned throughout his career. Beginning with a number of commentaries written in the last decade of the fourth century, Augustine became a prolific exegete after the year 400 with the writing of his final commentary on the book of Genesis and the publication of his sermons on the Psalms and the Johannine writings.[37] Given the importance of Augustine's use of Scripture, I will examine the manner in which he approaches the sacred text with particular emphasis on how the content of Scripture and the methods Augustine used to unlock that content affected his understanding of humility and greatness. Both Jewish and Christian Scripture plainly support the importance of humility to human greatness, and Augustine's exegetical methodology served to reinforce that support.

Following my description of Augustine's use of Scripture in support of his view concerning humility and greatness I will discuss the anthropological and moral principles Augustine draws from Scripture to sustain that view. The primary anthropological principle affecting Augustine's understanding of humility and greatness is his view of the human person as created in the image and likeness of God (Gen 1:26–27). This principle is critically important to the discussion, as it is in Augustine's view the highest honor to which the human person is called.[38] This image and likeness, how-

---

35. Plotinus, *Enn.* I.2.2.

36. Augustine, *Conf.* 3.5.9.

37. Bonner, "Augustine as Biblical Scholar," 543–44.

38. Augustine, *Trin.* 12.3.16.

ever, has been deformed by sin. The wound created by sin is, in Augustine's view, truly profound.[39] The roots of that sin are found in the disorder of pride, which Augustine conceives of as the choice of the person to pursue love of self in preference to love for God.[40] We will see that Augustine's view of pride as the foundation of sin is an important justification for his emphasis on the significance of humility as the principle opposed to self-serving love.

In chapter 3 I will present Augustine's understanding of humility within the context of the moral principles that shape his view of the principle. Augustine's moral theory borrows important elements from the eudaemonistic moral structures of his classical predecessors, yet is profoundly influenced by his reading of Scripture. In addition, his morality bears the marks of some of his most significant intellectual innovations. Augustine's understanding of knowledge, his emphasis on the importance of faith in relation to the moral life, his dynamic view of love as the key principle driving moral activity, his conceptual development of the will, the role of grace, his notion of pride, and his understanding of the end of human moral action as the intellectual possession of God are all significant developments beyond the moral thought he inherited from his Greek and Roman forerunners and each hold significant implications for Augustine's understanding of humility and greatness.

My investigation regarding the substance of Augustine's conception of humility in relation to morality will begin with an investigation of the words he uses to address the idea of humility. Following the terminological study, I will provide a description of the moral structure in which Augustine developed his understanding of humility. Augustine is well known for his understanding of the relation between grace and the moral life. It will be demonstrated that humility is a key aspect of Augustine's view regarding the necessity of grace for the human person's ability to choose the good and thus achieve perfection. Having described the specific role humility plays within the context of Augustine's moral structure, I will then treat the relation of humility with the different principles that comprise Augustine's moral thought. Augustine posits a significant function for humility in relation to faith, love, the will, virtue, and wisdom, all of which have bearing on his understanding of a person's highest calling.

---

39. Augustine, *Lib. Arb.* 1.11.22.

40. Augustine, *Gn. Adv. Mn.* 2.15.22.

Chapter 4 will examine Augustine's thought on the relationship between humility and greatness. Since Augustine views pride as the greatest impediment to greatness, I will begin by investigating Augustine's view of the manner in which humility is able to combat the vice associated with pride.[41] Following the description of the relationship between pride and humility, I will provide an account regarding the importance of Jesus to Augustine's understanding of humility and greatness. Christ is the epitome of both humility and greatness for Augustine and is therefore the personification of the relationship between the two principles. Lastly, I will discuss Augustine's paradoxical presentation of the relationship between humility and greatness, which culminates in the human person's ultimate honor as the image and likeness of the triune God.[42]

Although the theme of pride and humility is announced in the prologue of *The City of God* and runs throughout the course of that work, the relationship between the two receives its most explicit and systematic treatment in book fourteen. In chapter 4 I will provide an analysis of this text to highlight the themes Augustine presupposes and develops in relation to his understanding of humility and greatness. In addition to this textual analysis, the presentation of chapters 3 and 4 will use Augustine's sermons as the primary source from which I derive his understanding of humility and its relationship to human greatness. My focus on the sermons, based in part on Augustine's own encouragement to attend to his preaching rather than his written works,[43] is also based on the observations of contemporary authors who contend that Augustine's doctrinal and polemical works, although essential to understanding his thought as a whole, sometimes present only a partial view of that thought in their mission to argue a particular point of view. His pastoral writings, in their view, often present a more balanced and fuller articulation of doctrinal matters.[44] This is particularly the case for the presentation of humility and greatness in Augustine's sermons, which is both insightful and extensive.

More importantly for the purposes of my study, Augustine's sermons are focused upon the ideas of humility and greatness for three separate but related reasons and are thus particularly suited to be the primary source for a study on the topic. From a pastoral perspective, humility is critical to

---

41. Augustine, *En. Ps.* 58 (2).5 (WSA III/17:171).

42. Augustine, *Trin.* 12.3.16.

43. Augustine, *Cat. Rud.* 15.23.

44. Drobner, "Studying Augustine," 19–20.

the relationship of the individual believer with his or her God. Since the purpose of Augustine's sermons is to draw the members of his flock closer to God, he often highlights the importance of humility in that process.[45] The relation of humility to greatness is also important as an encouragement for the believer to embrace the humility that will lead to an enriched relationship with God. The second reason the sermons are a fruitful source for Augustine's view on humility is their Christological focus. Augustine's emphasis in his sermons on Christ has been characterized as the most pronounced of any Patristic author.[46] Since Christ is, for Augustine, the preeminent example of both humility and greatness, his presentation in the sermons often addresses these aspects of Christ's mission and person. Lastly, Augustine's sermons are frequently, if not predominantly, concerned with elaborating the passages of Scripture, which often address the idea of humility and its relation to exaltation. As a result, Augustine takes up many scriptural themes concerning humility and greatness throughout his preaching. In addition to the central role of the sermons, I will also make significant use of his doctrinal treatises to describe the moral context in which Augustine addresses humility and greatness. I will also use them where they are helpful to articulate the arguments concerning humility and greatness presented by the sermons.

In chapter 5, I will address the thought of David Hume and Friedrich Nietzsche as the most influential modern philosophers to write about humility and human excellence. In the presentation of his moral thought, David Hume takes the unprecedented step of applying the experimental method of Francis Bacon to the study of human nature, using that methodology as the criteria through which he evaluates morality.[47] The cautious and meticulous observation called for by this method is applied by Hume to the observation of human behavior, which would serve as the foundation of his approach to morality. This method, combined with the influence of seventeenth-century skepticism, serves to detach Hume's thought from that of his ancient and medieval predecessors. In that context, Hume replaces the rationalist approach to morality that dominated the thought of medievalists and ancients alike with a sentimentalist approach that focuses

45. Cf. Augustine, *Doc. Chr.* 4.4.6 for a sample text of his view regarding his role as preacher. Cf. Kolbet, *Augustine and the Cure of Souls,* 159–60, who characterizes Augustine's view of a catechist's role as only providing a spur through which audience members might embrace the love of Christ, the sole remedy capable of overcoming human pride.

46. Doyle, "Introduction to Augustine's Preaching," 13.

47. Norton, "An Introduction to Hume's Thought," 4.

on moral feeling and emotion as the criteria distinguishing good from bad action.[48] We will see that the focus on moral feeling has a direct impact on Hume's view of humility, which he characterizes as bad due to the negative emotions it arouses.[49] Hume's rejection of the relationship between religion and morality[50] (which again distinguishes him from classical philosophers who did not generally exclude the divine from their moral deliberations), the ethically normative role played by the views of society in his thought,[51] and his understanding of utility as the principle determining the moral value of social virtue and vice[52] all serve to shape his view of humility and human greatness in a markedly different way than that of Augustine.

Following Hume, I will introduce the aspects of Friedrich Nietzsche's thought that bear on the relationship between humility and greatness. One could characterize much of Nietzsche's moral thought as a reflection on the meaning of human greatness. There are no counterintuitive or paradoxical arguments in Nietzsche's understanding of that greatness, however. The human person's drive to express power is the principle that guides the moral thought of Nietzsche[53] and is the ultimate foundation of his view concerning human excellence. Nietzsche's will to power is expressed throughout his moral theory, which proposes an irrational view of the virtues[54] and is noted for the construct of a master and slave morality based on Nietzsche's critique of both Jewish and Christian moral thought.[55] Nietzsche's notions of irrational virtue and master and slave morality both contribute to his view of human greatness and his repudiation of humility as having any positive value in its regard. A last aspect of Nietzsche's thought with significant impact on his understanding of humility and greatness is his famous proclamation of the death of God.[56] Nietzsche contends that it is only with the removal of God that the human person can reach his or her greatest

---

48. MacIntyre, *Short History of Ethics*, 169.

49. Hume, *Treatise of Human Nature* 2.1.5.

50. Cf. Hume, *Enquiry Concerning the Principles of Morals* 9.1.1 for a sample text articulating Hume's opposition to the use of religious thought as a source to derive moral principles.

51. Hume, *Enquiry Concerning the Principles of Morals* 5.2.42.

52. Ibid., 5.1.4.

53. Nietzsche, *The Nietzsche Reader*, 318.

54. Hunt, *Origin of Virtue*, 81.

55. Nietzsche, *On the Genealogy of Morality* 1.7, 1.10.

56. Nietzsche, *The Gay Science* 5.343.

destiny. Simply stated, the Nietzschean view of humility and greatness is in radical opposition to that of Augustine.

In the final chapter, I will present a closing analysis in which I assess the most significant differences between approaches to human greatness that include humility and those that exclude it. I will begin that analysis with the most obvious difference between the modern thinkers and Augustine, which is their atheistic approach to morality as opposed to Augustine's decidedly theistic approach. An initial examination of the debate might conclude that this division is an insuperable barrier to a meaningful comparison between the thought of Hume and Nietzsche on the one hand and that of Augustine on the other. While the relation of God to the understanding of humility is obviously of great importance, opposing perspectives on the view of this relationship do not completely preclude meaningful comparisons between these authors. Such comparisons, if not made on the basis of a person's understanding of God, can still be articulated through other shared principles of moral discourse. One might counter that authors such as Augustine and Nietzsche have so little in common, comparisons on the basis of shared principles would be meager indeed. Yet despite their great differences, there are a number of contexts in which Hume and even Nietzsche may be compared with Augustine.

Following the discussion regarding theistic and atheistic approaches to humility and greatness, I will offer a reflection on the compatibility, or lack thereof, between Aristotle's understanding of magnanimity and Augustine's view of humble greatness. The reflection will first note the parallels between magnanimity and humble greatness and will then focus on the significant differences between the two concepts. In a second analysis I will provide a comparison between Augustine and the modern authors of the study regarding their varying conceptions of humility and greatness. Beginning with Hume's account of human excellence and then moving to that of Nietzsche and Augustine, the analysis will draw out the implications of each author's moral principles for the elaboration of their view of greatness and will subsequently comment on how well each conception depicts that greatness. The study will then conclude with a final reflection on Augustine's unique contribution to the understanding of humility and its importance to the heights of human excellence.

1

Classical Views of
Humility and Greatness

THE VIEWS OF ANCIENT Greek and Roman philosophers regarding humility and greatness are important to my study for two primary reasons. First, they form the philosophical foundation from which Western medieval and modern ethical theory developed. The philosophers of classical antiquity established the context in which human excellence would be understood by subsequent generations of thinkers. Human excellence, as we will see, was conceived of as moral excellence in the eudaemonistic context in which the cultivation of virtue led to happiness. Such an approach included implicit assumptions regarding humility and greatness that not only served as foundations for the advances of thinkers such as Augustine, but also served as foils against which modern philosophers, such as Hume and Nietzsche, would react. An example of these assumptions includes the idea that the moral life—the life of virtue—was grasped and acquired through the rational faculties of the human mind. A further example is the moral self-sufficiency asserted by classical Greek philosophers that became a principle Augustine would consciously reject in developing his understanding of humility and greatness. A third example can be seen in the social aspects latent in Aristotelian magnanimity and Ciceronian glory (magnanimity and glory in these contexts were very much concerned with honor and the opinion of others), which would also have significant impact on later thinkers concerned with human excellence.

The second reason classical philosophical thought is important to this study is the influence Greek and Roman philosophy specifically had on the thought of Augustine. Although the large majority of Augustine's education was mediated through Latin culture and language, the Greek philosophical tradition had a significant effect upon his thinking. The impact of ancient philosophy upon Augustine can hardly be overemphasized.[1] Whether it was Cicero's *Hortensius* directing him toward the study of philosophy or neo-Platonic philosophy laying the foundation for his rejection of Manichaeism and eventual conversion to Catholicism, classical philosophy was to have considerable influence on Augustine's thought throughout his life. Augustine's moral positions have been characterized as Stoic interpretations of Platonic philosophy. Augustine combines the insights of the two schools, which yields an understanding of happiness in which virtue becomes beatitude once a person has achieved intellectual union with God.[2] Given the importance of Stoic and neo-Platonic philosophy to the development of Augustine's moral thought, it is necessary to examine the principles of these schools as significant influences upon Augustine's view of humility and greatness.

In addition to Stoic and neo-Platonist thought, I will also examine Aristotelian morality. Despite the relatively indirect exposure of Augustine to Aristotle's writing, it is important to include his thought for two reasons. First, Aristotle's moral theory is one of the strongest expressions of an approach to morality that includes a focus on virtue and the importance of external goods, both of which he applies to his understanding of moral excellence in his depiction of magnanimity. The inclusion of such external goods in the consideration of moral greatness provides a position that Stoic approaches to the topic react against (although, as we'll see later, Cicero does not do away with it entirely) and sets a precedent for Augustine's approach as well. Second, given the merit of Aristotle's thought, one must account for his description of magnanimity to provide a thorough treatment of the relation between humility and greatness. Working forward chronologically, I will first treat Aristotle's thought on magnanimity and will then take up Stoic thinking and Cicero's view of *gloria* before treating neo-Platonic influences on Augustine, which will focus on the writings of Plotinus.

---

1. See Kenney, *Mysticism of Saint Augustine*, 49–57 for a discussion of classical philosophy's influence on the thought of Augustine. Further reflections on the influence of ancient philosophy on Augustine's thought can be found in Armstrong, *St. Augustine and Christian Platonism* and Wetzel, *Limits of Virtue*.

2. Wetzel, *Limits of Virtue*, 68.

Magnanimity as the Crown of Aristotelian Virtue

Despite the important role Aristotle's ethics played in the development of modern and contemporary moral thought, even the most cursory examination reveals marked differences between him and the philosophers that have shaped the modern moral discussion. Aristotle's eudaemonist approach to morality is significantly different from modern deontological and utilitarian approaches. However, it has significant parallels with the morality of the Stoic and neo-Platonist philosophical traditions so influential in the development of Augustine's thought. The eudaemonist tradition views morality as the pursuit of a final or supreme good, which is identified with human happiness.[3] Happiness, for Aristotle, has two basic elements. The first lies in the ability of a person to function properly as a human being. Proper functioning for Aristotle includes and is defined by the excellence of the function. Thus, in his view, the good or happiness of the human person is an activity of the soul in conformity with excellence, where virtue is seen as the embodiment of such excellence.[4] In addition to the happiness achieved through virtue, Aristotle asserts that happiness also depends on the possession of external goods, without which a person is unable to pursue the good of virtue.[5] Magnanimity, as Aristotle's crown of virtue,[6] incorporates both aspects of Aristotelian happiness. To be magnanimous one must not only be virtuous, but one must also be concerned with the external good of honor. The conception of human greatness resulting from this combination of elements has little to do with what might be considered humility and has been interpreted by many to be in opposition to Christian notions of humility.[7] In the examination to follow, I will describe Aristotle's understanding of magnanimity as the crown of the moral virtues and subsequently highlight the moral principles upon which he bases this conclusion.

3. Tessitore, *Reading Aristotle's Ethics*, 20.

4. Aristotle, *Nicomachean Ethics* 1098a7–18. Excellence is a translation of the Greek word *arête*, which has a long history in Greek moral discourse. Its meaning evolved over time, but came to be understood as the functional excellence of any person or thing. The English word virtue is often used as a translation as well.

5. Aristotle, *Nicomachean Ethics* 1099a31–32.

6. Ibid., 1124a1.

7. See Arnhart, "Statesmanship as Magnanimity," 263–83 for a discussion supporting the opposition between Aristotelian magnanimity and Christian humility.

Aristotle on *Megalopsychia*

In book four of the *Nicomachean Ethics*, Aristotle addresses the virtue of *megalopsychia*, which is typically translated in English as magnanimity or high-mindedness, and its associated vices. The magnanimous person achieves the happiness Aristotle associates with virtue and external goods because the magnanimous person holds all the virtues and is in possession of the greatest external good, which is honor. Despite the praise he casts upon the magnanimous person, many commentators have found Aristotle's treatment of magnanimity arrogant and even repugnant.[8] Aristotle's view that the high-minded person is justified in looking down on others is but one example of magnanimity's less attractive features.[9] MacIntyre attributes the alleged repugnance of Aristotle's magnanimous person to the social context in which he taught and developed his thought.[10] Whether his thought on the issue is repulsive or not, it is certainly the case that Aristotle developed his position on magnanimity within the context of his moral theory. He defines magnanimity as a mean between extremes, but like all virtues, it is also an extreme in relation to the good. It participates in the unity of the virtues and is also more opposed to one of its extremes than the other. Aristotle's teaching on magnanimity, despite its offensive nature to some, is clearly consistent with the principles of his ethics.

Aristotle begins his discussion by describing the magnanimous person as one who thinks he is deserving of great things and is correct in that estimation. "A man is regarded as high-minded when he thinks he deserves great things and actually deserves them."[11] He compares this type of person to someone who deserves little and thinks he deserves little. This is the description of someone who is aware of his limitations. Despite the contrast between these two types of character, Aristotle does not offer the person aware of his limitations as an extreme on one end of magnanimity's moral spectrum. Magnanimity is a mean in regard to the accuracy of the claim to greatness rather than the grandeur of that person's own virtues. As a consequence, Aristotle places the magnanimous person as the virtuous agent between the extremes of the vain person who thinks he deserves great things

8. A discussion of the offensive features of Aristotle's teaching on magnanimity can be found in Curzer, "Aristotle's Much Maligned Megalopsychos," 131–51.

9. Aristotle, *Nicomachean Ethics* 1124b5.

10. MacIntyre, *Short History of Ethics*, 78. Cf. Curzer, "Much Maligned Megalopsychos," 135–36 for a critique of MacIntyre's characterization.

11. Aristotle, *Nicomachean Ethics* 1123b1–2.

but doesn't and the small-minded person who underestimates himself. Thus, the magnanimous person represents a mean in regard to the accuracy of his claim and an extreme in regard to the greatness of his virtue.[12]

For Aristotle, the magnanimous person is truly virtuous in every respect. Since the high- minded person deserves what is greatest or best, it follows that she must possess the greatest character:

> A truly high minded person must be good. And what is great in each virtue would seem to be the mark of a high-minded person . . . If he were base he would not even deserve honor, for honor is the prize of excellence and virtue, and it is reserved as a tribute to the good. High-mindedness thus is the crown, as it were, of the virtues: it magnifies them and it cannot exist without them. Therefore, it is hard to be truly high-minded and, in fact, impossible without goodness and nobility.[13]

Here we see Aristotle presenting magnanimity as the summit of the moral life. Its possession implies a person holds all the other virtues, which are then enhanced by that magnanimity. The exercise of magnanimity makes the virtuous moral agent truly great.[14]

In his description of magnanimity Aristotle spends much effort describing how the high-minded person views honor, and due to this emphasis, there seems to be a tension in his presentation between the magnanimous person being solely focused on honor and being focused on honor in a more moderate fashion. In four different instances, Aristotle asserts that the primary concern of the high-minded person is honor.[15] His assertions seem to place the magnanimous person in a bad light. His characterization brings to mind the image of a superficial and self-serving person who cares only about what others think of him. In three other instances, however, Aristotle also asserts that the magnanimous person has the right attitude toward honor, deriving only a moderate amount of pleasure from honors.[16] This is the case because honor, even as the greatest of external goods, can never match the value of virtue.[17] Given Aristotle's priority of virtue over external goods and the fact that he views the magnanimous person as su-

---

12. Ibid., 1123b1–15.

13. Ibid., 1123b29–1124a4.

14. Holloway, "Christianity, Magnanimity, and Statesmanship," 581.

15. Aristotle, *Nicomachean Ethics* 1123b22, 1124a5, 1124a12, 1125a35.

16. Ibid., 1123b21–22, 1124a7, 1124a16.

17. Ibid., 1124a8.

premely virtuous, it stands to reason that his understanding of the high-minded person is not one in which such a person values honor over all else. It is difficult to conceive of a virtuous person who cares about honor in such a fashion. A more reasonable interpretation would be the high-minded person is unavoidably concerned with honor since as the greatest of external goods, it is the most likely good (next to virtue) to be worthy of the magnanimous person's attention. This does not change the fact that such a person would value virtue—his own virtue in particular—more highly than honor. Aristotle goes on to assert that the high-minded person despises dishonor, trivial honors, and honors offered to him by ordinary people. His disgust with these types of honors and dishonor is based on the fact that he deserves more and implies that the magnanimous person has the ability to be discriminate in his desire for praise.[18]

After his discussion regarding honor, Aristotle continues his description of the high-minded person with a list of attributes that do little to rehabilitate the image of the magnanimous person. The high-minded person is justified in looking down on others because she knows that she is superior to most people, which is the correct appraisal of her standing compared to others.[19] She dislikes charity because it makes her look inferior to someone else and will consequently return favors with greater good in order to gain the upper hand in a relationship.[20] She undertakes few actions because most actions are beneath her, but the few she does undertake are grand in scope and value.[21] She is open in her hatred and love of others because to be otherwise would manifest timidity unbecoming of the magnanimous person's stature.[22] Perhaps the only attribute that sounds somewhat positive in the remaining list is the fact that the high-minded person will be unassuming when mingling with others of more moderate means. To assert her virtue among the lower class would be crude. She will, however, show her stature among the people of eminence because it is appropriate to do so in such a context.[23] A last feature of the high-minded person is the tendency for such a person to possess things of beauty rather than useful things because beautiful objects will more clearly demonstrate the magnanimous person's

18. Ibid., 1124a9–10.
19. Ibid., 1124b5–6.
20. Ibid., 1124b8–12.
21. Ibid., 1124b25.
22. Ibid., 1124b26v27.
23. Ibid., 1124b18–22.

self-sufficiency.[24] Implied in this comment and presupposed in much of Aristotle's ethical theory is the idea that the virtuous person is the person least in need of assistance.

Turning to Aristotle's descriptions of the vices surrounding magnanimity, we see him take the position that vanity—the extreme in which a person thinks too highly of himself—is less opposed to magnanimity than the small-minded person who thinks too little of himself. He dismisses the vain as fools who do not know themselves and make a public display of that fact.[25] A small-minded person, on the other hand, is not considered evil, but only mistaken. This is because he deprives himself of the good he deserves, thinking he is unworthy of that good.[26] He is unable to assess his own value accurately. This inaccuracy is particularly troublesome because it discourages the small-minded person from pursuing noble acts and even external goods.[27] Aristotle concludes that small-mindedness is more opposed to high-mindedness because of its tendency to inhibit noble behavior and because it occurs more frequently than vanity.[28] Looking to the later sections of my work where I deal with Augustine's thought, we will see that the inaccurate self-vision of the Aristotelian small-minded person will be an impediment to a facile equation of people with such character to those that are humble in an Augustinian sense.

Aristotle's understanding of the magnanimous person is a direct result of his view of moral excellence. The magnanimous person has formed her character through deliberately chosen activity that gives rise to the excellence of virtue. That excellence is not limited to one virtue, but through the influence of practical wisdom, participates in the unity of all the virtues. The high-minded person has cultivated all the moral virtues and is thus in the position to cultivate the virtue of magnanimity as the virtue that brings the others to perfection. In addition, the magnanimous person is not only focused upon the intrinsic good of virtue, but is also concerned with the external good of honor. Honor, as the highest external good, reinforces the

---

24. Ibid., 1125a11–12. This aspect of Aristotle's thought provides a clear contrast to that of Augustine who asserts all people are dependent upon God's grace in their pursuit of the good. We will see that Augustine's position, developed on the basis of Hebrew and Christian Scripture, sees virtuous self-sufficiency as a fiction and a quite problematic feature of Greek morality.

25. Aristotle, *Nicomachean Ethics* 1125a27.

26. Ibid., 1125a19–20.

27. Ibid., 1125a25–26.

28. Ibid., 1125a34.

high-minded person's pursuit of virtue because Aristotle views the achievement of the mean with regard to any virtue as an accomplishment worthy of honor,[29] and thus it is even more appropriate to honor the person who holds all the virtues with magnanimity as their crown.

It is Aristotle's positive view of external goods such as honor that the Stoics take greatest issue with in general. In the Stoic personification of moral excellence, the sage, one sees a complete absence of concern for any external good. External goods are, for the Stoics, always a matter of indifference. From this perspective, the Stoic account of morality and moral excellence is much more akin to the views of Augustine, and it is to that account that I will now turn.

Stoic Thought on Moral Excellence

As I noted earlier, despite Augustine's reluctance to read Greek, the influence of the Greek philosophical traditions on his thought was quite significant. Third and fourth century Platonism—or Neo-Platonism as modern scholars would categorize it—was instrumental in his turn away from the Manichaean sect. Outside of Christian Scripture, no school of thought had greater influence on Augustine's moral theory than that of the Stoics. Stoicism was founded as a school of thought around 300 BCE by the Platonic philosopher Zeno. Diogenes of Babylon was a prominent Stoic philosopher who led the school during the second century BC and is the likely inspiration of Cicero's *De Finibus Bonorum et Malorum*.[30] I will use the *De Finibus* of Cicero as a guide to highlight the primary elements of Stoic moral theory in relation to the Stoic depiction of moral excellence in its understanding of the sage and as a prelude to Cicero's own understanding of *gloria*.

Emotion and Natural Goods in the Stoic View of Virtue

Written between the years 46 and 44 BCE, Cicero's *De Finibus* is a treatise on the major moral systems of his day: Epicureanism, Stoicism, and the ethics of the Academy, led at the time by Antiochus.[31] Book III provides an exposition of Stoic ethical thought in the context of the previous book's

29. Ibid., 1106b24–30.
30. Cicero, *De Finibus* xvii.
31. Ibid., xi.

critique of Epicurean morality. Having eliminated pleasure as a possible answer to the question regarding the nature of the chief good the human person seeks, Cicero raises the question of that in which the chief good, or final end, consists. He begins the book's treatment asserting that any answer regarding the chief good must include the idea of virtue, which is the height of human excellence.[32] Cicero then presents the Stoic version of the greatest good through a dialogue between himself and M. Cato in which Cato takes on the challenge of articulating the whole of the Stoic ethical system.

For the Stoics, excellence of virtue is achieved through the absence of emotion for natural goods and the presence of emotion a person should feel toward virtue. Cato begins his treatment of the Stoic ethical system by asserting that upon birth the human person experiences his first impulse, which is the impulse of self-preservation. Impulse is a fundamental category the Stoics use to explain their ethics. Following the Socratic position in Plato's *Protagoras*, the Stoics see impulses and all motivations to action as forms of belief.[33] As a motion of the soul in which assent is given, an impulse is necessary for action. The Stoics assert that no one can have an impulse without acting on it. This is the case because an impulse contains everything that is necessary to commence an activity. It is an evaluative judgment toward a particular situation that leads to immediate action.[34] Emotions are a species of impulse and are the basis for the many irrational moral choices people typically make. What frequently distinguishes emotions from other impulses is the fact that they assign the value of good or evil to some object of nature that is merely neutral in situations where the belief of the person falls short of knowledge. Emotions typically consist of an inaccurate assessment of an object where the assessment is false because its value neither rises to the level of goodness nor sinks to that of evil.[35]

Emotions are typically erroneous evaluations because they do not recognize that most objects of nature are indifferent rather than good or bad. In the Stoic understanding of morality, there is only one thing that is truly good, which is virtue, and only one thing that is truly bad, which is vice. Virtue is the only thing sought for its own sake. No other object of nature is intrinsically desirable.[36] Stoic teaching regarding the indiffer-

32. Ibid., 3.1.

33. Brennan, "Moral Psychology," 259–60.

34. Ibid.," 267.

35. Ibid., 269.

36. Cicero, *De Finibus* 3.22.

ence of natural objects demonstrates the school's roots in the traditions of both the Cynics and the Platonists. The Cynics proposed that there is only one good, which consists in virtue. Zeno adopted this assertion from the Cynics, but also modified it to correct the position's inability to distinguish the value of anything that fell outside the goodness of virtue. Adapting the thought of Polemo regarding external goods to his teaching, Zeno taught that objects of nature, while neither rising to the level of good nor sinking to the level of evil, do manifest limited value.[37] In the dialogue of *De Finibus,* Cato maintains that things in accordance with nature deserve to be selected due to their possession of a certain amount of positive value. Those things not in accordance with nature have negative value and should therefore be rejected. [38] Both positive and negative natural objects have no effect on a person's happiness (only the good of virtue or the evil of vice can have such an effect), but this does not deprive them of all value.[39] Appropriate action in regard to these objects is neither good nor bad. The criteria Cicero sets out in the words of Cato to describe appropriate action is that of reason. The selection or rejection of a natural object is deemed appropriate if a reasonable account can be rendered for its performance.[40] For example, if one were to undertake exercise to promote the object of health, it would be considered an appropriate act because reason has determined that exercise helps to promote health. An erroneous emotional evaluation of this action, on the other hand, would hold health as a good to be pursued and the feelings of emotion would arise due to the valuing of health as a good. Since health is not virtue and therefore not a good, such an evaluation must be inaccurate. Such inaccuracy would cause the person to assent to falsity, which is more repugnant to the Stoics than virtually anything else that is contrary to nature.[41]

Cicero's Cato not only makes it clear that natural objects do not rise to the level of the good; he is also unwavering in his commitment to equating human excellence—the chief good—with moral virtue. According to Cato, moral conduct or moral worth is the end to which all other things are ordered. The harmony that ought to govern human behavior is more important than any natural object. It is the chief end and is to be desired

37. Sedley, "The School," 10.
38. Cicero, *De Finibus* 3.20.
39. Ibid., 3.50.
40. Ibid., 3.58.
41. Ibid., 3.18.

for its own sake. The things that are the objects at which a person's actions aim are to be chosen or selected without desire. The manner in which we act in the pursuit of that aim, however, should be the object of desire because it is the one thing that is truly good.[42] Cicero provides two different rationales for this conclusion. First, he notes that the Stoics assert an intimate relationship between that which is good and that which is morally honorable. They reason that whatever is good is also praiseworthy. Things that are praiseworthy must be morally honorable; therefore, the good is that which is morally honorable.[43] A second justification for their conclusion of the good consisting in virtue stems from their understanding of the relationship between pride and a happy life. The Stoics insist that one can only be proud of a happy life. A happy life must be morally honorable because one could not take pride in such a life were it not honorable. They believe, therefore, that the happy life is a morally honorable life. If such is the case, it follows that moral value as the foundation of happiness must be the chief and only good.[44]

Stoic Virtue and the Progress toward Moral Excellence

The Stoic conception of virtue is based upon their beliefs concerning the divine reason that governs the cosmos, belief or knowledge concerning that reason, and the emotions and impulses that drive people to choose particular actions. Cicero asserts that the harmony governing conduct is the chief human good.[45] It is not what we do, but how we do things that constitutes human greatness, otherwise known as virtue. Zeno taught that virtue is nothing other than reason—reason that is consistent, firm, and unchangeable.[46] The reason he is referring to is that of the divine will governing the universe. By obeying reason, the human person obeys the same divine reason that rules the cosmos.[47] To be in conformity with reason is to conform to the truth of the natural surroundings we experience on a daily basis. As a result, the Stoics often described virtue as living consistently

---

42. Ibid., 3.21.

43. Ibid., 3.27.

44. Ibid., 3.28.

45. Ibid., 3.21.

46. Schofield, "Stoic Ethics," 241.

47. Ibid., 246.

or in accordance with nature.[48] It is important to recognize that the Stoics did not consider living in accordance with nature as merely responding to natural human impulses, like the impulse to self-preservation. Rather, one lives in accordance with nature by applying the experience of the course of natural events to one's own actions.[49] Through the experience of life one learns the wisdom of the reason that guides the universe. Virtue is the application of that reason by an individual to his or her behavior.

Asserting a Socratic understanding regarding the intellectual nature of moral motivation, the Stoics state that the knowledge one develops through the experience of reason is critical to the moral development of the individual. Knowledge plays an indispensable role for the sage as the exemplar of Stoic excellence. The importance of knowledge to the ability of a person to engage in virtuous activity can be seen in the Stoic equation of virtue to wisdom.[50] It is the sage's wisdom or knowledge—i.e., his virtue—that distinguishes him from the non-sage. The sage, by virtue of his knowledge, pursues what is truly good, as opposed to the non-sage who pursues what is only apparently good.[51] The knowledge of the sage has two morally relevant aspects. First, because of his familiarity with reason, the sage knows what is truly good and will consequently pursue the good (which alone is virtue) as that which is good and will treat indifferent things with the detachment of appropriate action. The goal of virtue, according to Aristo of Chios, a student of Zeno, was to treat all things between virtue and vice with indifference.[52] The sage's knowledge of reason empowers him to do just this. The second morally relevant aspect of the sage's knowledge is his knowledge of things indifferent. Since most objects of choice confronting the sage are indifferent—that is, they are neither good nor bad because they are not virtue or vice—the way the sage handles such objects becomes crucial to his ability to be virtuous. Since it is not the objects the sage chooses but the way in which he chooses those objects that constitutes his virtue, the sage must have a thorough knowledge of indifferent things so as to handle them in a virtuous manner. His virtue consists in his knowledge of indifferent

48. Ibid., 242, 244.

49. Ibid., 244.

50. Sharples, *Stoics, Epicureans, and Sceptics*, 100.

51. Brennan, "Moral Psychology," 291.

52. Schofield, "Stoic Ethics," 247–48.

things, which enables him to choose among them with the expertise and detachment appropriate to a sage.[53]

It is through the influence of knowledge and belief that the sage is able to correct her natural impulses, replacing the emotions of the non-sage that lead to false conclusions and misery with the emotions of the sage, which lead to truth and happiness. It is the knowledge of the difference between indifferent objects and virtue or vice that allows the sage to choose actions in accordance with nature. Such choices will associate choosing with desire to choices involving virtue and selection without desire to choices concerning indifferent goods. The sage does not experience emotion when choosing indifferent goods. When acting virtuously, on the other hand, she does experience emotion because the good of virtue elicits an emotional response. The emotions of the sage differ from those of the non-sage because they are accurate, while those of the non-sage lack accuracy. One becomes a sage, then, by replacing emotional choice with dispassionate selection when considering indifferent objects[54] and by choosing with emotion when pursuing virtuous action.

Given the Stoic understanding of virtue, ethical progress (the transition from being a non-sage to being a sage) is the goal of human moral striving. Ethical progress from moral corruption to perfect goodness is one of the fundamental characteristics of Stoic moral theory.[55] The virtue of the sage requires, according to the Stoics, great thought and involves lifelong steadfastness, strength, and consistency.[56] Cicero depicts four separate stages through which a person advances in the process of developing virtue.

> The first "appropriate act" (for so I render the Greek *kathekon*) is to preserve oneself in one's natural constitution; the next is to retain those things that are in accordance with nature and to repel those that are the contrary; then when this principle of choice and also of rejection has been discovered, there follows next in order choice conditioned by "appropriate action;" then, such choice becomes a fixed habit; and finally choice is fully rationalized and in harmony with nature. It is at this stage that the Good properly so-called emerges and comes to be understood in its true nature.[57]

---

53. Brennan, "Moral Psychology," 287.

54. Ibid., 272.

55. Kidd, "Moral Actions," 247.

56. Cicero, *De Finibus* 3.50.

57. Ibid., 3.20.

The Stoic understanding of moral progress not only provides a goal after which each person can strive, it is the context in which they understand the greatness to be achieved by the human person. The Stoics believe that a fundamental power of a person is the ability to develop the character that responds appropriately and virtuously to the situations experienced in life. We will see in later chapters that, despite their significant influence on Augustine's thought, the Stoic belief in a person's ability to improve his or her moral character differs significantly from that of Augustine.

Stoic moral thought is typically remembered for its focus on *apatheia*, the absence of feeling or emotion.[58] While *apatheia* is certainly a distinctive aspect of Stoic morality, it does not capture the full meaning of Stoic moral excellence. Moral excellence for the Stoics is virtue, where virtue is understood as living a life in conformity with reason as an expression of the divine will that governs the universe.[59] Such virtue is achieved through the knowledge of experience with goods of indifference or natural goods and the goods of virtue. The person of virtue adapts his character to experience emotion for the goods of virtue while withholding emotion for indifferent goods. The sage, the Stoic paragon of virtue and height of human excellence, holds no emotion for the latter while desiring with emotion the good of the former. The Stoic notion of human greatness, then, not only includes *apatheia* for natural goods, but also incorporates the emotional pursuit of the good that is only available in the acquisition of virtue.

Aristotelian and Stoic Morality: Commonality and Divergence

Before addressing Cicero's conception of *gloria* as another classical perspective on human greatness, I will provide a comparison between the Aristotelian and Stoic traditions to highlight the distinctive aspects of the classical views of greatness, which will in turn provide contrasts to Augustine, Hume, and Nietzsche on the issue. A first distinction between Aristotelian and Stoic thought that impacts the morality of each perspective is their differing views of God and the relation of God to the world of human experience. The God of Aristotle, the unmoved mover, has little bearing on his ethics because ethics for Aristotle concerns things achievable through

58. Cf. Cicero, *De Finibus* 3.35 for a description of how the wise person is always free from the influence of emotion.

59. Schofield, "Stoic Ethics," 246.

human agency, which consequently excludes the unmoved mover.[60] Unlike Aristotle's position, God has enormous influence on the morality of the Stoics because the virtuous person must conform herself to God's reason in order to become virtuous. As a result of this difference, each school views human excellence differently. The height of moral activity for Aristotle is magnanimity, the crowning virtue bringing to perfection the moral agent who is in possession of all the other virtues.[61] For the Stoics, human greatness consists in developing virtue so that one may live life in accordance with the reason of the divine will that governs the universe.[62] Thus the Stoic conception of God shapes their view of morality and human excellence, while that of Aristotle affects only the intellectual virtues that can contemplate the divine[63] and has little bearing on moral excellence.

An aspect of ethics in which Aristotle and the Stoics converge lies in their understanding of morality and virtue. This is not to say there are no differences between Stoic and Aristotelian understandings of virtue. There are differences, some of which are significant. An example of their differences, and perhaps the most important, is the view each school takes toward goods external to the human person, or what the Stoics call objects of indifference. Aristotle and the Stoics view morality through the lens of virtue, asking moral questions in the context of how one ought to live and what character one ought to develop in order to live a happy life. Despite this similarity in framework, the Stoics argue that their view of the chief good lying only in virtue to the exclusion of all else is significantly—even profoundly—different than Aristotelian thought. Aristotle argues that the happiness of the human person consists primarily in the operation of virtue, but that external goods also have a secondary role in the provision of happiness. He puts it rather forcefully, "Those who assert that a man is happy even on the rack and even when great misfortune befalls him, provided that he is good, are talking nonsense, whether they know it or not . . . happiness also needs fortune."[64] Cicero's Cato likewise argued the Stoic position with vehemence.

60. Aristotle, *Nicomachean Ethics* 1096b30–34.

61. Ibid., 1123b29–1124a4.

62. Diogenes, *Lives of Eminent Philosophers* 2.7.86–87. In this text, Diogenes reports Zeno's teaching on the subject as one who lives life in accordance with reason is living the natural life and to live life in agreement with nature is to be virtuous.

63. Aristotle, *Nicomachean Ethics* 1177a11–18.

64. Aristotle, *Nicomachean Ethics* 1153b19–20.

Moral Worth (is) the only good and Moral Baseness the only evil. All other philosophical systems—in varying degree no doubt, but still all—that reckon anything of which virtue is not an element either as a good or an evil do not merely, as I hold, give us any assistance or support towards becoming better men, but are actually corrupting to the character. Either this point must be firmly maintained—that Moral Worth is the sole good—or it is absolutely impossible to prove that virtue constitutes happiness. And in that case, I do not see why we trouble to study philosophy. For if anyone who is wise could be miserable, I should not set much value on your vaunted and belauded virtue.[65]

The Stoics regard the external goods of Aristotle as so insignificant that their addition to the happiness produced by virtue is utterly negligible. In the words of Cicero, they are like "a drop of honey . . . lost in the vastness of the Aegean sea."[66] In addition, they assert that the wise man can indeed be happy on the rack because pain is subject to a person's state of mind. For the right reason, one can tolerate great pain; therefore the virtuous person can be happy even in a state of bodily torture.[67] Despite this debate and other differences, however, the Stoic and Aristotelian views of virtue agree in one salient aspect that is contrary to Augustine's position. The Aristotelian understanding of virtue presupposes a person's ability to form the virtues necessary to become a person of good character. Likewise, the Stoic teaching regarding the moral progress a person makes in becoming a sage explicitly asserts that the human person is capable of improving himself on the basis of his own natural resources. These two positions differ from Augustine's view of virtue and a person's ability to improve morally. In the following chapters, we will see that Augustine holds it is only through the assistance of divine grace that a person can improve his or her moral character.[68]

---

65. Cicero, *De Finibus* 3.11.

66. Ibid., 3.45.

67. Ibid., 3.42.

68. Augustine, *Nat. et Gr.* 7.7.

Cicero's Conception of *Gloria*

Despite Cicero's profession as a follower of the Academy's skeptical philosophy[69] and perhaps as a result of his skeptical philosophic method, many Stoic ideals can be found in his writing.[70] In his presentation of human glory, one can see a strong connection between the position of Cicero and the Stoic view of virtue. *Gloria* is the Latin term Cicero used to describe the person worthy of great honor, the rough equivalent of Aristotle's high-minded person.[71] It was an idea that held a prominent place in Cicero's thought. He develops his perspective on it in a number of different works, even devoting an entire treatise to the topic—*De Gloria*, which is now lost.[72] For Cicero, *gloria* is a priceless gift that lasts beyond the grave. It is a pledge to immortality, taking on greater importance than the vicissitudes of mortal life on earth.[73] Cicero's understanding of *gloria* deepened over time and combined a number of different elements. Transitioning in his earlier days from a view of *gloria* as merely fame and popular reputation, Cicero ultimately associated it with service to the state and virtue. In his final formulations, he asserts that many are misled by a fleeting false glory, but true glory is substantial and lasting. In addition, we'll see that Cicero mentions elements implying some common ground between his understanding of *gloria* and Augustine's view of humility and greatness.

In one of his earliest works, Cicero describes *gloria* as widespread popularity.[74] Over the course of his political career and through his philosophical reflection, Cicero would move away from this as a true definition of *gloria*, but would retain it as the basis for his definition of false glory to which many people fell prey. In his *Tusculan Disputations,* Cicero acknowledges the popular belief that glory is the fame associated with military command and high civic office and observes how the noblest of men are attracted to these laurels in their quest for honor. He asserts, however, that they are chasing nothing but a phantom.[75] The false glory of public reputation is, for Cicero, filled with pretense and dissembling speech. It is a

---

69. Powell, "Cicero's Philosophical Works," 18.

70. Ibid., 24.

71. See Arnhart, "Statesmanship as Magnanimity," 265–71 for a discussion of the relation between Aristotle's understanding of magnanimity and Cicero's view of glory.

72. Cicero, *De Officiis* 2.31.

73. Sullivan, "Cicero and Gloria," 391.

74. Cicero, *De Inventione* 383.

75. Cicero, *Disputationes Tusculanae* 3.2.

glory that fades quickly due to human mortality and the short memory of succeeding generations. "Nor will any man's reputation endure very long, for what men say dies with them and is blotted out with the forgetfulness of posterity."[76] True glory, on the other hand, differs from false both in its longevity and its content. True glory, according to Cicero, is not ephemeral, but takes root in a person's life and continues to grow.[77] It is a real substance, as opposed to false glory's phantom nature, which he defines as nothing other than the agreed approval of good men.[78] Authentic glory, as opposed to false glory, is permanent and can only be appraised by one of virtuous character rather than the inaccurate opinion of the masses.

The question remains, however, what it is that meets with the approval of the aforementioned good men. In what does glory actually consist or how does one participate in glory? Cicero consistently identifies two general elements that must be present for a person to attain glory: public service and virtue. Cicero believes that great men concern themselves with the political community.[79] People who aspire to great service in politics are well-suited to glory because public service is the primary context in which greatness of spirit may be displayed.[80] Public service provides both a stage and the opportunity to display the merits that win a person glory. Public debates—whether before jurors, the people, or the senate—are all forums in which a civic official can demonstrate the eloquence so important to winning the admiration of others.[81] The challenge of public administration is also an opportunity for the great statesman to risk his own welfare for the sake of the republic's citizens.[82] Glory will accrue to the leaders of public affairs who forget their own advantage and pursue that which will benefit their fellow citizens.[83] For Cicero, the path to the immortal glory of heaven is open to those who have served their country well.[84]

If public service provides the opportunity for a person to earn glory and the admiration of others, it is virtue that actually causes others to

76. Cicero, *De Republica* 6.23.

77. Cicero, *De Officiis* 2.43.

78. Cicero, *Disputationes Tusculanae* 3.2.

79. Cicero, *De Officiis* 2.46.

80. Ibid., 1.70, 1.72.

81. Ibid., 2.49.

82. Ibid., 1.83.

83. Ibid., 1.85.

84. Cicero, *De Republica* 6.24.

admire the public servant. In the *Dream of Scipio* (found in the last book of *The Republic*), Cicero asserts that it is virtue itself that leads to true glory.[85] There is no other inheritance for which one could wish than the glory of virtue.[86] Cicero articulates three factors that are particularly important in attaining glory. The first is the fact that the good will of others is aroused by the reputation of kindly service. Others will admire a person who is known to be beneficent, just, gentle, and faithful in his commitments. Since the virtues of kindness please most people, those that demonstrate having such characteristics will be loved by most people.[87] Cicero breaks the second element necessary for glory into two qualities: good sense and justice. People have faith in and admiration for someone who is capable of arriving at solutions for the problems presented by his station in life. This admiration and faith, however, will only be given if the competence exhibited by the person is accompanied by the virtue of justice, which enables one to trust the person of good sense. Of the two qualities, justice is the more important because good sense without justice is reduced to cunning, which will inspire neither faith nor glory.[88] The last element necessary for glory is the actual judgment of others that a person is worthy of honor and admiration. Such honor and admiration is chiefly reserved for a person of exceptional virtue. A person endowed with the moral fiber to cling to reason in the face of the allures of pleasure and the fear of pain cannot fail to be admired.[89]

Cicero concludes and summarizes his analysis by reiterating the importance of justice to glory. The virtue of justice is essential to glory because it is on the basis of justice that one is chosen to rule, thereby making it possible to manifest the virtues that arouse admiration.[90] It is also on the basis of justice alone that one is called good.[91] Cicero sees virtue, in particular the virtue of justice, as the true content of *gloria*. "For true glory is a thing of real substance and clearly wrought, no shadowy phantom: it is the agreed approval of good men, the unbiased verdict of judges deciding honestly the question of pre-eminent merit; it gives back to virtue the echo of her voice."[92]

---

85. Ibid., 6.23.
86. Cicero, *De Officiis* 1.121.
87. Ibid., 2.32.
88. Ibid., 2.33–34.
89. Ibid., 2.36–37.
90. Ibid., 2.42.
91. Ibid., 2.38.
92. Cicero, *Disputationes Tusculanae* 3.2.

Of interest to my study is the fact that humility, while not a primary element of Cicero's thought concerning *gloria*, is mentioned in connection with the idea. Cicero observes that when a public official meets with success it is critically important for the official to avoid haughtiness, scorn, and anger.[93] This is based on his previously articulated principle that a person deserving of glory should carry himself according to virtue and reason when faced with either the temptation of pleasure or the fear of pain. Lack of virtue is manifest in an overreaction to success, which would in turn diminish the official's glory. Cicero contends that a person who has become over-confident through repeated success must be educated regarding the frailty and variability of human affairs. He concludes that the more one excels, the more humbly that person should behave.[94] Humility is thus conceived as an element of wisdom that corrects the ignorance associated with lack of failure. The wise and virtuous person will have humility to the extent that it allows him to see his own limitations and the fortuitous aspects of his success.

Plotinus as a Precedent to Augustine's Moral Thought

A last school of philosophy with significant parallels in the thought of Augustine was the Platonist school that emerged in the third century and was to have significant influence on fourth-century Christian thinkers. Plotinus (b. 205) was a Greek Egyptian who initially studied in Alexandria under the philosopher Ammonius. Viewed by modern scholars as the founder of the neo-Platonic school of thought, Plotinus was the leading expositor of Platonism in the third century and was of great influence in the Milanese Christian circles to which Augustine was exposed prior to his conversion to Catholicism in 386 AD.[95] Plotinus is an eloquent exponent of the Platonic hierarchy of existence, which provides the context in which he situates his description of human excellence. Developing the thought of Plato and Aristotle, the metaphysical system proposed by Plotinus explains existence as a process of emanation in which the existence of lower beings is generated and explained by the existence of higher principles.

The metaphysical hierarchy of Plotinus provides the principles through which he portrays the pursuit and achievement of human greatness. For

93. Cicero, *De Officiis* 1.90.

94. Ibid.

95. Cf. Brown, *Augustine*, 81–85 for a description of the late fourth century Milanese intellectual culture.

Plotinus, humans as composite beings must turn from the lower realities of matter and sensible existence toward the forms of intellect and the unity of the One if they are to achieve their highest destiny, which is union with the One. In doing so, the person becomes, in the words of Plotinus, like to God.[96] To demonstrate the process in which one becomes god-like, I will first discuss Plotinus' conception of the indeterminateness of evil that a person must overcome in his pursuit of the good. Having examined the Plotinian conception of evil, I will then turn to Plotinus's discussion of the mechanism through which a person rises above evil to become god-like, which is virtue.

Moral Evil as the Antithesis of Human Excellence

Plotinus's metaphysical hierarchy holds strong implications for his notion of evil and his understanding of human greatness. He begins the treatment of his view of evil by noting that opposites are known by one and the same knowledge. This being the case, he proposes to examine evil by first giving attention to its opposite, the good.[97] Plotinus asserts that intellect is the first act of the One, or the good, so goodness can be equated to the many forms that comprise intellect.[98] Since goodness is comprised of form, it follows that its opposite—evil—is the absence of form. He concludes that form is better than its absence, and therefore, privation of form is evil:[99]

> Evil cannot be included in what really exists or in what is beyond existence; for these are good. So it remains that if evil exists, it must be among non-existent things as a sort of form of non-existence, and pertain to one of the things that are mingled with non-being or somehow share in non-being. Non-being here does not mean absolute non-being but only something other than being.[100]

Matter as completely indefinite is the absence of form and thus can be equated to evil in Plotinus's system.[101] In the absence of form, matter (con-

---

96. Plotinus, *Enn.* I.2.1.

97. Plotinus, *Enn.* I.8.1. See also O'Brien, "Plotinus on Matter and Evil," 175–78 for a discussion on the opposing relationship between matter and form.

98. Plotinus, *Enn.* I.8.2.

99. Ibid., I.8.1.

100. Ibid., I.8.3.

101. O'Brien, "Plotinus on Matter and Evil," 176.

sidered in itself) is absolutely deficient. Matter is essential evil for Plotinus because it has no contact with the good of form and intellect.[102]

Returning to the hierarchical scheme of Plotinus, we remember that matter is the lowest level of existence, so low that it barely fits the description of being. Within the Plotinian hierarchical context, matter is in contact with soul, the next higher level of being. Through matter's reception of form from its contact with the soul, individual sensual beings are generated. Soul, as a higher level of existence and unlike matter, is intellectual due to its participation in and contact with intellect. Yet soul, even though it is generated from the higher realm of the intellect, still chooses to mingle itself with matter. Plotinus poses an answer to the question of how it is that soul as the generated product of intellect, which is the foundation of goodness, would choose the indeterminacy and evil of matter. For Plotinus, the cause of the soul's fall or its turn to evil lies in the soul's audacity. The soul comes to be in sensible existence through its desire to belong to itself. Delighted with its own independence, the soul turns toward matter,[103] thus enabling it to become part of a composite being.[104] Plotinus uses the term *tolma*, understood as the soul's willful desire for otherness and self-determination, to designate the motive driving the soul to embrace matter and involve itself in temporal processes.[105] As an element of a composite being, the soul mistakenly delights in other composite beings, which are lower than the good of intellect. Plotinus asserts that the soul's inclination toward matter as opposed to a movement toward the good of intellect constitutes its own ugliness. The ugly and impure soul is dragged downward toward objects of sense, is focused upon bodily concerns, and consorts much with matter. A soul sunken in matter is dissolute and unjust, full of lusts, sunk in fear and petty jealousy, and is consumed by impure pleasures and bodily sensations.[106] Such is the face of moral evil, the antithesis of human greatness, in the thought of Plotinus.

102. Plotinus, *Enn.* I.8.5. Cf. *Enn.* II.4 for a discussion on the nature of matter and its relation to evil.

103. Plotinus, *Enn.* V.1.1.

104. Plotinus, *Enn.* I.8.14.

105. Plotinus, *Enn.* V.1.1.

106. Plotinus, *Enn.* I.6.5.

Virtue as Likeness to God

Plotinus addresses ethics explicitly in his treatises *On Virtue* (*Ennead I.2*) and *On Beauty* (*Ennead I.6*), which despite its name principally concerns morality rather than aesthetics.[107] The goal of the moral life for Plotinus is for an individual to become like to the good, or as he more frequently puts it, to be like to God:[108] "Our concern . . . is not to be out of sin, but to be God."[109] It is sometimes difficult to distinguish what Plotinus means by God since he uses the term in reference to both intellect and the One. In *On Virtue,* the discussion in reference to God seems to imply intellect, especially in the dialogue concerning the absence of virtue in God.[110] In *On Beauty,* on the other hand, God likely refers to the One since Plotinus discusses God as the ultimate end of the soul and the end referred to is one in which principles are joined into a unity (e.g., the good and beauty are the same in God) rather than a diversity of principles.[111] From a practical perspective, however, the distinction is not crucial because the soul seeking the good will continue on past intellect to the One in the same manner that it had been seeking intellect. Contact with the One is achieved through intellect, which is the path a person must take to realize his or her potential excellence.

The moral life, or the mission to become godlike, starts with the soul that is mired in the indeterminateness of matter. Despite the fact that the soul for Plotinus is generated by intellect—the source of all goodness in the sensible universe—he goes so far as to say that the soul is evil when entirely mixed with the body.[112] Plotinus makes this assertion on the basis of his distinction between the higher and lower soul. The lower soul as an image of the higher is mixed with the indeterminateness of matter and becomes the source of evil for the higher. In order to free itself from evil, the lower soul must reverse its orientation and begin its ascent up the chain of being to the height of goodness in intellect and the One. The first step in this process is to reject the formlessness of matter and return to pure form.[113] Since matter is located in external sensible beings, the turn away from matter consists in

---

107. Dillon, "Ethic for Antique Sage," 319.

108. Plotinus, *Enn.* I.2.1.

109. Ibid., I.2.6.

110. Ibid., I.2.1.

111. Ibid., I.6.6.

112. Ibid., I.2.3.

113. Dillon, "Ethic for Antique Sage, 329.

the turn of attention from things external to what is internal to the soul.[114] By turning inward toward the soul, a person is also turning toward the soul's origin in intellect, which is the source of goodness. Plotinus characterizes this inward turn away from matter as purification. The soul is purified when it draws away from the body and is completely unaffected by bodily disturbances. The soul that can distance itself from all pleasures, pains, passions, emotions, fears, and desires of the body will be pure and can begin to contemplate the purity of form.[115] Rather than wallowing in the mud and filth of matter, the pure soul, like gold that has been removed from the earth and cleansed of all debris, is beautiful in its purity.[116]

Following Plato's lead in the *Phaedo*, Plotinus goes on to equate purification with virtue.[117] It is through the virtues that the soul purifies itself:

> Since the soul is evil when it is thoroughly mixed with the body and shares its experiences and has all the same opinions, it will be good and possess virtue when it no longer has the same opinions but acts alone—this is intelligence and wisdom—and does not share the body's experiences—this is self-control—and is not afraid of departing from the body—this is courage—and is ruled by reason and intellect, without opposition—this is justice. One would not be wrong in calling this state of the soul likeness to God, in which its activity is intellectual, and it is free in this way from bodily affections.[118]

It is by means of virtue that the soul detaches itself from bodily concerns. This is to say, virtue is the mechanism that enables the soul to turn from the sensible and approach the intelligible.[119] Wisdom aligns the soul with the forms of intellect rather than the opinions of composite beings. Self-control or temperance allows the soul to detach itself from bodily pleasures. Courage conquers the fear of death common to composite beings. Justice allows the soul to rule its behavior by the dictates of reason and intellect rather than those of the body.[120]

---

114. Plotinus, *Enn.* I.6.9.

115. Ibid., I.2.5.

116. Ibid., I.6.5.

117. Gerson, *Plotinus*, 199.

118. Plotinus, *Enn.* I.2.3.

119. Ibid., 6.9.

120. Ibid., 2.3.

Plotinus maintains that it is the desire of every soul to ascend to the good.[121] The ascent to the good consists in the soul's ability to see the forms of intellect.[122] Such vision is impossible without the purification of the soul, and since Plotinus equates purification with moral virtue, it is by means of moral virtue that the soul begins the ascent. Virtue is required for the soul to turn away from the body and its affections and begin its interior trek toward the good. One cannot turn toward intellect and the One without the purification effected by virtue. Purification, i.e., virtue, turns the soul to the intelligible realm.[123] The purification of moral virtue is critical to the soul's pursuit of the good because the unpurified soul is incapable of seeing the good. To see the beauty of form, the soul must put on the beauty of virtue, and in this way, become like to form, or become god-like.[124]

Despite its importance, however, moral virtue is not the means by which the soul attains the good. Moral virtue is a process of purification that aims at something beyond itself.[125] It is a prerequisite for achieving the good; that is, the good cannot be achieved by a person who lacks moral virtue. The good, however, transcends moral virtue; as a consequence, moral virtue does not constitute happiness for Plotinus.[126] This is the case for two reasons. First, moral virtue, which results from training and habit, is a reality belonging to the composite nature of the lower soul and the body. It is not by the moral virtues that one sees the forms of intellect. This is the province of the intellectual virtues, which belong to the higher soul.[127] The virtue of wisdom contemplates the forms of intellect,[128] and in so doing, enables the soul to become god-like.[129] It is the intellectual nature of the higher soul and its virtue that provides the link to intellect itself.[130]

---

121. Ibid., 6.7. Cf. Gerson, *Plotinus*, 188 who characterizes the position of Plotinus as an assertion that it is only in union with the One that the desires of the soul can be satisfied.

122. Plotinus, *Enn.* I.6.9.

123. Ibid., 2.4. Cf. Gerson, *Plotinus*, 199.

124. Plotinus, *Enn.* I.6.9.

125. Gerson, *Plotinus,* 199.

126. Ibid., 191.

127. Plotinus, *Enn.* I.1.10.

128. Ibid., I.2.6.

129. Ibid., I.2.2.

130. See Gerson, *Plotinus,* 200 for a discussion of Plotinus' distinction between lower and higher virtues.

The second reason the good transcends moral and even intellectual virtue is the fact that virtue is a state of the soul by which it participates in form, but it is not a characteristic of intellect. Intellect, according to Plotinus, has no states. The intellectual activity of soul relies on virtue for its proper functioning. This is not the case for intellect. There is no virtue in intellect.[131] The forms of intellect are the foundations for the virtues of the souls, but in themselves are beyond the virtues.[132] For example, the existence of justice in the soul is a virtue, but it exists as an archetype in intellect. The soul participates in the principle of justice existing in intellect by way of the virtue of justice; but again, this does not necessitate the presence of virtue in intellect. It merely illustrates the dependence of the lower principle—in this case the virtue of justice—upon the higher, which is intellect's archetype of justice. Thus, virtue—both intellectual and moral—is for Plotinus the means through which the soul pursues the good. The soul's participation in form and its ability to become god-like is dependent upon the purification of the soul through the moral virtues, which in turn enables the intellectual virtues to see and participate in the good.

The ethical thought of Plotinus was certainly in continuity with the eudaimonistic approach characteristic of classical philosophy. Like other Greek ethicists, Plotinus offers an intellectual and other-worldly morality.[133] Although his ethical approach ignored many of the primary issues raised by Aristotle in the *Nichomachean Ethics* (virtue as the mean, practical syllogisms, etc.), he does concur with Aristotle's position positing the end of the human person as the life of contemplation.[134] This is despite Plotinus's consideration that Aristotle's view of the unmoved mover as self-thinking thought mistook intellect for the One.[135] With its focus on indifference toward external goods (composite beings and matter for Plotinus), Stoic morality seems to play a more significant role in his ethical thought. Plotinus adds to this indifference the notions of purification[136] and

131. Ibid., 199.

132. Plotinus, *Enn.* I.2.3.

133. Dillon, "Ethic for Antique Sage," 319, 331. Cf. Brown, *Augustine*, 84, for a discussion of Platonism's other-worldly character. Cf. Kenney who asserts Platonism's importance in offering philosophical support for immaterial reality. Kenney, *Mysticism of Augustine*, 51.

134. Dillon, "Ethic for Antique Sage," 331.

135. Plotinus, *Enn.* V.1.9.

136. Whittaker, *Neo-Platonists*, 91.

the transcendence of becoming god-like through virtue.[137] In the debate regarding the role of the external goods in relation to morality, Plotinus clearly sides with the position of the Stoics rather than that of Aristotle, viewing such goods as peripheral to virtue and morality.[138]

The moral thought and views of human greatness held by the classical philosophers examined in this chapter (with the exception of Aristotle) set a portion of the foundation upon which Augustine builds his own moral theory and view of human excellence. The following chapter will detail the presuppositions to Augustine's moral thought not primarily derived from the eudaemonistic ethics of his Greek and Roman predecessors. Those presuppositions find their roots in Augustine's interpretation of sacred Scripture, which forms the anthropological and moral principles that shape his view of humility and greatness.

137. Dillon, "Ethic for Antique Sage," 320.
138. Ibid., 331.

2

Foundations for Augustine's View of Humility and Greatness

Scripture, the Image of God, and Sin

IN MY EXAMINATION OF Augusine's view on greatness and humility, we will see that despite the important influence of classical philosophy on Augustine's thought, the preeminent influence on his thinking, especially as it developed and matured, was that of sacred Scripture. Scripture shaped Augustine's views on any number of topics, not least of which was his view of the relation between humility and human excellence. Also of great significance to his understanding of humility and greatness was Augustine's view of the human person as created in the image and likeness of God. Greatness for Augustine is defined by the person's status as God's image. Likewise, of great import for my topic is Augustine's view of the damage done to that image through sin and especially through the sin of pride. In Augustine's view, it is the evil of pride that humility must overcome if the human person is to achieve the greatness offered by creation in the image and likeness of God.

Links to Humility in Augustine's Interpretation of Scripture

Due to the pervasive presence of scriptural sources in Augustine's later work and in the development of his mature thought, one must examine not only the content of Scripture that shaped his views on humility and greatness, but also the methodology Augustine uses in his application of scriptural principles to those ideas. The principles he relies upon for his general understanding of Scripture, which include ideas such as the unity of Scripture and his figurative method of interpretation, also provides important insights to his view of humility and human excellence. In addition, while it is important to remain cognizant of the significance of Scripture to Augustine's understanding of humility, it is also beneficial to examine the role humility plays in his understanding of Scripture.

Augustine's Exegetical Methodology and its Relation to Humility

Over the course of Augustine's career as an exegete, one can discern a number of principles upon which he repeatedly depends to derive his understanding of Scripture's passages. The unity of Scripture is one such principle.[1] Augustine asserts that ". . . a believing eye finds both in the New Testament what they accuse in the Old and in the Old what they praise in the New."[2] Augustine's methodology in unlocking the meaning of obscure biblical texts manifests his consistent dependence upon the unity of Scripture as a presupposition to his exegesis. Augustine also explains the presence of obscure passages in addition to the plain texts of Scripture, observing that the latter satisfy a person's hunger for truth, while the former serve to stimulate one's appetite.[3] He asserts that ambiguities in Scripture should be clarified by reference to the context of the passage and through

---

1. Augustine accepted the unity of Scripture as he emerged from his adherence to Manichaean belief. The neo-Platonic position in which lower levels of reality image the truth contained in higher levels of existence helped Augustine overcome the Manichaean literalism that prevented him from seeing the unity of the Old and New Testaments. See Plotinus, *Enn.* V.9.4 for a sample text supporting the neo-Platonic view of the relation between lower sensible reality and higher intelligible reality. With that background, Augustine could approach the words of Scripture, understood to be imaging the higher truth of God, and not be tied to a literal interpretation of the words that seemed to separate the two testaments. See Augustine, *Mor.*, 1.14 (9) (WSA I/19:37) for one of many examples in which he relies on that unity by citing Pauline literature with the support of the Old Testament. See *Mor.* 1.34, 1.39, 1.42 for further examples of Augustine's use of Old Testament texts with that of the Pauline corpus. Cf. de Margerie, *History of Exegesis* and *Saint Augustine*, 12.

2. Augustine, *c. Adim.* 27 (WSA I/19:221). See also Freeman, "Figure and History, 320, for Augustine's view that the New Testament lies hidden in the Old and the Old is revealed in the New.

3. Augustine, *Doc. Chr.* 2.6.8.

the examination of its translation, which included the study of the original language of the passage and the comparison of different translations.[4] Augustine advocates bringing knowledge of history, natural science, and philosophy to bear in the effort to interpret a particular passage. His preference, however, is to use clear passages of Scripture to interpret the ambiguous texts.[5] The most skillful interpreters of Scripture, then, will be familiar with the whole of Scripture.[6] Augustine asserts that since everything relating to faith and morals can be found in the clear teachings of Scripture, one should first study the rules of life and faith as related by the biblical texts.[7] Once a person is familiar with the rules of the faith, the obscure passages can be approached using the rules as a guide for interpreting the texts that lack clarity.[8] Augustine's use of Scripture to interpret Scripture and his assertion that such is the best method to clarify ambiguous texts demonstrates his commitment to Scripture's underlying unity. Were Scripture to lack an underlying meaning and purpose, using passages from its disparate parts to clarify confusing texts would only add to that confusion rather than resolve it.

An example of this methodology applied to his treatment of humility can be seen in Augustine's teaching regarding the poor in spirit. Addressing the beatitude of Matthew's Gospel in which Jesus asserts that the poor in spirit will inherit the kingdom of heaven (Matt 5:3), Augustine asks what being poor in spirit might actually mean. His answer is taken from Luke's Gospel (Luke 14:11). In that passage, Jesus clearly asserts that anyone who humbles himself will be exalted. Equating exaltation with gaining the kingdom, Augustine asserts that the poor in spirit are those who humble themselves.[9] This is just one of many examples in which Augustine clarifies the meaning of an opaque text regarding humility through recourse to a passage clearly annunciating the importance of humility. In this manner, Augustine is able to mine many texts not explicitly mentioning humility for insights into its nature.[10]

4. Ibid., 3.4.8.

5. Ibid., 3.28.39.

6. Ibid., 2.8.12.

7. Ibid., 2.9.14.

8. Ibid.

9. Augustine, S. 53.1 (WSA III/3:66).

10. See Augustine, S. 137:4 (WSA III/4:374), S. 169:9 (WSA III/5:227–28), S. 179:3 (WSA III/5:299) for further examples of texts without explicit statements on humility being interpreted to emphasize the importance of humility.

In addition to using the texts of Scripture to interpret different passages, Augustine also espouses allegorical interpretations of Scripture and the development of figural understandings to some of Scripture's passages.[11] Such an approach is supported by neo-Platonic metaphysics, a context within which the sensible words of Scripture are understood as allegorically representing an interior, intelligible truth of Scripture.[12] Ambrose, whose spiritual interpretation of the Law and Prophets was instrumental to Augustine's conversion, provided a precedent for Augustine's own work with the biblical texts. Recalling in the *Confessions* his delight in hearing Ambrose preach, Augustine remembered Ambrose advocating a Pauline verse as a principle for the interpretation of Scripture: "The letter kills, the Spirit gives life" (2 Cor 3:6).[13] Due in part to the influence of Ambrose, Augustine comes to the conclusion that a blind adherence to the letter of the text is the equivalent of subjecting spiritual reality to that of the flesh. "It is surely a miserable slavery of the soul to take signs for things, and to be unable to lift the eye of the mind above what is corporeal and created, that it may drink in eternal light."[14]

Augustine frequently uses allegorical interpretive methods in support of his view of humility when preaching on the parables of Jesus. An example can be seen in his interpretation of Christ's parable concerning the rich man and Lazarus (Luke 16:19–31). Augustine takes this parable to be a vindication of humility. He notes the incongruity in the fact that the poor Lazarus is brought to his reward in the bosom of Abraham, who was a man of significant means in his mortal life. Augustine asserts that it is not the poverty of Lazarus that draws him to Abraham's bosom, but the fact that he, like Abraham, is a person of humility. Augustine sees the humility of Abraham in Abraham's profession of faith in God, which led to his justification. Abraham, like all who are saved, is justified not by his own presumption, but by the grace of God. Augustine declares that the justification of Lazarus is likewise achieved through his humility, just as the condemnation of the rich man is not made on the basis of his material wealth but on the basis of

11. See Augustine, *Doc. Chr.* 3.5.9, 3.8.12 for texts that support the legitimacy and importance of figurative scriptural interpretation. See also *Doc. Chr.* 3.10.14, 3.11.17, 3.12.18 for principles that guide Augustine's figurative interpretation of Scripture.

12. Bonner, "Augustine as Biblical Scholar," 552.

13. Augustine, *Conf.* 6.4.6.

14. Augustine, *Doc. Chr.* 3.5.9.

the pride that wealth fostered.[15] For Augustine, the parable is a clear support for humility and an equally clear condemnation of pride.

The usefulness of figurative interpretation does not, however, give license to spiritual interpretation of any or all scriptural passages. If it is a mistake to interpret a figurative text literally, Augustine also asserts as mistaken the interpretation of a literal text figuratively.[16] Augustine distinguishes between figurative and literal texts by applying a criterion in which a literal interpretation cannot be held if such an interpretation would undermine purity of life or sound doctrine.[17] Thus, a passage that seems to attribute sin to God or a person of holiness must be interpreted in a figurative sense.[18]

Another manner in which Augustine applies the methodology of figural interpretation is through the establishment of a connection between two historical events or persons separated by time. The first event/person signifies itself, while simultaneously implying the later event/person, while the latter event/person is seen as the fulfillment of the first. Both events are regarded as historical, but imply a deeper meaning given their relationship.[19] An example of such figural exegesis can be seen in the relationship Augustine establishes between the rejection of Saul as king and his replacement by David and the later replacement of the Old Covenant in favor of Christ and the New Covenant.[20] Here we see the fruits of both Augustine's figurative interpretation of Scripture and his belief that disparate parts of Scripture are the best mechanisms through which to interpret its different texts.

Such manner of figural interpretation is yet another mechanism through which Augustine applies the teaching of scripture to his view of humility and greatness. For example, Augustine links David as a type to Christ, doing so in the context of the humility and greatness of each. David won his greatest victory—the defeat of Goliath—through his humble dependence on God.[21] Augustine explicitly links the humility of David as

15. Augustine, *S.* 14.4 (WSA III/1:318). See also Augustine, *S.* 15A:5 (WSA III/1:335–36) for a nearly identical interpretation of the same parable.

16. Augustine, *Doc. Chr.* 3.10.14.

17. Ibid.

18. Ibid., 3.12.18.

19. Auerbach,, "Figura," in *Scenes from the Drama of European Literature* (Minneapolis: University of Minnesota Press, 1984), 53 as cited in Freeman "Figure and History," 320.

20. Augustine, *City of God* 17.4.

21. Augustine, *S.* 32.12, 26 (WSA III/2:143, 148–49).

the shepherd of God's flock with the humility of Christ coming as a second shepherd to feed God's people. Distinguishing between Christ's divine and human natures, Augustine asserts that it is in the self-emptying of Christ as the eternal Son of God, it is by becoming human in the incarnation, that Christ plays the role of shepherd in the tradition of David's shepherding role. Augustine further declares that in his role as servant Christ is lifted up to the right hand of the Father, and he has "bestowed on him a name that is above every name" (Phil 2:9).[22] David's humility and exaltation is a figure of the humility and exaltation to be revealed in Christ's inauguration of the new covenant.

Scriptural Themes in Augustine's understanding of Humility

Augustine's thought on humility springs from his reading of both the Old and New Testaments. He asserts that divine doctrine directs the human pursuit of heaven by way of humble piety[23] and also observes that God teaches humility through both the words and examples contained in Scripture.[24] His references to Old Testament texts in regard to humility focus mainly on the wisdom literature with the Books of Psalms, Proverbs, and Sirach providing the most prominent support.[25] Augustine does not restrict himself, however, from other areas of the Old Testament as he also relies on figures such as Hannah, the mother of Samuel,[26] David,[27] and Abraham to confirm his positions on humility.[28]

Augustine derives some of his most important views regarding humility from Old Testament texts. On their basis, he asserts that God is especially

---

22. Augustine, *S.* 47:20 (WSA III/2:314–15).

23. Augustine, *Civ. Dei* 1.31.

24. Augustine, *S.* 218C.4 (WSA III/6:196).

25. As I examine Augustine's presentation of humility in his sermons, I will depict his significant dependence on the wisdom literature. The teachings of *Proverbs* and *Sirach* are particularly important as they provide explicit principles regarding the nature of pride and God's view of the humble person that Augustine sees as fundamental to his argument concerning humility.

26. Augustine, *Civ. Dei* 17.4.

27. Ibid., 17.20.

28. Augustine, *S.* 14:4 (WSA III/1:318).

concerned for the downtrodden and lowly of heart (Ps 145:14).[29] He also raises the epistemological aspect of humility in the context of Old Testament passages, contending that it is through humility that a person can learn God's law and so understand the nature of justification (Ps 119:71).[30] Augustine cites the book of Sirach (Sir 10:13) as the most prominent Old Testament text condemning the sin of pride,[31] but also uses the book (Sir 3:17-20) to support the relationship between humility and greatness.[32] Possibly the most frequently cited Old Testament text Augustine uses in regard to humility is Proverbs 3:34, which proclaims that God resists the proud, but gives aid to the humble.[33] Given his focus on the unity of Scripture, it is not surprising to see that Augustine uses the above texts to support and further the claims of the New Testament regarding humility.

Augustine's reliance on the texts of Scripture in support of humility only increases as we turn to the use he makes of the New Testament. Applying his distinction between the words and examples of Scripture that uphold the value of humility can help catalogue the many instances in which Augustine relates the importance of humility via his reading of the New Testament. Turning first to the words of Scripture, we see Augustine refer to both the explicit teachings of Jesus, as well as his many parables to reinforce his emphasis on humility. For example, Augustine cites the importance of humility in the focus of Jesus on the value of children. It is only by humbling oneself like a small child that a person can achieve heavenly glory (Matt 18:2–4).[34] Augustine maintains that the parable of the tax collector and the Pharisee is a potent depiction of the power of humility. The Pharisee, he contends, is the picture of pride who will not participate in the justification received by the tax collector humiliated by his sin (Luke 18:9–14).[35] Augustine also makes indirect use of Proverbs 3:34 in his references to the Letter of James and the First Letter of Peter in which each of the New Testament authors derive their advocacy for

---

29. Augustine, *Conf.* 11.31.41.

30. Augustine, *S.* 25:5 (WSA III/2:84).

31. Augustine, *S.* 346B.3 (WSA III10/82).

32. Augustine, *S.* 292.4 (WSA III/8:140).

33. Augustine, *Civ. Dei* Preface Book 1. See also Augustine, *Conf.* 1.1.1, 4.15.26 and Augustine, *S.* 218C.4 (WSA III/6:196).

34. Augustine, *S.* 82.6 (WSA III/3:372).

35. Augustine, *S.* 115.2 (WSA III/4:199–200).

humility from the idea that God resists the proud and bestows favor on the humble (Jas 4:6, 1 Pet 5:5).[36]

In addition to the teachings of Jesus, Augustine sees examples of humility in many of the most important figures of the New Testament. He considers Paul, Barnabas, and Peter all to be models of humility.[37] In the case of Paul, his earlier identity as Saul—the prideful persecutor of the Church—is transformed when Saul receives the garment of humility.[38] In his interpretation of Paul's conversion story, Augustine attributes the stumbling of Saul to the blindness caused by the tumor of his pride, which is healed by the humility of Christ.[39] Augustine sees Peter as a symbol of humility both in the accounts of Peter's denial of Jesus (Matt 26:69–75, Mark 15:66–72, Luke 22:54–62, John 18:15–17, 25–27) and in Christ's post-resurrection command for Peter to tend to his flock (John 21:15–19). In Peter's denial of Christ prior to the crucifixion, Augustine sees a scene in which God briefly abandons Peter as a humiliation that will spiritually fortify him in the future.[40] Augustine similarly interprets Christ's charge for Peter to tend his sheep as implying humility. Christ is directing Peter to follow in his own footsteps as the shepherd that guides his flock in the humility and the ignominy of his passion and death.[41] In his *Commentary on Galatians*, Augustine further notes Peter's superlative humility in accepting the public rebuke of Paul in the midst of the controversy concerning gentile observance of the Jewish Law.[42] John the Baptist is yet another New Testament figure Augustine singles out as a role model for humility. Augustine refers to the Gospels of both Matthew and John as he describes the humility embodied in the Baptist. Augustine notes John's humility in his attempt to subordinate himself to Christ as Christ approached him for baptism (Matt 3:13–16).[43] He also places John in the company of Jesus as one who has come to show the way of humility. This is demonstrated in the Baptist's assertion that he is not worthy to lift the sandal of the one who is to come after him (John 1:27).[44] We can see through the above examples

---

36. Augustine, *S.* 23A.4 (WSA III/2:70). Augustine, *S.* 218C.4 (WSA III/6:196).

37. Augustine, *S.* 198.13 (WSA III/11:190-91).

38. Augustine, *S.* 168.6 (WSA III/5:220).

39. Augustine, *S.* 169.9 (WSA III/5:228).

40. Augustine, *S.* 229/O.1(WSA III/6:323–24).

41. Augustine, *S.* 137.4 (WSA III/4:374).

42. Augustine, *Augustine's Commentary on Galatians*, 2.11.

43. Augustine, *S.* 292.4 (WSA III/8:140).

44. Augustine, *S.* 293A.3-4 (WSA III/11:254–55).

that Augustine does not hesitate to promote humility through the words and actions of the major figures of the New Testament. As I will show later in my study, this is most truly the case in Augustine's interpretation of the words and deeds of Jesus himself.

The Image of God and Its Impact on Anthropological and Epistemological Elements in Augustine's View of Humility and Greatness

Two presuppositions to Augustine's moral thought that have important ramifications for his understanding of humility and greatness are his view of the human person as created in the image and likeness of God (Gen 1:26–27) and his distinction between knowledge and wisdom. The human person's imaging of God has a direct impact on Augustine's understanding of humility and greatness both in its trinitarian and Christological aspects. For Augustine, the imaging of the triune God by the human person constitutes its greatest honor and dignity.[45] In addition, he sets the humble example of Christ as the paradigm both for the humility that the human person should imitate and the greatness that flows from such humility. Turning to Augustine's view of the relation between knowledge and wisdom, one sees an understanding that sets him apart from his Greek predecessors[46] and serves as a critical link between his understanding of morality and the human person's greatest good in the intellectual possession of God. For Augustine, the transition from the knowledge of earthly things to the conception of things divine that constitutes wisdom is a transition from the humble things of earthly existence to the sublimity of eternal existence.

Augustine's View of the Human Person as Created in the Image and Likeness of God

Unlike his Greek and Roman predecessors, Augustine views the human person as created by and for the God of Jesus Christ. He succinctly articulates the implications of this view in his famous statement to God at the beginning of the *Confessions*, "You have made us for yourself, and our heart

---

45. Augustine, *Trin.* 12.3.16.
46. Ibid., 14.1.3.

is restless until it rests in you."[47] Augustine's anthropology is founded upon the assertion in the text of Genesis that the human person is created in the image and likeness of God (Gen 1:26–27). He makes extraordinary use of this idea in *The Trinity*, where he uses the concept of the human person imaging his creator, the *Imago Dei*, as the mechanism through which to explore the nature of the triune God. It is in this context that Augustine details his view of the human person's image of and likeness to God. Referencing the plural language of the Genesis account, he asserts that the human person is created in the image of the Trinity.[48] In contrast to the human imaging of the Trinity, Augustine distinguishes the manner in which the Son is an image of the Father within the Holy Trinity. The Son as image of the Father is born of the Father and is perfectly equal to the Father.[49] Christ, the Son, images the Father by being the divine light that illuminates all created beings.[50] Human persons, on the other hand, are made by the Father through the Son. Humans are images of God because they are illuminated by Christ's divine light. In addition, the human person images the triune God through his mind rather than his body[51] and is preserved in God's image by remaining oriented toward God, who provides the illumination that constitutes the human image of the divine.[52]

In *The City of God* Augustine provides a summary of the nature of the human person's image of God:

47. Augustine, *Conf.* 1.1.1.

48. Augustine, *Trin.* 12.2.6.

49. Although I have emphasized the continuity between the thought of Plotinus and Augustine, the equality of the Father and Son is one among many points where Augustine's Christian theology clearly contradicts the philosophy of Plotinus. In this case, the parallel relationship in Plotinus of the One to intellect (as opposed to the Christian relationship of the Father to the Son) clearly subordinates intellect to the One (e.g., *Enn.* V.1.6).

50. Augustine, *Trin.* 7.2.5.

51. Ibid., 12.3.12.

52. Ibid., 12.3.16. Augustine's above portrait of God's image in the human person draws its foundations from Christian scripture, Neo-Platonic metaphysics, and Stoic ethics. The idea of the human person's image of God is taken from the text of Genesis (Gen 1:26–27), but is supported by Plotinus's use of the idea of image as the relation between lower and higher levels of existence (*Enn.* V.2.2). The orientation of the person toward God as the act that maintains the image is likewise supported by the Plotinian idea that lower levels of existence image the higher by looking toward and being illuminated by the higher (*Enn.* V.2.2). The emphasis of the value of eternal goods over temporal goods echoes the Stoic preference for virtue over external goods (*De Finibus* 3.11) and has direct links to Plotinus's call to value eternal goods over those of body and matter (*Enn.* I.6.5).

> Contemplating His image in ourselves, therefore, let us, like that younger son of the Gospel, come to ourselves, and arise and return to Him whom we had forsaken by our sin. In Him our being will have no death, our knowledge will have no error, and our love will know no check. In our present state, we believe that we possess these three things—being, knowledge, and love.[53]

For Augustine, the trinitarian image of God in the human person consists in that person's existence, the person's knowledge of their existence, and the love the person has for both her existence and the knowledge of her existence.[54] Since the human person images God through her mind, it is in the function and operation of the mind that the person most truly participates in the image and likeness of God. The image reaches the apex of its likeness to God when it recollects God, understands God, and loves God on the basis of that understanding.[55]

Due to the fact that the image of God in the human person is manifest in the intellectual capacity of the mind, Augustine's theory of knowledge sheds important light on his understanding of the image and his understanding of human greatness. Within Augustine's distinction between knowledge and wisdom, we see yet another area where the continuity between humility and greatness is pertinent. It is within the intellectual structure of the image that Augustine develops his moral thought. As a result of Augustine's focus on the human mind as the image of God, the principles through which he envisions the human person pursuing his end of intellectual union with God become faith, love, and wisdom. It is in loving and knowing that the person undertakes the moral activity necessary for the intellectual possession of God, which Augustine sees as the source of human happiness and the height of human dignity.[56]

Knowledge and Wisdom in Augustine's Morality

Many have asserted that the notion of love is the factor that drives Augustine's moral thought.[57] It is plainly true that one cannot give an account of Augustine's conception of morality and virtue without recourse to the

53. Augustine, *Civ. Dei* 11.28.

54. Ibid., 11.26.

55 Augustine, *Trin.* 14.4.15.

56. Augustine, *Eighty-Three Different Questions* 35.1.

57. Carney, "Structure of Augustine's Ethic," 28.

central role played by love in his thought. As a result, the majority of the analysis I will offer regarding Augustine's morality will focus on the concepts and interrelations of love, will, and virtue. Despite the importance of love and these related concepts, one cannot give a coherent explanation of Augustine's moral thought without addressing the critical roles played by faith and the truth of wisdom. In his essay "The Structure of Augustine's Ethic," Frederick Carney asserts that truth plays a role as significant as that of love in Augustine's moral thought. For Carney, truth and love form a "double matrix" of principles around which Augustine constructs his ethic. They operate in parallel, neither being reducible to the other.[58] Whether one agrees with Carney regarding the importance of truth relative to love in Augustine's morality or not, his argument that truth plays a critical role in that morality is certainly valid. In my examination of Augustine's moral thought, we will see that the knowledge of faith is an early way station on Augustine's path of moral perfection, which ends in wisdom understood as true knowledge of God.

Carney's description, however, does not address two significant features of Augustine's thought regarding the cognitive aspects of morality. The first is the division Augustine asserts between knowledge and wisdom, which is grounded in St. Paul's distinction between the spirit of wisdom and the spirit of knowledge (1 Cor 12:8).[59] Augustine describes the relation between the two in the context of an inward turn away from the nature humans share with animals—what he calls the outer person—toward the cognizance of intelligible and eternal being. On the path to eternal intelligible things one encounters the rational apprehension of temporal objects.[60] The thought concerning transitory things through which a person makes good use of temporal objects is a function of the lower soul, which Augustine labels *scientia*, or knowledge.[61] Such intellectual activity is distinct from both the activity of beasts and the apprehension of eternal truth. The understanding of eternal, unchanging truth, on the other hand, belongs to Augustine's category of wisdom, *sapientia*. As the highest function of the human mind, wisdom grasps the supreme truths of intelligible reality.[62]

---

58. Ibid., 28–29.

59. Augustine, *Trin.* 12.4.25, 12.4.22.

60. Ibid., 12.4.25.

61. Ibid., 12.4.22, 12.4.25.

62. Ibid.

The second feature absent from Carney's account is the Plotinian aspect of Augustine's moral thought in which love builds the foundation upon which wisdom stands in its acquisition of the human person's end in the vision of God. Recalling the Gospel of Matthew where the evangelist asserts that only the pure in heart will see God (Matt 5:8), Augustine asserts that love working through the virtues purifies the human person and thus enables the person to know God, which represents the pinnacle of human wisdom.[63] In similar fashion to Plotinus, Augustine advocates for a purification of the soul achieved through the development of virtue that enables a person to see the divine. Knowledge (in particular the knowledge of faith), love, and the truth of wisdom each represent a stage in Augustine's moral thought through which every person must pass in the pursuit of happiness.

In my analysis of the relations between humility and faith and humility and wisdom, we will see the flowering of the love for God in which the humble knowledge of faith is transformed into the sublimity of eternal wisdom, which consists in the knowledge of God. Before addressing that transition, however, we must also account for the moral implications of sin's effect on the human person's image of God. Sin, for Augustine, and its foundation in the sin of pride, establishes another important context for his understanding of humility and its importane to moral greatness as the antithesis of pride.

Sin: The Historical Condition of the Image

According to Augustine, the image of God in the human person is deformed when the person turns from the eternal good of God and chooses temporal goods in preference to God's goodness.[64] His view takes its starting point from Adam's fall in the account of Genesis and the disastrous consequences brought on by that fall. For Augustine, sin's effect on the image of God in the human person is truly profound. Sin deforms and disables the very functions provided to the person by God's image. The human person's knowledge of truth is diminished by sin, and the will lacks the ability to love what is good. Augustine asserts that the punishment for sin carries the loss of the power to know what is right. In addition, the will to do what is right is impaired due to the resistance of carnal habit, which is built up

63. Cf. Augustine, *Trin.* 8.3.6 regarding love's purificatory effect. See also Augustine, *Mor.* 15.25 for Augustine's view of virtue as the perfect love for God.

64 Augustine, *Trin.* 14.5.22.

through sinful activity.[65] In Augustine's view, the inescapable effects of sin are truly bewildering and corrupting. Through sin,

> . . . lust dominates the mind, despoils it of the wealth of its virtue, and drags it, poor and needy, now this way and now that; now approving and even defending what is false as though it were true, now disapproving what it previously defended, and rushing on to other falsities; now refusing assent and fearing clear reasoning; now despairing of fully discovering the truth and clinging to the deep obscurities of stupidity; now struggling into the light of understanding and falling back again from weariness. Meanwhile, the reign of lust rages tyrannically and distracts the life and whole spirit of man with many conflicting storms of terror, desire, anxiety, empty and false happiness, torture because of the loss of something that he used to love, eagerness to possess what he does not have, grievances for injuries received, and fires of vengeance. Wherever he turns, greed amasses, extravagance wastes, ambition entices, pride bloats, envy twists, sloth buries, obstinacy goads, submissiveness harasses, and all the other innumerable things that throng and busy themselves in the kingdom of lust.[66]

Although in his earliest works Augustine views evil lust as the source of sin,[67] he later makes the transition to placing sin's origin in the disordered love of self he understands as pride.

The nature of evil is one of the earliest and most significant issues Augustine seeks to address in his philosophical thought. Shortly after reading Cicero's *Hortensius*, Augustine's effort to understand why the human person commits acts of evil led him to embrace the Manichees and their teaching on good and evil.[68] The dualism of the Manichees, which seeks to protect the goodness of God from evil by positing a second original principle from which all evil derives, later gives way in Augustine's mind to the Platonist conception of good and evil. In the metaphysical structure of Plotinus and the neo-Platonists, evil consists in a turning away from the

---

65. Augustine, *Lib. Arb.* 3.18.52.

66. Ibid., 1.11.22.

67. Ibid., 1.4.10.

68. Felix the Manichean gives a defense of the dualistic Manichean approach to good and evil Augustine had accepted in his youth in Augustine's *c. Fel.* 2.2 (WSA I/19:299–300). Cf. Augustine, *Conf.* 3.7.12 which mentions the notion of evil as one of the issues to which Augustine assented during his time as a Manichee. Cf. Brown, *Augustine*, 35 for an account of Augustine's attraction to the Manichees on the basis of their teaching concerning evil.

One and intelligibility toward formlessness and non-being.[69] Augustine formulates his notion of sin by placing his understanding of love within the context of this conception of evil as the turning away from eternal and spiritual good toward the non-being of temporary goods. To love God, the eternal good, and order one's actions in accordance with that love is to do good. To represent the love of God, Augustine most often uses the term *caritas*. To do evil, or sin, on the other hand is to desire a temporary good for itself—i.e., to love that temporary good. Such love Augustine labels *cupiditas*, which he understands to be a wrongful desire, and it is *cupiditas* that the early Augustine identifies as the root of all sin.[70]

Augustine's depiction of *cupiditas* is focused on its intrinsic disorder and the negative consequences to which it inevitably leads. He does not consider the temporary goods that are the object of *cupiditas* evil. Anything that exists, as a product of God's creative activity, is to a certain extent good.[71] Evil lies in the will's choice to love such goods for themselves.

> The will, however, commits sin when it turns away from immutable and common goods, toward its private good, either something external to itself or lower than itself. It turns to its own private good when it desires to be its own master; it turns to external goods when it busies itself with the private affairs of others or with whatever is none of its concern; it turns to goods lower than itself when it loves the pleasure of the body. Thus a man becomes proud, meddlesome, and lustful; he is caught up in another life which, when compared to the higher one, is death.[72]

Cupiditas, for Augustine, is a disordered love that leads to unhappiness. As love, *cupiditas* moves the person toward the object of its desire. This movement is problematic because the temporary objects to which *cupiditas* is ordered cannot provide happiness to the human person. Since temporary goods can always be lost or taken from a person against her will, Augustine observes that desire for such goods is always accompanied by fear.[73] Augustine considers the fear associated with love of temporal objects to be

69. Plotinus, *Enn.* I. 8.3.

70. Augustine, *Lib. Arb.* 1.4.10. Augustine, *Mor.* 19.36. See also Babcock, "Cupiditas and Caritas," 47.

71. Augustine, *Lib. Arb.* 2.20.54.

72. Ibid., 2.19.53.

73. Augustine, *Div. Qu.* 33.

incompatible with true happiness.[74] In addition, Augustine does not admit that such goods provide happiness even when they are possessed. They lead only to false happiness, greed, and extravagance.[75] In addition to its failure to provide happiness, *cupiditas* is a degradation of a person's dignity. Following Stoic lines of thought in which desire for external goods makes a person dependant upon those goods for her happiness, Augustine asserts that love subjects a person to the thing that she loves. The human person—constituted in part by a spiritual soul—therefore becomes subjected to lower, material objects.[76] Still another harmful effect of *cupiditas* for Augustine is its promotion of conflict between one person and another. Due to the fear aroused by the possible loss of temporal goods, the lover of such goods will endeavor to eliminate any impediment that might hinder her from enjoying the goods she desires. Since often times the impediments to material goods are other people, lovers of these goods resort to evil and crime against others in order to safeguard or acquire possession of those goods.[77]

Augustine also sees evidence in Scripture for the condemnation of the desire for material goods. He cites Paul's First Letter to Timothy as support for that condemnation. Paul states that the desire for money or material goods is the root of all evil (1 Tim 6:10). Given Augustine's neo-Platonic conception of evil supporting the iniquity of *cupiditas*, its many negative effects on the human person, and Paul's denunciation of material desire, Augustine concludes in his early writing that *cupiditas* is indeed the foundation of human sin.[78]

Pride as the Source of Sin

Cupiditas, for Augustine, will remain one of the most important aspects of his understanding of sin throughout his writing career. Yet it loses its stature as the source of all sin as Augustine writes his commentaries on the narrative of Adam and Eve in Genesis and under the influence of his many philosophical/theological engagements over the course of his career.[79] In

74. Augustine, *B. Vita* 2.11.

75. Augustine, *Lib. Arb.* 1.11.22.

76. Augustine, *Mor.* 21.39.

77. Augustine, *Lib. Arb.* 1.4.10.

78. Ibid. See also Augustine, *Mor.* 19.36.

79. See also Burns, "Augustine on the Origin and Progress of Evil," 73 for his discussion of Augustine's transition between a material source of sin to a spiritual source; also

the depiction to follow, I will describe the intellectual context in which Augustine shifts his search for the source of sin from *cupiditas* to pride, or *superbia*, and will then depict Augustine's conception of pride and its relation to sin and *cupiditas*.

Augustine's shift to the idea of pride as the origin of sin is plainly rooted in his interpretation of Genesis. In addition to that interpretation, one can identify a number of intellectual influences that would lead Augustine to consider *superbia* as the source for sin rather than *cupiditas*. The Plotinian concept of *tolma* in which Plotinus identifies audacity and the willful desire for self-determination as the source of evil is a significant parallel to Augustine's understanding of *superbia*.[80] The influence of the Pauline corpus is also significant for Augustine's view of pride, especially in his interpretation of the Genesis text. In that interpretation, Augustine sees a parallel in the role of the command of God not to eat of the tree and the Pauline understanding of the role of the Law in revealing sin to human consciousness (Rom 7:7). Both the command and the Law function to manifest sin that would otherwise remain hidden.[81] Augustine's interpretation of the various controversies that engaged him over the course of his career also lends support to his focus on pride. Augustine sees elements of pride at work in the Manichaean denial of all moral responsibility and in the Donatist assertion that the merit of their bishops rather than God's grace was the foundation of the church's purity.[82] He also sees pride as the foundation of Pelagian perfectionism, the Platonist rejection of the incarnation, and in Rome's drive for glory and lust for domination.[83] Pride even makes the otherwise unfathomable reasoning behind Augustine's adolescent theft of the pears comprehensible, if not reasonable. Augustine admits no particular wrongful desire for the stolen pears. It is the perverse desire to act with impunity and autonomy along with the companionship of his fellow thieves that drives

---

80–82 for a description of Augustine's interpretation of events in support of *superbia* as the root of sin.

80. Plotinus, *Enn.* V.1.1. See Torchia, "Superbia," 66–80 for a discussion regarding the relation between *tolma* in the thought of Plotinus and *superbia* in Augustine's thought.

81. Augustine, *Civ. Dei* 14.13. God's command not to eat of the tree in paradise allows the spiritual transgression of Adam and Eve to be seen. See Burns, "Augustine on the Origin of Evil," 78 for a discussion of the revelatory aspect of the command in the Genesis narrative of humanity's fall.

82. Burns, "Augustine on the Origin of Evil," 80–81.

83. Ibid., 81–82.

him to the theft.[84] In the end, Augustine sees pride's persistent presence in the difficulties of human experience as a more likely candidate to account for the ubiquitous phenomenon of sin than the notion of *cupiditas*.

Pride: Love of Self Rather than Love for God

Augustine first identifies pride as the source of human sin in his work *De Genesi Adversus Manicheos*. Holding closely to the words of Genesis, he asserts that it is to Eve's and Adam's pride that the serpent appeals when he promises they would be like gods if they eat the forbidden fruit:

> We see from these words that they were persuaded to sin through pride, for this is the meaning of the statement "You will be like gods." So too he said, "For God knew that on the day that you eat from it, your eyes will be opened." What does this mean but they were persuaded to refuse to be under God and to want rather to be in their own power without God?[85]

Later in *The City of God,* Augustine maintains that the sin of pride exists in Adam and Eve prior to their outward act of disobedience. Augustine claims this to be the case because it is not credible from his perspective that an otherwise chaste mind would respond to the temptations of the serpent. Only a darkened and weakened will could take the serpent's words as truth. An evil will precedes their evil act and the source of this evil, for Augustine, is pride: a desire for a perverse elevation of self at the expense of God. Augustine cites the Book of Sirach (Sir 10:13) where pride is condemned as the source of sin in his justification of the premise that it must have been pride that first stirred the will to evil desire.[86] He also notes pride as the motivation for the excuses Adam and Eve offer to justify their transgression. In their dialogue with God, they do not humble themselves and seek God's pardon for their misdeed. Rather, they seek to assign the blame to another—in Eve's case the serpent and in Adam's his companion, Eve. Augustine asserts that it is pride that seeks to avoid blame for an evil deed.[87]

---

84. Augustine, *Conf.* 2.4.9. Cf. Burns, "Augustine on the Origin of Evil," 79–80.

85. Augustine, *Gn. adv. Man.* 2.15.22.

86. Augustine, *Civ. Dei* 14.13.

87. Ibid., 14.14.

Augustine declares that the love of self, or love of the self's excellence,[88] that constitutes *superbia* leads to further sin because it cuts the will off from God, its source of perfection. When turned toward God, the will is illuminated by God's light and given the fire of God's love to know and choose that which is good. Once the will turns to the self, it is cut off from the light and fire of God. In this chilled and darkened state, the will turns aside from the good and seeks its own pleasure:

> For it is a perverse kind of elevation indeed to forsake the foundation upon which the mind should rest, and to become and remain, as it were, one's own foundation. This occurs when a man is too well pleased with himself; and he is too well pleased with himself when he falls away from that immutable good with which he ought rather to have been pleased than with himself. This betrayal occurs as a free act of the will. For if the will had remained unshaken in its love of that higher and immutable Good by Which is bestowed upon it the light by which it can see and the fire by which it can love, it would not have turned aside from this Good to follow its own pleasure.[89]

The consequence and punishment for the sin of pride is the division of the human person against herself. Pride is the origin of the conflict between body and soul. The higher element, the soul, is now subjected to the lower, which is the body. "Man, who would have become spiritual even in his flesh had he kept the commandment, now became fleshly even in his mind."[90] Thus pride leads to the desire of bodily goods and can therefore be considered the root of *cupiditas* and all other sin. Both *superbia* and *cupiditas* are crucial to Augustine's understanding of sin. It is pride, however, or love of self, that is the source from which the evil desires of *cupiditas* spring.

Pride: An Ever-Present Danger

Not only does Augustine view pride as the source of sin, he also sees it as an insidious evil, able to corrupt and undermine any good human action. Augustine sees evidence for pride's uniquely corrosive effect in the cases of both the Pelagians and the Platonists. Augustine spends much of his later career combatting what he considered to be the dangerous form of pride

88. Augustine, *S.* 354.6 (WSA III/10:159).

89. Augustine, *Civ. Dei* 14.13.

90. Ibid., 14.15.

manifest in the teachings of Pelagius and his followers. He notes how the Pelagians justified their opinion that the grace of God is merited on the basis of a person's turning to God. Citing Scripture's support (Zech 1:3, 2 Chr 15:2), the Pelagians assert that grace will be given to the one who approaches God, thus placing the initiative for a person's relationship to God with the human person rather than with God.[91] Augustine counters that such passages are addressed to a person's will, but do not rule out the priority of God's grace in the relationship between God and the human person. He asserts that to interpret such passages as proving grace is merited is to ignore the overwhelming testimony of Scripture that the human turning to God is itself a gift from God.[92] Augustine considers the claim of the Pelagians to be particularly prideful because they are claiming the gifts of God by which they are justified as their own. The logic of the Pelagian position leads (in Augustine's view) to the most debilitating form of pride: that of self-righteousness. The source of a person's justification is now derived from his own human nature rather than the grace of God.[93]

Turning to the Platonists, we see that Platonic thought is, for Augustine, the best thought classical philosophy has to offer. The Platonists, after all, are the philosophers that had drawn closest to a Christian perspective, even discerning the end toward which the human soul is ordered.[94] Despite their achievement in seeing the nature of that end, however, according to Augustine they only see it from a distance and do not know the means by which to attain it.[95] In addition, pride serves to subvert the very achievements of the pagan philosophers. As they develop virtue and the ability to temper their emotions, they become proud and exult in that virtue. Through pride in their virtue, their haughtiness grows and ultimately yields persons bereft of any emotion—who have lost their humanity in a false tranquility.[96] Thus, pride is corrosive even of virtue's goodness. Platonism's great claim to the possibility of human perfection is dashed upon the rocks of human pride.[97] For Augustine, none but Christ escape the shadow of sin

91. Augustine, *Gr. et Lib. Arb.* 5.10–11.

92. Ibid., 5.10. Augustine cites the psalms among other scripture passages that demonstrate God as the agent turning the human will toward himself.

93. Burns, "Augustine on Origin of Evil," 81.

94. Augustine, *Civ. Dei* 8.5.

95. Augustine, *Conf.* 7.20.26.

96. Augustine, *Civ. Dei* 14.9.

97. Rist, *Augustine*, 18.

in this life (Rom 5:12).[98] Even the greatest among the human race, and many times the greatest in particular, are stalked by the sin of pride.

Pride's Antidote: Humility

Such are the ramifications of pride and sin for the human person, from Augustine's perspective. The ills, sorrows, and hardships of the present age are the just consequence of sin, which is also the cause of life's ultimate limitation in death.[99] In a sense, the existence of sin gives purpose to the moral life as conceived by Augustine because the purpose of the moral life is to restore the image of God in the human person who has been deformed by sin. The restoration of that image will yield happiness and immortal life.[100] Augustine understands the beginning of this restoration as God's gift of grace that establishes the humility of the human person in relation to God. The restoration of the image of God in the human person is the result of grace working with a person's free will to cure the debility of sin through a steady process of renewal.[101] It is within this context that Augustine establishes the importance of humility for the human person's destiny of eternal bliss in union with God. For Augustine, the only way to combat pride and achieve this destiny is the way demonstrated by Christ in his incarnation and death. God demonstrates his humility both by becoming human and by his death on the cross.[102] It is through Christ's humility that the tumor of human pride can be healed.[103] In the following chapters, I will describe Augustine's understanding of humility, the importance he places on it in the context of his moral thought, and how for Augustine, it is humility that enables a person to achieve his greatest calling.

98. Augustine, S. 165.7 (WSA III/5:205).

99. Augustine, Trin. 13.5.20.

100. Cf. Augustine, Trin. 13.3 for a discussion on the relation between happiness and immortality.

101. Augustine, Trin. 14.5.23.

102. Augustine, S. 68.11 (WSA III/3:230-31).

103. Augustine, Trin. 8.3.7.

3

Humility in Augustine's Moral Thought

AUGUSTINE'S NOTION OF PRIDE seems to take precedence over what he understands to be its antidote, the virtue of humility.[1] For Augustine, pride is the foundation of all sin and certainly takes a prominent role in his thought as that foundation.[2] Yet, while Augustine's focus on humility is by no means disconnected from his understanding of pride, pride is not the only perspective from which he approaches the idea of humility. Humility for Augustine has a significant, positive role to play both in his thought and in the lives of those entrusted to his pastoral care. Humility is a multi-dimensional concept that lies at the foundation of his moral theory.

Augustine derives his interest and dependence on the idea of humility from many of the principles I have discussed in my previous chapter. Pride, as I have mentioned, plays an important role in setting the context for his understanding of humility. So, too, does Augustine's interpretation of Scripture. As we will see in this chapter, Augustine's understanding of morality is also of fundamental importance to his position on humility and greatness. Augustine's views of faith, love, the will, grace, virtue, and wisdom all have consequences for his understanding of humility, and in turn, are affected by that understanding.

My goal in this chapter is to demonstrate the role humility plays within Augustine's moral thought. My demonstration will proceed through

1. Augustine, *Trin.* 8.3.7. Cf. Augustine, *S.* 123.1 (WSA III/4:244) and Augustine, *S.* 341.4 (WSA III/11:285). Each of the above texts is a sample in which Augustine characterizes humility as the medicine or mechanism through which pride is overcome.

2. Augustine, *Gn. Adv. Man.* 2.14.21–15.22. Augustine, *Civ. Dei* 14.13. Cf. Mac-Queen, "*Contemptus Dei*," 252–53.

four stages. In the first stage, I will evaluate the words that Augustine uses to describe the idea of humility. Secondly, I will describe the distinctive manner in which Augustine adapts and interprets the eudaemonistic moral tradition to which he is heir. Augustine's understanding of knowledge, love, and the human will distinguish his eudaemonist conception of morality from its classical antecedents. These concepts, along with Augustine's use of Scripture and his notion of pride, provide a critical role for humility in his moral structure that is absent in the thought of his Greek and Roman predecessors. Third, having described the moral structure of Augustine's thought, I will depict the role humility plays within that thought. As a primary effect of God's grace, humility is indispensable to Augustine's account of the manner in which a person pursues her high calling as the image and likeness of God. Lastly, I will describe the way Augustine's view of humility affects his understanding of the elements that comprise his moral thought. Faith, charity, the will, virtue, and wisdom are all interpreted and understood by Augustine in the light shed by his understanding of humility.

Humilitas in Augustine's Discussion of Humility

Augustine's training as a rhetorician and his voluminous writing gave him a facility with words matched by few. Despite his exceptional command of language, however, he was remarkably consistent in his use of the word *humilitas* when approaching the idea of humility. An examination of the manner in which he addresses humility in his sermons reveals his almost repetitive use of the word to represent the idea of humility. A query of *humilitas* and its cognates in the *Library of Latin Texts Series A* database reveals Augustine uses the word in excess of 1,600 times throughout his literary corpus.[3] Confining the query to Augustine's sermons, including his reflections on the psalms and Johannine writings, one finds *humilitas* used more than 1,100 times. It most frequently appears in connection with Christ (over 250 instances), *superbia* (more than one hundred times), and with various terms representing human greatness (just under ninety references).[4] Despite Augustine's consistent use of *humilitas*, he does make use of other synonyms when discussing humility. When he does use synonyms for *humilitas* they are usually drawn from scriptural sources. *Cor* (sixty-five references), *mitis* (fifty-two references), *pauper/paupertas* (twen-

3. Library of Latin Texts—Series A, http://clt.brepolis.net.proxycu.wrlc.org/.

4. Ibid.

ty-two references), *pius* (sixteen references), *infirmitas* (twelve references), and *paruuli* (six references) are all words Augustine uses in conjunction with *humilitas* to help fill out the meaning of particular arguments.[5] For example, Augustine typically combines the ideas of meekness and humility of heart in reference to Christ's admonition to be meek and humble of heart (Matt 11:29). [6] A similar example is his use of *paruuli*, or little ones, as the humble to whom God reveals the truth, as opposed to the wise from whom truth is hidden (Luke 10:21, Matt 11:25).[7] A last example of a frequently used term in relation to *humilitas* is *infirmitas*. The context of Augustine's use is again scriptural (2 Cor 12:9–10), and marks one of the more frequent ways in which Augustine links humility to greatness.[8] Despite Augustine's use of these related terms, *humilitas* is the dominant word he uses when discussing humility, particularly when discussing the humility of Christ (*humilitas Christi*).[9]

Augustine's Moral Structure as the Context for His Understanding of Humility

Augustine's view of morality is founded upon his understanding of the relationship between God and the human person revealed in sacred Scripture. Within this context, Augustine (like his classical forebears) is profoundly affected by the eudaemonist moral tradition of ancient Greek philosophy; that is to say, Augustine's ethical positions are structured around the question of the ultimate human good, which he identifies with human happiness.[10] Yet if Augustine can be classified as a eudaemonist, we must distinguish him from his Stoic and neo-Platonic predecessors and characterize him as a eudaemonist with a difference. That difference, of course, was rooted in his application of Christian Scripture to the moral framework he adopts from the Greek philosophers.

5. Ibid.

6. Augustine, *S*. 45.7 (WSA III/2:256).

7. Augustine, *S*.67.8 (WSA III/3:219).

8. See Augustine, *S*. 163.8 for Augustine's discussion of Paul's temptation to pride and the weakening God provides him to fight the temptation. See Augustine, *Trin*. 4.1.2 for an example of the link between *infirmitas* and *humilitas*.

9. See Augustine, *S*. 123.1 (WSA III/4:244) for a typical formulation concerning Christ's humility.

10. O'Donovan, *Self-Love in St. Augustine*, 16.

Scripture plays an enormous role in Augustine's understanding and articulation of the moral categories he adopts from classical philosophy. Examples of Scripture's influence on Augustine's morality are numerous and significant. Augustine moves beyond the Aristotelian notion of the highest good as an activity of the human person (i.e., the activity of contemplation) to the objective end of the transcendent Christian God.[11] Under the influence of Scripture's twofold command to love God and neighbor, Augustine integrates a Christian understanding of love with a characteristically eudaemonistic structure of happiness achieved through the cultivation of virtue.[12] In addition, submission to the commands of Scripture introduces an element concerned with obedience into Augustine's moral thought that was lacking in classical sources.[13] Through his anthropological confrontation with Pelagius and his followers, Augustine honed his view on the relation between nature and grace and its implications for the moral life on the basis of Scripture. The Pelagian controversy reinforces the most significant distinction between Augustine's approach to morality and that of Greek philosophy: the human person's inability to choose the good without the help of God's grace.[14] Lastly, Augustine's focus on pride as the original source of the human person's fall into sinfulness provides an important role for the virtue of humility that was quite foreign to classical morality.[15]

As a thinker who viewed true philosophy in distinctly theological terms, it is not surprising to find Augustine's morality to be an integration of both philosophical and theological principles. In tracing the broad outlines of his moral thought, one must begin with the foundation of that thought in Augustine's conception of the human person as created in the image and likeness of God (Gen1:26–27), which for Augustine, is the person's highest honor:

> For man's true honor is God's image and likeness in him, but it
> can only be preserved when facing him from whom its impression
> is received . . . And thus, since his honor consists in being like
> God and his disgrace in being like an animal, man established in

11. Ibid., 17.

12. Cf. Augustine, *Mor.* 15.25 for his assertion that virtue is the highest form of love for God.

13. Cf. Augustine, *Div. Qu.* 35.2 for an example of Augustine's emphasis on the importance of the great commandment to love God with one's whole strength.

14. Augustine, *Gr. et Lib. Arb.* 4.7.

15. Cf. Augustine, *Civ. Dei* 14.13 for Augustine's assertion that pride is the beginning of all sin.

honor did not understand; he was matched with senseless cattle and became like them (Ps 49:12).[16]

The image, as the above citation implies, has been deformed through sin,[17] which finds its root in pride.[18] Following the teaching of Paul (Rom 5:12), Augustine asserts that as descendants of Adam all people have sinned[19] and are thus heir to the sin of pride, which causes each person to turn to herself to satisfy the desire of love rather than choosing God to be the object of that love.[20] Augustine identifies the human will as the mechanism through which a person succumbs to *superbia*, or love of self. It is through free will that a person turns from the fire and light of God's love to the lower goods of earthly existence. In its darkness, the will directs its affection to temporal and material goods.[21] Such goods, however, cannot render a person happy due to the fear of their loss, which Augustine asserts is incompatible with true happiness.[22] The result of this fear is a life of moral evil in which the human person resorts to sin and crime in the effort to protect and secure material goods from the threat posed by others seeking those same goods.[23] Moral evil, according to Augustine, is the product of pride's initial turn from God, which culminates in the sin, sorrow, and death that mark the human condition.

The will, as the source of a person's moral evil[24] and the foundation of pride, is the faculty of the soul that must be healed to prevent the disastrous consequences of sin. In Augustine's view, such healing is not a work that can be done on the basis of human nature alone. The human will deforms itself in its fall by turning away from God as the source of goodness, and only grace can restore the will to its proper orientation toward God.[25] Indeed, God's grace is of such fundamental importance to the human moral

---

16. Augustine, *Trin.* 12.3.16.

17. Ibid., 14.5.22.

18. Augustine, *Gn. Adv. Man.* 2.15.22. Cf. MacQueen "*Contemptus Dei*," 252–53.

19. Augustine, *Nat. et Gr.* 41.48. Cf. Augustine, *Trin.* 13.4.16.

20. Augustine, *Civ. Dei* 14.13.

21. Ibid.

22. Augustine, *B. Vita* 2.11. Cf. Babcock, "Early Augustine on Love," 42.

23. Augustine, *Lib. Arb.* 1.4.10.

24. Ibid., 2.19.52–53.

25. Augustine, *Trin.* 14.5.22.

life that Augustine asserts a person is completely unable to choose any good without the help of that grace.[26]

Through the healing action of grace, and specifically the healing action of humility, the human will is re-oriented toward God and empowered to love that which is truly good. The re-orientation that is God's initial gift of grace yields the further grace of faith in God. It is in the knowledge conferred by faith that a person can begin to love the good of God above the temporal goods of sensible reality.[27] The love of God that finds its source in faith, however, is not something that spontaneously uproots the evil customs built over the course of a person's life through the operation of *superbia* and *cupiditas*. He sees such uprooting as a process of renewal in which grace and free will collaborate together to overcome carnal habit and restore the image of God in a particular person.[28]

> To be sure, this renewal does not happen in one moment of conversion . . . . The first stage of the cure is to remove the cause of debility, and this is done by pardoning all sins; the second stage is curing the debility itself, and this is done gradually by making steady progress in the renewal of this image . . . . So then the man who is being renewed in the recognition of God and in justice and holiness of truth by making progress day by day, is transferring his love from temporal things to eternal, from visible to intelligible, from carnal to spiritual things; he is industriously applying himself to checking and lessening his greed for the one sort and binding himself with charity to the other. But his success in this depends on divine assistance; it is after all God who declares, *Without me you can do nothing* (John 15:5).[29]

The gradual process of moral renewal that restores the image of God in the human person reaches its zenith in the establishment of virtue. Virtue, for Augustine, is the perfect love of God.[30] Virtue replaces the vice built by *superbia* and *cupiditas* when the will, through the love of God developed on the basis of faith, submits itself to ". . . the immutable rules and lights of those virtues which dwell incorruptible in truth."[31] Augustine sees

26. Augustine, *Gr. et Lib. Arb.* 4.7.

27. Augustine, *Trin.* 8.5.13.

28. Augustine, *Gr. et Lib. Arb.* 4.7.

29. Augustine, *Trin.* 14.5.23.

30. Augustine, *Mor.* 15.25.

31. Augustine, *Lib. Arb.* 2.19.52–53.

the foundation of true virtue in the will's choice to submit itself in love to God alone. Virtue then becomes the mechanism through which the human person is purified and empowered to achieve his or her greatest happiness, which is the possession of God through the function of the soul's intellect. The purification achieved through virtue and the perfection of love it makes possible yield the knowledge of God, or wisdom, which fulfills every desire of the human heart.[32] The end of the moral life, for Augustine, is achieved through virtue but resides in the intellectual possession of God in the Beatific Vision.

The challenge of the moral life, for Augustine, is the reversal of the evil brought on by the sin of pride. Humility is the gift of God's grace that begins the process of moral renewal in which pride is overcome. Humility's importance to overcoming pride and sin stems from this initial role, as well as its importance to the human person throughout the various stages of moral renewal. The process through which a person develops the love that will enable the possession of God's eternal goodness is, in Augustine's view, inescapably tied to humility.

Humility: God's Initial Gift of Grace to the Human Person

One of the primary outcomes of the Pelagian controversy is Augustine's development and refinement of his doctrine of grace. In that teaching, Augustine repeatedly and emphatically asserts that the human person is incapable of good action without the assistance of God's grace.[33] The human person, according to Augustine, is only able to choose that which is good through the interaction of grace and the will.[34] The initiative for that interaction lies on the side of God's grace. God prepares the will for the reception of grace and then subsequently assists the will to choose the good as well. In describing God's mercy in assisting the will, Augustine declares, "God . . . makes the good will ready to help and helps it when it has been made ready."[35] Grace precedes even the gift of faith (which is also a gift of

---

32. Babcock, "Early Augustine on Love," 54.

33. Augustine, *Gr. et Lib. Arb.* 4.7.

34. Ibid.

35. Augustine, *Ench.* 9.32.

grace) and is the result of God's mercy.[36] God offers grace to the human will, weighed down by sin, and through that offer a person is able to overcome the pride that separates him from God.[37]

As the perfection of love that enables one to turn from the self-love of pride and be opened to the love of God, humility is a critical aspect of the grace without which a person is incapable of choosing the good. The human person is able to love God and overcome the dominance of his self-love because God first loved the human person. Augustine addresses this fundamental aspect of humility in a number of different contexts. Using Paul's metaphor of grafting to the olive tree (Rom 11:19–23), he asserts that humility is the mechanism by which God joins the human person to himself. The power to be grafted onto the tree lies not with the human person, but with God.[38] As the branch now connected to the tree, the humble person is able to receive the nourishment God as the trunk offers in his grace. Augustine likewise maintains that it is through the gift of humility that a person is able to receive the Holy Spirit.[39] Humility is the cause that enables a person to be born of God's Spirit because it is when a person is humbled—when the person is crushed in heart—that the Lord will draw near to her (Ps 34:18). It is only through such lowliness of heart that a person can be born of the Spirit because it is in that lowliness that a person turns from herself and looks to God for fulfillment.[40] In still another sermon, Augustine contends that Jesus heals the person through humility since pride is the root sin to be confronted. As an experienced doctor, Christ knows the underlying cause of the human disorder. Rather than treating the symptoms, Jesus cures the human person with his own humility, which heals the initial sin of pride.[41] Augustine even asserts that it was through humility that Jesus was able to reveal himself to people prior to his incarnation in the flesh. Augustine states that as the humble mediator Jesus had never failed anyone who had sought him in humility. He ascribes such humility to the great figures of the Old Testament, including persons such as Melchizedek and Job, who though not numbered among the Hebrews, were considered

36. Augustine, *Gr. et Lib. Arb.* 14.28.

37. Augustine, *Trin.* 8.3.7.

38. Augustine, *S.* 162A.9 (WSA III/5:161). Cf. Augustine, *Tractates on the Gospel of John* 16.6 (106).

39. Augustine, *S.* 270.6 (WSA III/7:294).

40. Augustine, *Tractates on the Gospel of John*, 12.6 (2).

41. Augustine, *S.* 159B.11 (WSA III/11:156–57).

to be righteous. Their righteousness, according to Augustine, was achieved through humility. God reveals himself only to the humble, and it is only the humble that are purified and saved by the Lord.[42]

Augustine's position regarding the necessity of grace in the will's ability to choose good and his designation of pride as the source of sin lead to the conclusion that the grace of humility is at the foundation of salvation for the human person. Robert Dodaro asserts that ". . . for Augustine humility is fundamental to the gift of grace itself."[43] The supreme instance of this grace is the humility of Christ through which the love of God has drawn close to mortal human beings.[44] For Augustine, no one is excused from learning the humility of Christ,[45] which has been revealed as the way to eternal salvation.[46] As we'll see in the next section, it is in Christ's gift of humility that the faith through which a person is saved begins to grow.

The Importance of Faith to Augustine's Moral Thought

Augustine views the knowledge offered to the human person's intellect by faith as critical to a person's ability to love God, and as a result of that love, live a life of virtue. In the context of sin's devastating effect on the image of God in the human person, Augustine presents an understanding of morality in which faith plays an early and vital role in the pursuit of the good that leads to happiness. For Augustine, moral renewal and the reformation of God's image in the human person takes place as that person transfers his love from temporal objects to things eternal.[47] Since God is the human person's primary and final good, Augustine reasons that to live well is to love God, as Scripture tells us, with all of one's heart, soul, and mind.[48] Loving God in the present condition of the human race, however, raises difficulties for Augustine. Citing the testimony of St. Paul, Augustine reminds us that we do not yet see God face to face in this life (1 Cor 13:12), since we still walk by faith and not by sight (2 Cor 5:7). Given that lack of vision

42. Augustine, *S.* 198.38 (WSA III/11:209).

43. Dodaro, "The Secret Justice of God," 90.

44. Schlabach, "Augustine's Hermeneutic of Humility," 316.

45. Augustine, *S.* 164.7 (WSA III/5:191).

46. Augustine, *S.* 123.3 (WSA III/4:245).

47. Augustine, *Trin.* 14.5.23.

48. Augustine, *Mor.* 25.46.

and the intellectual uncertainty brought on by sin, Augustine concludes that we initially do not know God in the sense of beholding and clearly grasping him with the human mind.[49] Yet he also asserts that one cannot love something of which he has no knowledge.[50] The two assertions present Augustine with the problem of how the human person can come to love God if that person does not know God. He solves the apparent contradiction through his understanding of faith.

Augustine asserts that it is through the knowledge of faith that a person can come to love God.[51] He makes this assertion in the context of placing the act of faith within the domain of temporal knowledge rather than that of eternal wisdom.[52] Despite the fact that the object of faith is God, the foundation and pinnacle of eternal truth, Augustine maintains that God has become an object of temporal knowledge through the incarnation of Jesus. Christ, in Augustine's view, bridges the epistemological gap between knowledge and wisdom. As the eternal Word, Christ "is without time and without space, coeternal with the Father and wholly present everywhere; and if anyone can utter a true word about this, as far as he is able, it will be a word of wisdom."[53] As the Word made flesh, however, Augustine ascribes the actions taken and suffered by Jesus during his earthly life to knowledge rather than wisdom.[54] On the basis of this distinction, Augustine concludes that through faith in the earthly deeds and teaching of Christ, one can come to know God indirectly. Paul asserts that the knowledge of God gained through faith provides an indistinct vision of God. It is a vision of his image present in the earthly actions of the Word made flesh, Jesus Christ. The incarnation provides initial knowledge of God that is true but falls short of wisdom because of the temporal and finite aspect of the Son's existence as a human being. In the person of Jesus, one sees the image of God as one could see a reflection in a mirror (1 Cor 13:12). For Augustine, such knowledge not only provides the basis upon which the human person can love God, but it is also the path through which one achieves true wisdom. Knowledge is inferior to wisdom but still allows for an authentic and true relationship between God and the human person. "Our knowledge there-

49. Augustine, *Trin.* 8.3.6.

50. Ibid., 10.1.1.

51. Ibid., 8.3.6.

52. Ibid., 13.6.24.

53. Ibid.

54. Ibid.

fore is Christ, and our wisdom is the same Christ. It is he who plants faith in us about temporal things, he who presents us with the truth about eternal things. Through him we go straight toward him, through knowledge toward wisdom."[55] Here we find a reformulation and manifestation of Augustine's principle that one must first believe in order to understand.[56] By believing in the knowledge we have of the earthly Christ, we can begin our journey toward the knowledge of God's eternal reality present in human wisdom. Faith, then, in Augustine's view, provides the knowledge necessary for the human person to establish a loving relationship with God.

The Humility of Faith

In the introduction to Book Four of his translation of *The Trinity*, Edmund Hill describes Augustine's view of faith as ". . . a hard form of intellectual humility, which . . . purifies us of pride and makes us morally fit for contemplation."[57] The lack of understanding Augustine associates with pride of intellect is overcome through the humility of faith. Augustine asserts that it is humble to believe by authority what cannot be demonstrated to the mind.[58] The intellectual humility of faith becomes a crucial turning point in Augustine's own conversion. As a result of Augustine's failure to penetrate the mysteries of life through reason alone, faith in the authority of the church and Scripture becomes his path to understanding the truth about God and God's relationship to the human person. Stepping down from the pride of his intellect, Augustine is able to understand God's truth through the humility of belief.[59]

Augustine also presents the establishment of the knowledge of faith in a person's mind as a function of humility. The capacious aspect of humility, which I will develop further in my discussion of humility and the will, plays an important role in this establishment. Humility's function of making space for God's love and grace to enter the human will becomes the grounds and condition in which faith is made possible. We see this principle manifest in Augustine's interpretation of the parable concerning the Pharisee and the tax collector (Luke 18:10–14). Faith, Augustine says,

55. Ibid.

56. Ibid., 8.3.8.

57. Hill, "Introductory Essay," 150.

58. Augustine, *Conf.* 6.5.7.

59. Augustine, *Trin.* 8.3.8.

". . . belongs not to the proud, but to the humble."[60] Augustine's notion of pride as a love of excelling is personified in the character of the Pharisee.[61] Indeed, there are few who illustrate pride better. Augustine observes how the Pharisee goes up to pray to God and does nothing but praise himself. The Pharisee in his self-love requests nothing from God, placing faith in himself, the ultimate object of his love.[62] The tax collector, on the other hand, is the personification of humility. He stands a long way off, beating his breast, without even the strength to raise his eyes.[63] His downcast vision contemplates his own emptiness.[64] It is in the acknowledgement of his emptiness that is the capaciousness of his humility that the tax collector finds God's grace. In admitting he is empty, the tax collector has something.[65] And it is on this foundation, the foundation of humility, that he can make his request to God. Humility, then, is the initial moment of grace where the love of pride is overturned,[66] making room for God's love. It is in the presence of this grace that the gift of faith begins to grow, which is the reason Augustine asserts that faith belongs to the humble.[67]

Augustine uses the Gospel stories concerning the Canaanite woman (Matt 15:21–28) and the Roman centurion (Matt 8:5–13; Luke 7:1–10) to demonstrate two further dimensions of the relationship between faith and humility. In both circumstances, Jesus recognizes the act of faith through the humility of the woman's and the centurion's actions. Jesus acknowledges the faith of the Canaanite woman and praises the strength of that faith on the basis of the radical humility she demonstrates in accepting her lower status relative to the children of Israel.[68] In similar fashion, Augustine observes how Jesus discerns the faith of the centurion through his humble

60. Augustine, S. 115:2 (WSA III/4.199).

61. Augustine, S. 354:6 (WSA III/10:159).

62. Augustine, S. 115:2 (WSA III/4:199).

63. Ibid.

64. Augustine, S. 36:11 (WSA III/2:181).

65. Ibid.

66. Augustine discusses the role of humility overturning pride in many passages including: Augustine, Trin. 13.5.21; 13.5.22; Augustine, S. 4A.1 (WSA III/1:214); S. 123.1 (WSA III/4:244); S. 398.6 (WSA III/10:448). Cf. Schlabach, "Hermeneutic of Humility," 316 for a discussion of Christ's humility as the supreme instance of grace that serves as a first principle to heal the will maimed by sin.

67. Augustine, S. 115:2 (WSA III/4:199). Cf. Dodaro, "Gift of Humility," 89 for a discussion of humility's role in conditioning faith.

68. Augustine, S. 77.11 (WSA III/3:322).

assertion that he is not worthy for Christ to enter under his roof.[69] Faith and humility are linked in humility's ability to reveal an interior faith. Similar to the function of God's command revealing Adam's pride,[70] humility is able to shine light on the interior act of believing in God. In addition to this revelatory aspect, Augustine also asserts on the basis of these two stories that an already existing faith is made great by humility. In the case of the centurion, Augustine asserts that his faith is bolstered by his humility. It is through humility that Christ enters the door of the centurion's heart so he can reside there more fully. The faith of the centurion was not only made possible by humility but is further strengthened by it as well.[71] Likewise, Augustine sees the Canaanite woman's faith made great by her profound humility.[72] Again, using the metaphor of the olive tree, Augustine observes that Christ did not find such great faith in the people of Israel, who were broken off from the olive tree due to their pride. The greatness of faith these new believers possess, he asserts, finds its source in their humility.[73]

Augustine sees the interaction of grace and humility as the foundation of the moral life. For Augustine, grace is the reward of grace.[74] Putting names on each of these graces, then, we can see that the grace of faith is the reward of the grace of humility. It is on the foundation of these two gifts that Augustine asserts the person can begin to do good works. This is the case because it is through humility and faith that a person can petition God for the grace to fulfill the dictates of the Law. The person's ability to fulfill the Law and be justified by grace is accomplished through humble faith (Eph 2:8).[75] In addition, not only are humility and faith the basis on which the person petitions God for help, they are also the interior principles through which the love for God grows. The humility of faith is the basis for Augustine's conception of love that drives his moral thought.

---

69. Augustine, *S.* 62:3 (WSA III/3:157).

70. Augustine, *Civ. Dei* 14.13.

71. Augustine, *S.* 62A.2 (WSA III/3:171).

72. Augustine, *S.* 203.2 (WSA III/6:96).

73. Augustine, *S.* 77.12 (WSA III/3:323).

74. Augustine, *Gr. et Lib. Arb.* 8.20.

75. Ibid.

Love, Will, and Humility in Augustine's Understanding of Morality

The idea of love is critically important to Augustine's thought in general and of particular importance to his moral thought. Like my earlier characterization of Augustine's view of humility, his understanding of *caritas* is complex and quite rich.[76] That view encompasses features ranging from the acquisitive aspect of love developed in Greek philosophy to the notion of God as love depicted in the pages of Scripture. The focus of my discussion will center on the role played by love in Augustine's moral thought as the connection between the knowledge of faith and the knowledge of wisdom. Love, according to Augustine, is the link that bridges the gap between temporal knowledge and knowledge of the eternal.[77] This function is made possible through the orientation given to a person's love through the operation of the human will. The will can turn a person's love to God's eternal good, and in so doing, enables love to acquire the knowledge of God all people desire; the greatest end to which every person aspires.[78] We will see, however, that will and love can only lead to such greatness through the operation of humility. Without humility, the will turns to serve itself, and love is mired in the temporal goods that lead only to unhappiness and death.[79] Will and love are the powers of the human person that will lead the person to God if and only if the person is given God's gift of humility.

The section's discussion will begin with an examination of the terms Augustine uses in reference to love. Following the terminological study, I will describe Augustine's conception of love and its orientation toward knowledge, which culminates in the knowledge of God love provides to the human person. After addressing the relation of love to knowledge of God, I will examine Augustine's notion of the will and its fundamental role in orienting love toward God, thus making knowledge of God possible. The section will conclude by describing the importance of humility to the proper functioning of both the will and love.

---

76. Cf. Burnaby, *Amor Dei,* 92 for commentary on the complexity of *caritas* in Augustine's thought.

77. Augustine, *Trin.* 13.6.24.

78. Augustine, *Civ. Dei* 14.13.

79. Augustine, *Lib. Arb.* 2.19.53.

Caritas and its Cognates in Augustine's Thought

Although there is significant scholarly debate regarding the precise meaning of the various Latin words Augustine employs regarding love, recent scholarship has recognized some general trends regarding his terminology on the basis of his use of the words and the descriptions he provides in their regard. Turning first to the words Augustine uses in reference to what he considers disordered love, Augustine observes that use of the words *cupiditas* and *concupiscentia* without precisely stating an object of desire implies a love or desire in a bad sense.[80] *Cupiditas* is the converse of *caritas* in its effect of dragging a person's affection down toward earthly and temporal goods, whereas *caritas* lifts a person's desire toward spiritual goods.[81] Turning to the terms that can indicate a rightly ordered love, Augustine asserts as synonymous the words *amor*, *dilectio*, and *caritas*.[82] While he does use the three terms interchangeably at times (e.g., he attributes the same meaning to *amor dei* and *caritas*), this use does not deny the presence of nuances in each of the three words lacking in the others.[83] Ragnar Holte has characterized the Latin *amor* as indicating love in the largest sense—a natural, spontaneous sentiment[84]—while John Burnaby observes a neutral aspect to it, where it can apply to love of both good and evil.[85] Augustine points out that *dilectio*, too, can be directed toward good and evil on the basis of its use in the Latin text of Scripture.[86] *Dilectio* at times takes on the meaning of love associated with conscious preference.[87] *Dilectio* is also understood to express in relation to virtue a just choice between natural objects.[88] *Caritas*, on the other hand, takes on the most elevated meaning of the three love terms in Augustine's use.[89] It is the word used in Scripture most frequently to designate love for God[90] and takes on the character of divinity because of

---

80. Augustine, *Civ. Dei* 14.7.

81. Burnaby, *Amor Dei*, 94.

82. Augustine, *Civ. Dei* 14.7. Cf. Holte, *Beatitude et Sagesse*, 262.

83. Burnaby, *Amor Dei*, 92, 99. Cf. Dideberg, *Saint Augustin*, 177.

84. Holte, *Beatitude et Sagesse*, 261.

85. Burnaby, *Amor Dei*, 95.

86. Augustine, *Civ. Dei* 14.7.

87. Burnaby, *Amor Dei*, 115.

88. Holte, *Beatitude et Sagesse*, 263.

89. Ibid., 261.

90. Dideberg, *Theologie de l'Agape*, 177.

its use in 1 John 4:8, 16 as an expression of God's nature.[91] *Caritas* can also refer to the love of the human person for God or for neighbor and is less likely to be used in reference to base desires.[92]

Caritas and *Voluntas* as the Foundation for Augustine's View of Humility

Augustine declares that to love something is to desire it for its own sake.[93] He describes love as a desire possessed by the mind that permeates all the functions of the soul.[94] It is a principle of motion, moving the person possessed of that love toward the object of his desire. [95] Oliver O'Donovan notes the intrinsic dynamism to Augustine's notion of love, contending that his view implies an innate force that drives the person toward a particular object.[96] In the same way that fire rises and oil floats on water, love is the human person's principle of movement. It is the weight by which a person moves.[97] For Augustine, love is never idle in the soul. It necessarily causes the movement of the human person.[98] "It is love that asks, love that seeks, love that knocks, love that reveals, love, too, that gives continuance in what is revealed."[99]

Augustine's notion of love, however, is not merely an egocentric acquisitiveness as Anders Nygren famously asserts.[100] For Augustine, authentic human love is subjected to God's love,[101] a subjection that is achieved through humility and always has a reference to the common good rather than the

91. O'Donovan, *Self-Love in Augustine*, 11.

92. Ibid. Cf. Mayer, *Augustinus-Lexikon*, 294 for a description of the positive and negative use Augustine makes of *caritas*. Almost always used in reference to love of something good, usually God or neighbor, the Lexikon does list two citations (cf. S. 349.1–4; S. Lambot 5) in which Augustine orients *caritas* negatively as seen in the formulations *caritas illicita* and *caritas mundi*.

93. Augustine, *Sol.* 1.13.22.

94. Cf. Holte, *Beatitude et Sagesse*, 252–56 for a description of the threefold differentiation of love in Augustine's thought that is grounded in the classical view of the soul's threefold power.

95. Augustine, *Div. Qu.* 35.2. Cf. Augustine *Civ. Dei* 14.7.

96. O'Donovan, *Self-Love in Augustine*, 20.

97. Augustine, *Conf.* 13.9.10.

98. Augustine, *En. Ps.* 121.1 (WSA III/20:13).

99. Augustine, *Mor.* 17.31.

100. Nygren, *Agape and Eros*, 499.

101. Burnaby, "Amor in St. Augustine," 181–82.

merely private good of fulfilling individual desires.[102] John Burnaby points out that love, in Augustine's view, does not only seek. In its pursuit and acquisition of God's eternal good, the love of the soul finds its rest and happiness in the eternal possession of God.[103] Such happiness is not simply a feeling but represents the eudaemonist conception of the blessed life as the fulfillment of human existence.[104] Such an understanding of love encompasses all of the soul's powers—its sensual, active, and intellectual capacities.[105]

Augustine's view of love, although encompassing the soul's sensual and active desires, finds its fulfillment in the desire of intellect. For Augustine, true knowledge of an object comes through the acquisition and enjoyment of that object, both of which are products of the person's love. The limited knowledge presupposed by desire of an object is deepened and brought to fulfillment through love's acquisition and enjoyment of the object.[106] The intimacy achieved between the subject and object of love confers knowledge of the object to the subject. For Augustine, one cannot know the extent of an object's goodness without enjoying the object.[107] This is the case not only for temporal things, but even in the human love for God himself. It is through the experience of love that a person can come to know God.[108] Despite the somewhat unfamiliar formulation of loving one's love, Augustine emphasizes that in loving one's love, a person comes to authentic knowledge of God:

> Let him love his brother, and love that love; after all, he knows the love he loves better than the brother he loves. There now, he can already have God better known to him than his brother, certainly better known because more present, better known because more inward to him, better known because more sure. Embrace love which is God, and embrace God with love . . . If a man is full of love, what is he full of but God?[109]

It is only the power of love that can truly unlock the knowledge of God that is the final end of each human person.

102. Ibid., 183.

103. Augustine, *S.* 71.8 (WSA III/3:256). Cf. Burnaby, *Amor Dei*, 92.

104. Augustine, *Sol.* 1.1.3. Cf. Burnaby, "Amor in Augustine," 181.

105. Holte, *Beatitude et Sagesse*, 254.

106. Augustine, *Trin.* 10.1.1.

107. Augustine, *Div. Qu.* 35.1.

108. Augustine, *Trin.* 8.5.12.

109. Ibid.

Achieving knowledge of God, however, can only be achieved if the person's will turns the desire of his love toward God. Augustine characterizes love as *caritas* when it is ordered toward the higher intellectual or spiritual goods and in love's highest calling in its desire and enjoyment of God. The disordered love of *cupiditas*, on the other hand, drags a person's desire toward temporary goods incapable of making the person happy.[110] Augustine places the blame for a person's ability to succumb to the love of *cupiditas* on the function of *voluntas*, the human will. It is in the will's capacity to choose poorly that love may be misdirected. For Augustine, the difference between the righteous love of *caritas* and the degrading love of *cupiditas* originates in the will's free choice. It is in the freedom of *voluntas* that we can see the critical role humility plays in orienting the will toward God, enabling a person to possess the love of *caritas* rather than that of *cupiditas*. One can understand the importance of humility to the proper functioning of the will by examining the basic role Augustine's notion of *voluntas* plays in relation to love.

There are strong parallels between the concepts of will and love in Augustine's thought. He describes *voluntas* in *De Duabus Animabus* as "an uncompelled movement of mind either to acquire or to avoid losing some object."[111] Augustine's emphasis on the will's movement toward objects brings to mind his emphasis on the acquisitive aspect of love's desire for objects. He consistently points to a close relationship between the two ideas, asserting in another context that what a person chooses to love is a function of his will.[112] Like his description in *The Morals of the Catholic Church* where love asks, seeks, and knocks, Augustine maintains in *On Free Will* that it is by means of the will that one seeks, asks, and tries.[113] A similar parallel arises between *The Trinity* and Augustine's *Confessions*, where he uses the idea of a weight to describe the movement associated with will in the former and the same metaphor to describe the reality of love in the latter.[114] Given the close relation in Augustine's thought between the two principles, the difference between them becomes an important and somewhat subtle distinction to make. That difference lies in the will's role of

110. Augustine, *Lib. Arb.* 2.19.53.

111. Augustine, *Duab. An.* 10.14. Cf. Babcock, "Augustine on Sin and Moral Agency," 96.

112. Augustine, *Lib. Arb.* 1.16.34.

113. Ibid., 3.20.58.

114. Augustine, *Trin.* 11.4.18, *Conf.* 13.9.10.

deciding, as opposed to love's role as the force that moves a person toward a particular object. Both love and will are involved when a person loves an object. Love, on the one hand, is the force that draws the person to the object. Will, on the other, provides the consent or refusal to love the object.[115] Will functions as the arbiter that allows the person to persist in and enjoy the love of an object or to reject that love.

In Augustine's view, the fundamental choice made by the will in regard to love is its choice to love God or to love the self in place of God.[116] The choice for love of self that constitutes pride is of fundamental moral importance to both the individual and to the community. The will or person who chooses love of self over love for God will be mired in the desire of temporary goods and will reap the unhappiness to which such desires lead.[117] In the social setting, Augustine's distinction between love of self and love of God becomes the foundation characterizing and separating the earthly city from the heavenly city.[118] The emphasis Augustine places upon will and its corrupting turn to love of self provides the context in which humility plays such a crucial role. It is the grace of humility operating upon the human will that can turn a person from *superbia* and *cupiditas* to *caritas*. Humility, for Augustine, is the fundamental orientation that allows a person to direct her love toward God and thus develop the knowledge of God to which she is drawn. An examination of the interactions between humility and the will and humility and love reveals how humility executes such an important role in relation to both principles.

Humility and the Will's Approach to God

The will, having turned away from God's eternal good, can only be healed and reoriented toward that good through the intervention of divine grace as the gift of humility.[119] Augustine's thought on the manner in which humility joins the human person to God can be approached from the perspective of the humility God exhibits in the activity of Jesus Christ and from that of the human person's possession of humility. God's humility is well expressed by

---

115. Augustine, *Gr. et Lib. Arb.* 3.5. Cf. Rist, *Augustine*, 176–77 for a discussion of the understanding of will's role as consent in relation to love.

116. Augustine, *Civ. Dei* 14.13.

117. Ibid. Cf. Augustine, *Lib. Arb.* 1.11.22.

118. Augustine, Civ. Dei 14.13.

119. Augustine, *Trin.* 14.5.22.

Nygren's formulation of *agapé*.[120] The descent of God's superabundant love for sinners is made manifest in the incarnation of Jesus. The self-abasement of the divine Son into human form is the epiphany of God's humble love. The revelation of God's humility in the incarnation not only demonstrates his love for humanity, but also enables the will of the person to turn away from the love of self and temporary goods to the love of God and eternal goods. For Augustine, it is the grace of Christ's humility that teaches and empowers the human person to humble himself and choose the love of God over love of self.[121]

From the perspective of the human person, humility is the source of grace that joins a person's will to God. Augustine frequently cites the scriptural principle that asserts God's resistance to the proud and special care for the humble (Prov 3:34, 1 Pet 5:5, Jas 4:6).[122] The high and mighty of the world are distant from God's love and grace.[123] Augustine maintains that a person must humble himself if he is to make contact with God.[124] Perhaps the most significant expression of how the will of a person embraces God through humility can be seen in the confession of sin. For Augustine, there is nothing nearer to God's ear than a confessing heart.[125] Confession of sin is one of the most prevalent acts Augustine associates with humility.[126] He stresses that repentance of sin is accomplished through humility,[127] and it is in the humiliation of acknowledging one's sin that God will bestow grace to a person. Augustine turns to the figure of King David to illustrate his point. David overcomes his sins through ". . . a piety so great, and a penitence of

120. Nygren, *Agape and Eros*, 212.

121. Cf. Augustine, *S.* 4a.1 (WSA III/1:214), *S.* 50.11 (WSA III/2:350), *S.* 30.9 (WSA III/2:128), *S.* 51.4 (WSA III/3:23), *S.* 70A.1 (WSA III/3:243–44), *S.* 123.1 (WSA III/4:244), *S.* 218C.4 (WSA III/6:196), *S.* 340A.5 (WSA III/9:298–99) for some of the many references in which Augustine emphasizes Christ's humility as the example and impetus for human humility.

122. Augustine, *En. Ps.* 18(1).8 (WSA III/15:200). Cf. Augustine, *Civ. Dei*, Preface to Book One, 11.33, 19.27.

123. Augustine, *S.* 70A.2 (WSA III/3:244); *S. 68.7* (WSA III/3:226-27).

124. Augustine, *S.* 45.7 (WSA III/2:256). Cf. *En. Ps.* 31(2).22 (WSA III/15:383).

125. Augustine, *En. Ps.* 31(2).18 (WSA III/15:380-81). Cf. Augustine, *Conf.* 2.3.5.

126. Cf. Augustine, *En. Ps.* 75:13, 95:9, 93:22, 141.13, 121.8, *Jo. Ev. Tr.* 3.2 (4), 14.5 (1) and *Ep. Jo.*, 1.6, 8.2 for sample texts of Augustine linking confession of sin to humility.

127. Augustine, *S.* 110.1 (WSA III/4:136). CF. Schlabach, "Hermeneutic of Humility," 321-22.

such wholesome humility."[128] God desires a contrite heart that is humble with the sorrow of penitence.[129] Such humility and contrition are desired by God so that he may fill the person's spiritual poverty with the grace of the Holy Spirit.[130]

Spiritual poverty is another significant feature of humility that Augustine develops in many of his sermons. He equates poverty of spirit with humility, the condition through which a person has room to accept God's grace.[131] Augustine describes this aspect of humility as spiritual emptiness or capaciousness.[132] He draws significantly on Scripture in support of the idea. Augustine cites the Psalms when asserting the humble of heart are God's house ready to be filled by his grace[133] and uses the emptiness of the tax collector to reinforce the point.[134] He cites Paul's teaching (Phil 2:12) when he asserts that the emotion of fear allows a person to be filled with God's grace.[135] For Augustine, humility is the principle that makes room for the presence of God in a person's will.[136] God withdraws from the person of pride because his self-love takes up the space that could otherwise be occupied by God's grace. The return to God must therefore come through the self-emptying of devout humility.[137] Humility's healing of the will puts a person in touch with God's grace and enables him to love God's good rather than earthly goods.

128. Augustine, *Civ. Dei* 17.2.

129. Ibid., 10.5.

130. Augustine, *S.* 270.6 (WSA III/7:294); *S.* 335J.4 (WSA III/9:253).

131. Augustine, *S.* 53.1 (WSA III/3:66).

132. Augustine, *S.* 270.6 (WSA III/7:294).

133. Augustine, *Conf.* 11.31.41.

134. Augustine, *S.* 36.11 (WSA III/2:181).

135. Augustine, *S.* 131.3 (WSA III/4:318).

136. Cf. Augustine, *Jo. Ev. Tr.* 25.15, 25.17 (FCNT 79:253, 256). This aspect of Augustine's view of humility was also shaped in part by his Platonic heritage. Phillip Cary notes that Augustine's understanding of the inner-self has its roots in Plotinian Platonism, which held that the interior soul is divine because of its contact with the forms of intellect. Augustine does not accept the neo-Platonic divinity of the soul, but holds on to a notion of the interior life of the soul that is under God. The Platonist turned inward and found God within the soul. Augustine also turned inward, but found God above the soul rather than in it. The common element between the two views is the fact that one must turn into the soul to find God. Within this context, humility can be seen as the virtue necessary to clear the inner space of the soul so that one can turn upwards to receive God's grace. Cf. Cary, *Augustine's Invention of the Inner Self*, 28–42.

137. Augustine, *Conf.* 3.8.16.

Humility as the Perfection of Charity

Having described the manner in which humility and the will work together to properly orient a person's love toward God, one can see the significance of humility in the support and encouragement of that love once it has been initially established. Due to the importance and intimacy of humility to Augustine's understanding of *caritas*, he often equates the two by presenting love as the antithesis of pride. In such instances, he asserts an inverse proportion between love and pride. The more the person is cured of pride, the more she is possessed by *caritas*.[138] Augustine declares that it is only in having a humble view of one's self that a person is able to love God.[139]

Humility, as an aspect of love, also participates in the relation between love and knowledge I have discussed in the preceding pages. Augustine notes that knowledge of earthly things is highly prized by human beings. The mind without humility ". . . sets out to explore or even knows already, the course of the stars, while ignorant of the course it should follow itself to its own health and strength."[140] Keeping in mind Augustine's principle that one must know an object in order to love it, *cupiditas* as the love of temporary external goods requires knowledge of earthly things. Such knowledge, without the humble orientation of a person's love toward God, serves only to reinforce a person's pride. Drawing from chapters eight and thirteen of Paul's First Letter to the Corinthians, Augustine often notes the relation of knowledge and the self-inflated nature of pride in contrast to the humility of love.[141] The knowledge of pride puffs up, while knowledge achieved through the humility of love builds authentic strength in a person:[142]

> So what, then? Must you run away from knowledge, and are you going to choose to know nothing, rather than be puffed up? . . . Why am I reminding you of what you know, introducing you to what you don't know, if knowledge is to be avoided, in case it should puff one up? So then, love knowledge, but put charity first. If knowledge is there by itself, it puffs up. But because *charity builds up* (1 Cor 8:1), it doesn't allow knowledge to be puffed up.

138. Augustine, *Trin.* 8.5.12.

139. Augustine, *S.* 142.2 (WSA III/4:414).

140. Augustine, *Trin.* Prologue 4.1.

141. A number of texts in which Augustine addresses the pride of knowledge and the humility of love include *S.* 142.12 (WSA III/4:421); *S.* 354.6 (WSA III/10:159); *Trin.* Prologue 4.1; 12.3.16; 14.1.3; *Conf.* 7.20.26.

142. Augustine, *Trin.* 12.3.16.

> So knowledge only puffs up, where charity is not building up; but
> where it is building up, knowledge is set firm and solid. There is no
> puffing up where the rock is the foundation.[143]

The love of God made possible by humility results in the knowledge of
eternal goods rather than earthly goods. In this relationship, one sees what
might be characterized as a virtuous cycle. Humility leads to love of God,
which leads to knowledge of God. Authentic knowledge of God leads to the
awe and gratitude from which humility springs,[144] which leads to a further
deepening of love for God. Humility, as the foundation of love for God,
becomes critical to a person's knowledge of God, as well.

Augustine also asserts humility as a central element in the love humans have for one another. Since love is the principle of motion moving a
subject toward an object of her love, it can be seen as the force that draws
people together, just as it is the force that draws a person toward God.[145] It
is in the context of love as a principle uniting persons that Augustine again
understands love as humility. The humble person, according to Augustine,
is simply unable to wish that harm befall other people. This is the case because humility in its orientation toward God's eternal good is disinterested
in the misfortune of others. Such misfortune contributes nothing to the
good of the humble person.[146] Humility's inability to wish another harm, or
put more positively, its ability to only wish good for others, enhances and
supports the love of neighbor. The charitable person, the person of humility, will only wish good for others due to the presence of God's love in that
person's will. The love of God not only requires love and concern for one's
neighbor (as manifested by the commandment to love one's neighbor) but
is also the end to which love of neighbor is ordered.[147] Given the orientation
of both love and humility toward the good of one's neighbor, Augustine
contends that encouraging humility is to advocate for love. Humility ". . .
is suggesting love, and the most genuine sort of love for one's fellows, love
without mixed motives, without conceit, without arrogance, and without
deceit."[148] Humility, for Augustine, is an absolutely necessary ingredient to

143. Augustine, S. 354.6 (WSA III/10:159).

144. Dodaro, "Gift of Humility," 90.

145. Augustine, *Div. Qu.* 35.2. Cf. Augustine *Civ. Dei* 14.7. Cf. O'Donovan, *Self-Love
in Augustine*, 20.

146. Augustine, S. 353.1 (WSA III/10:153).

147. Augustine, *Mor.* 26.48.

148. Augustine, S. 142:12 (WSA III/4:421).

love of neighbor, and its perfection is seen in the charity of Christ, which he contends is built on the foundation of humility.[149]

In *The Trinity*, Augustine makes one of his strongest assertions regarding the importance of humility to *caritas* when he states, "He (God) arranged it so that the power of charity is brought to perfection in the weakness of humility."[150] Augustine makes this assertion in relation to his understanding of love's fullness as depicted in John 15:13, which portrays that fullness as the laying down of one's life for the good of a friend. Augustine also reads this verse in conjunction with 1 John 3:16, which proclaims that believers should lay down their lives for their brethren just as Christ laid down his own life for the good of others. For Augustine, such sacrificial love can only be offered by one who is humble.[151] Augustine declares that the purest or fullest love is a humble love.[152] It is a love that expresses its strength in humility.[153] Christ, Augustine asserts, models this love when washing the feet of the disciples (John 13:3–11). Christ's act of washing the feet is not primarily concerned with cleansing; for Augustine it is an act of humility. In the description of Christ girding himself with a towel, Augustine sees a metaphor for the humble strength with which he accomplishes his mission.[154] The height of sacrificial love is dependent upon humility because it is through humility that we can be exposed to the full power of God's grace. Augustine articulates the principle when he declares on the basis of Paul's thought (2 Cor 12:9) that one must be weakened in order to be strengthened by the power of Christ. Such weakening, he teaches, is to be understood as putting no trust in oneself. Trust placed in the strength of God's grace is the process by which the love of the human person is fortified by the love of God.[155] Placing trust in God rather than oneself is the fundamental act of humility. In that act, the person turns to God and is given a strength of love beyond the capacities of human nature alone.

149. Augustine, *Conf.* 7.20.26.

150. Augustine, *Trin.* 4.1.2. Cf. *Ep. Jo.* 1.6 (WSA III/14:27).

151. Augustine, *S.* 28A.4 (WSA III/11:51).

152. Augustine, *S.* 142.12 (WSA III/4:421).

153. Augustine, *En. Ps.* 92.3 (WSA III/18:364).

154. Ibid.

155. Augustine, *Trin.* 4.1.2.

Virtue: The Perfection of Love

Given the close relation of humility to love in Augustine's thought, it comes as little surprise that humility also plays a significant role in relation to virtue, which Augustine views as the perfection of human love for God.[156] To illustrate this role, I will first describe Augustine's approach to virtue in relation to love and will then detail the manner in which humility and virtue interact.

Recognizing that the human person is composed of a body and soul, Augustine asserts that the chief good of the person must be beneficial to each of these constituent parts. In examining human nature more closely, however, Augustine observes that the greatest good of the body is a good soul. Thus, whatever is the good of the soul (i.e., perfective of the soul) will also be good for the body.[157] Having established that the soul is perfective of the body, Augustine asks what would perfect the soul in the same way that the soul perfects the body. For whatever gives perfection to the soul will also give perfection to the body, and thus the happiness of the person will be fulfilled.[158] Within his eudaemonistic moral context, Augustine remarks that no one questions the fact that virtue gives perfection to the soul. Presupposing the link between virtue and the perfection of the soul, he provides a description of how virtue exists outside of the human person and in what manner it is acquired by the soul.

> In the pursuit of virtue the soul follows after something, and this must be either the soul itself, or virtue, or something else. But if the soul follows after itself in the pursuit of virtue, it follows after a foolish thing; for before obtaining virtue it is foolish . . . . We must allow that the soul follows after something else in order that virtue may be produced in itself; for neither by following after nothing, nor by following after folly, can the soul, according to my reasoning, attain to wisdom . . . . This something else then . . . is . . . God . . . God then remains, in following after whom we live well, and in reaching whom we live both well and happily.[159]

The moral life for Augustine consists in living well, which in turn leads to happiness. He conceives of living well in the same terms as the Greek

---

156. Augustine, *Mor.* 15.25.
157. Ibid., 5.8.
158. Ibid.
159. Ibid., 6.9–10.

philosophical tradition—i.e., living well consists in the development of virtue. Augustine differs from much of the classical tradition, however, in the way he understands the role of love and the human person's relationship to God as fundamental to the person's cultivation of virtue and happiness. In Augustine's view, it is in reaching God that a person is happy and the moral life fulfilled. He describes the growth of a person's love for God as a person's quest to live well, which can only be achieved through love's increasing intimacy with the virtue and wisdom of God.

> If then we ask what it is to live well—that is, to strive after happiness by living well—it must assuredly be to love virtue, to love wisdom, to love truth, and to love with all the heart, with all the soul, and with all the mind; virtue which is inviolable and immutable, wisdom which never gives place to folly, truth which knows no change or variation from its uniform character. Through this the Father Himself is seen; for it is said, "No man cometh unto the Father but by me" (John 14:6). To this we cleave by sanctification. For when sanctified we burn with full and perfect love, which is the only security for our not turning away from God, and for our being conformed to him rather than this world.[160]

The moral life for Augustine is centered on the acquisition of God as the object of the person's love. It is in loving God that one acquires virtue.[161]

It is here that one can see the importance of the will for Augustine's understanding of virtue. Love turns to God through the will's choice to cleave to God alone. In the will's choice to subject itself to God, an act that can be described from Augustine's perspective as an act of humility, he sees the foundation of all human virtue.

> Man obtains virtues by adapting his spirit to the immutable rules and lights of those virtues which dwell incorruptible in truth itself and in common wisdom, to which the virtuous man has adapted himself and fitted his spirit. The man seeking virtue has determined to imitate this spirit, because it is endowed with virtue. Therefore the will, clinging to common and immutable goods, obtains the first and great goods of man, although it is itself only an intermediate good.[162]

---

160. Ibid., 13.22.

161. Ibid.

162. Augustine, *Lib. Arb.* 2.19.52–53 .

Love is the conduit through which a person may become virtuous, but only if the will directs that love to God.[163]

Augustine defines and understands the individual virtues within his conception of human love for God. Taking up the fourfold division of the virtues from Greek philosophy, he asserts that each virtue represents a different form of love.[164] Beginning with temperance, Augustine describes it as the virtue in which the integrity of a person's love for God is maintained and protected. It restrains the passions that might turn the person from God to the love of temporal things. Through temperance, one is able to scorn bodily delights and the applause of others, turning his thoughts and desires to the unseen things of God.[165]

Fortitude is the virtue that empowers the person to bear all things out of love for God. If temperance is the ability to forsake earthly goods for God, fortitude is the strength to bear the loss of any earthly good for the sake of God's love. Augustine observes the strength of love of those who value gold or praise or women above all else. Such persons seek the object of their desire even in the face of great peril with unflagging energy. If the fortitude of a lover can be displayed in the desire of these base goods, how much more so should the fortitude of those who love the greatest good, God, outstrip the love of inferior goods. In the human person's confrontation with fear and pain, ". . . there is nothing, though of iron hardness, which the fire of love cannot subdue. And when the mind is carried up to God in this love, it will soar above all torture free and glorious, with wings beauteous and unhurt, on which chaste love rises to the embrace of God."[166] It is the virtue of fortitude that steels the martyrs in the face of torture and death to hold on to their love for God. Fortitude, then, is the aspect of love—the virtue—which enables a person to overcome all obstacles in the soul's pursuit of the divine.

The heart of justice, Augustine asserts, lies in the worship of God in which love of God takes precedence over the desire for all other things. The person must love God as the highest good and must rule or use all other things as subject to himself. Augustine quotes *Deuteronomy* (Deut 6:13) in support of his assertion, but also maintains that this rule of life is supported

---

163. Babcock, "Early Augustine on Love," 53.

164. Augustine, *Mor.* 15.25.

165. Ibid., 19.36.

166. Ibid., 22.41.

by the authority of both the Old and New Testaments.[167] This formulation seems somewhat unrelated to the Greek definition of justice in which each person is given what is due to him. Augustine does not reject the Greek perspective on justice,[168] however, but merely incorporates it into his moral context of the human person's love for God. The love of God above all other things is the most just act a person can render, for as the highest of all goods, God is due the greatest of all devotion. Likewise, the subjection of all earthly goods to the human person renders justice to them since the human person takes up a superior position relative to them as the median between temporal reality and the eternity of God.

Like justice, Augustine uses the terminology of love to describe the importance and role of prudence in the moral life. It is the function of prudence to ". . . discern between what is to be desired and what is to be shunned."[169] Prudence is the ability to love what ought to be loved and reject what ought not to be loved. Augustine again uses Scripture as the primary backdrop in his description of the virtue. In Christ's many exhortations to watch and be alert (e.g., Matt 24:42), Augustine sees a call to prudence. So also in the Old Testament the believer is warned, "He who despises small things will fall little by little" (Sir 19:1).[170] It is the role of prudence to guide the person in choosing things that reinforce love for God and reject those things that would undermine that love. Again, despite the scriptural background and the use of Augustine's love language, one sees an understanding of prudence that holds much in common with Greek philosophy. Aristotle, for example, holds that prudence or practical wisdom is the ability to choose what actions are good or advantageous.[171] A second similarity lies in the fact that for both Augustine and Aristotle, prudence is the central virtue. It is the foundational virtue without which a person is unable to acquire the other virtues.[172]

The continuity between Augustine and Greek philosophy on the nature of the cardinal virtues is manifestly strong. As I noted earlier, however, Augustine's understanding of virtue and morality in general is not merely a

167. Ibid., 24.44.

168. Cf. Augustine, *Lib. Arb.* 1.13.27 for an example of his use of the traditional definition of justice.

169. Augustine, *Mor.* 24.45.

170. Ibid.

171. Aristotle, *Nichomachean Ethics* 1141a27 and 1140a25–26.

172. Augustine, *Mor.* 24.45. Cf. Aristotle, *Nichomachean Ethics* 1144b32–1145a2.

repetition of the Greek concepts. His use of Scripture, the idea of love, and the relationship of God to the human person change the context in which Augustine understands the virtues. Those elements also provide a context in which humility plays a significant role in relation to virtue.

Augustine on Humility's Role in Relation to Virtue

Augustine presents a number of ways in which humility makes an important contribution to the other virtues. Humility plays a role in the development of virtues, while also playing a fundamental role in its function to preserve virtue from the encroachments of pride. In its protection and promotion of virtue, one can also see the importance of humility for virtue's relation to wisdom and the vision of God. In regard to individual virtues, Augustine highlights the importance of humility to obedience and justice. I will first examine Augustine's treatment of the relation to obedience and justice before investigating its role regarding virtue in general.

Augustine emphasizes the importance of humility to the virtue of obedience due to the intrinsically close relation between the two virtues and their similarly close relation to love of God. In *The City of God*, Augustine defines obedience as the lifting up of one's heart to God, in contrast to the proud who lift their heart to their own self. Obedience belongs to the humble since it is only the humble person who expels love of self in favor of love of God.[173] In a later discussion, Augustine reinforces the relation between humility and obedience when he reiterates Paul's teaching that all should be humble since there is nothing a person can count as a possession that has not been given to her by God (1 Cor 4:7). For Augustine, one acts rightly by glorying in the understanding and knowledge of the Lord rather than in the temporal gifts bestowed by the Lord. Such a person will obey the commandments of the Lord, and through the humility of that obedience, will experience its reward, which is ". . . love out of a pure heart, and of a good conscience, and of faith unfeigned (1 Tim 1:5)."[174] For Augustine, obedience to God's commandments, as one of the primary scriptural criteria for the manifestation of authentic love for God, replicates the love of God in preference to love of self that constitutes humility.

Recalling my treatment concerning Augustine's view of justice, one can also see justice as closely related to his understanding of humility.

173. Augustine, *Civ. Dei* 14.13.

174. Ibid., 17.4.

The highest form of justice from Augustine's perspective is in the love and worship of God that takes precedence above all other concerns.[175] Such a definition of justice bears close resemblance to Augustine's understanding of humility in which humility is considered the preference for love of God over love of self.[176] If, in Augustine's view, it is in humility that a person clings to God as her greatest good,[177] it becomes hard to avoid positing a close relationship between it and his understanding of justice as the love of God above all other things.

Augustine's interpretation of the earthly actions of Christ reinforces his close association of the meanings of justice and humility. In two of his sermons, Augustine notes that the baptism of Jesus by John was primarily an act of humility.[178] Following the text of Matthew's Gospel, he asserts that Christ's baptism is an act of humility that fulfills all justice (Matt 3:15). "What is *all justice*? It was in the form of humility that he was urging justice upon us; the heavenly master and true Lord was urging justice upon us above all in the form of humility. That he was baptized, you see, was a matter of humility; and that's why, as he was about to do what was a matter of humility, he said, *Let all justice be fulfilled.*"[179] In neither sermon, however, does Augustine explain how humility should be understood as "all justice." In a related text of *The Trinity* concerning the death of Jesus, Augustine again links humility and justice, but in this instance, provides a rationale for the link. Augustine declares it is the humility of Christ that releases sinners from the power of the devil and achieves their justification. Through his humility, God became human and was thus capable of death. In the death of the innocent Christ, who the devil had no just cause to kill, it becomes eminently just that the remainder of sinners should be freed of their debt to the evil one. "In this way the justice of humility was made more acceptable, seeing that the power of divinity could have avoided the humiliation if it had wanted to; and so by the death of one so powerful we powerless mortals have justice set before us and promised us."[180] By taking the life of the innocent God-man, the devil forfeited his right to sinful humans. As Adam's pride became the foundation for the sin of all subse-

---

175. Augustine, *Mor.* 24.44.

176. Augustine, *S.* 142.2 (WSA III/4:414). Cf. Augustine *Trin.* 8.5.11.

177. Augustine, *S.* 142.2 (WSA III/4:414).

178. Augustine, *S.* 52.1 (WSA III/3:50), *S.* 292.4 (WSA III/8:140).

179. Augustine, *S.* 292.4 (WSA III/8:140).

180. Augustine, *Trin.* 13.4.18.

quent generations, Christ's humility became the foundation upon which all generations are made just.

Turning to the relationship between humility and virtue in general, Augustine appoints a significant role for humility in the human person's ability to overcome vice and establish virtue. In his *Confessions*, Augustine asserts that humiliation brings health to the soul of a proud person.[181] This is the case because vices are overcome through love of God, which is always the gift of God's grace.[182] Nothing but fixing desire on the supreme and immutable good of God will serve to eradicate vice.[183] Humility as the love for God that replaces pride's love of self is the mechanism through which the love for God is developed. The proud person can only be healed by stepping down from the position of pride and humbly turning his affection toward God.[184] Humility is an absolutely necessary attribute to enable a person to cling to God as his greatest good.[185] Augustine sees in the humiliation of Peter's denial of Christ an example of the soul healing function of humility.[186] Humility is of such power in Augustine's view that even the rich can overcome vice and be spiritually poor through it.[187]

Despite the importance Augustine placed on humility's role in overcoming vice and establishing virtue, its most prominent role in his thought concerning virtue lies in its preservation of virtue. Augustine asserts in a number of different venues that the temptations of pride present a subtle—and therefore powerful—attraction to the most virtuous of people. In his sermons, Augustine sounds a frequent refrain that one must not take pride in virtue because such pride will lead God to disqualify a person.[188] He raises the issue twice in relationship to the virtue of generosity. One should not have pride in giving,[189] nor enjoy the goodness of generosity over that of humility.[190] In addition, Augustine notes the tendency of the unjust to

181. Augustine, *Conf.* 4.1.1.

182. Augustine, *Civ. Dei* 21.16.

183. Ibid., 22.24.

184. Augustine, *S.* 125.6 (WSA III/4:257-58). Cf. MacQueen, "*Contemptus Dei*," 282-83.

185. Augustine, *S.* 142.2 (WSA III/4:414). Cf. Augustine *Trin.* 8.5.11.

186. Augustine, *S.* 229O.1 (WSA III/6:323).

187. Augustine, *S.* 14.4–5 (WSA III/1:318–19).

188. Augustine, *S.* 16B.2-4 (WSA III/1:363–65).

189. Augustine, *S.* 389.3 (WSA III/10:405–06).

190. Augustine, *S.* 209.3 (WSA III/6:116).

blame God for their sins, while taking credit for any good choices they have made. A first step to overcome such a dangerous state of mind is to attribute any good one may do to God as its source. This is not enough, however, especially if the person who does undertake morally good actions looks upon others who do not with scorn. Such pride in virtue will lead God to reject that person despite the good action they have previously taken. Augustine again cites the parable of the Pharisee and the tax collector to illustrate the point. The Pharisee, who avoids doing evil but fails in humility, leaves unjustified, while the humble tax collector finds favor with God.[191] In yet another passage, Augustine highlights the insidious nature of pride's influence by observing in his own experience how disdain for excessive pride can be the source for further pride.

> But the word proceeding out of the mouth and the actions which become known to the people contain a most hazardous temptation in the love of praise. This likes to gather and beg for support to bolster a kind of private superiority. This is a temptation to me even when I reject it, because of the very fact that I am rejecting it. Often the contempt for vainglory becomes a source for even more vainglory. For it is not being scorned when the contempt is something one is proud of.[192]

Augustine's solution to the longings of pride in virtue is for the person to focus on how far she has yet to go on the journey of justice rather than looking upon how far she has come.[193] One must not look to one's own merits but be cognizant of the gifts of God's grace.[194] It is the possession of such humility that enables the humble to see God[195] and thus cling to God as their greatest good.[196]

---

191. Augustine, *S.* 16B.3–4 (WSA III/1:364–65). Cf. *En. Ps.* 74.10 (WSA III/18:48–49).

192. Augustine, *Conf.* 10.38.63.

193. Augustine, *S.* 159B.15 (WSA III/11:160).

194. Augustine, *S.* 174.2 (WSA III/5:259). Cf. Burns, "Augustine on Origin of Evil," 81 for a discussion of the Pelagian notion of grace that is merited as opposed to Augustinian notion where the understanding of grace excludes the possibility of pride on the part of the human person.

195. Augustine, *S.* 68.7 (WSA III/3:227).

196. Augustine, *S.* 142:2 (WSA III/4:414).

The Summit of Love: Happiness as Wisdom

Having described Augustine's understanding of love, will, and virtue and their relation to humility, we can now approach the implications of those principles for Augustine's belief concerning the *telos* of human life, which he understands to be wisdom. *On the Happy Life*, written in 386 AD, is one of Augustine's earliest attempts to define human happiness and describe its contents. In it Augustine insists that every person desires to be happy, which consists in having what one wants.[197] Augustine also points out that an individual who seems to have what he wants may still be unhappy. To be happy, one must not only have what one wants; what one wants must also be conducive to happiness. That one can be mistaken about what makes a person happy is developed further in *The Trinity* where Augustine cites Cicero's support for the idea that all persons desire happiness. In the *Hortensius*, Cicero observes that some equate happiness to living as one wants. According to Cicero, however, to live as one wants can lead to great unhappiness if one wants what is not right.[198] Augustine accepts Cicero's view, stating that no one ought to call a person happy who lives a criminal and licentious life. He goes on to note,

> A man is made unhappy just by having a bad will alone, but much more so by the power to fulfill the desires of his bad will . . . . All who are happy have what they want, though not all who have what they want are *ipso facto* happy; but those who do not have what they want, or have what they have no right to want, are *ipso facto* unhappy. Thus no one is happy but the man who has everything he wants, and wants nothing wrongly.[199]

Happiness, as opposed to unhappiness, consists in the possession of ". . . that which always endures and cannot be snatched away through any severe misfortune."[200] To be happy, one must possess something permanent. In addition, one must possess that which is actually good. It is in desiring rightly and obtaining an object that is truly good that a person will find happiness.[201] For Augustine, the one reality satisfying both of these requirements is God. Having come to the conclusion that impermanent goods

197. Augustine, *B. Vita* 2.10.
198. Augustine, *Trin.* 13.2.8.
199. Ibid.
200. Augustine, *B. Vita* 2.11.
201. Augustine, *Trin.* 13.2.9.

cannot make one happy, Augustine quickly transitions to the view that the eternal existence of the Christian God most perfectly fulfills the required permanence necessary for human happiness.[202] Likewise, in *The Trinity* he concludes that God is the source of good, which makes the human person happy.[203] The person who possesses God is the person who is truly happy.

Although Augustine's presentation of human happiness in *The Happy Life* does not explicitly rely on it, the idea of love is implied and even provides the foundational structure for Augustine's argument. By equating happiness with the possession of something that someone wants, Augustine is placing love at the center of his understanding of happiness, which in turn makes love foundational to his eudaemonistic morality. Recalling Augustine's view that love is simply the desire that moves a person toward an object, it follows that Augustine's understanding of happiness can also be stated in terms of love. Happiness, for Augustine, is the acquisition of what one wants, what one desires, what one loves. Augustine explicitly links the ideas of love and happiness in another of his early writings, *The Morals of the Catholic Church*. In it Augustine reiterates his contention that all people desire to be happy. Yet, rather than using the word want (the Latin *volo*) as he does in *The Happy Life*, Augustine transitions to one of the love terms, *amo*.[204] While the meaning of the two formulations remains very similar, the new presentation signals the importance of love to Augustine's understanding of the moral life. Love plays a consistent and central role in Augustine's new description of happiness.

> The title happy cannot, in my opinion, belong either to him who has not what he loves, whatever it may be, or to him who has what he loves if it is hurtful, or to him who does not love what he has, although it is good in perfection . . . . In none of these cases can the man be happy. I find, then, a fourth case, where the happy life exists—when that which is man's chief good is both loved and possessed. For what do we call enjoyment but having at hand the objects of love?[205]

In Augustine's account, love is the critical dynamic that will lead to either happiness or unhappiness. Directed toward the good and eternal, love leads

---

202. Augustine, *B. Vita* 2.11.
203. Augustine, *Trin.* 13.3.10.
204. Augustine, *B. Vita* 2.11.
205. Augustine, *Mor.* 2.4.

to happiness. Love, however, will lead to misery when directed toward what is not right or toward temporary goods.

Since virtue is the highest form of human love, it becomes fundamental to Augustine's understanding of the relationship between love and knowledge of God. Augustine maintains that a person cannot truly know an object without loving it. "For who can know to what extent something is good when he does not enjoy it?"[206] It is in enjoying or loving an object in one's possession that a person can fully appreciate the goodness of the object. Thus, the perfect love of God—i.e., virtue—is critical to the person's ability to know God.

The question may be asked, however, how does wisdom as knowledge of God relate to Augustine's earlier assertion that happiness lies in the possession of God? Augustine answers the question in his description of the manner in which the human person can possess an eternal good, the possession of which is constitutive of human happiness. Augustine states that to live happily is to possess an eternal object by knowing that object:

> For the eternal is that in which alone one can rightly place his confidence, it is that which cannot be taken away from the one who loves it, and it is that very thing which one possesses solely by knowing it. For of all things, the most excellent is what is eternal, and therefore we cannot possess it except by that part of ourselves in which lies our excellence, i.e., by our mind. But whatever is possessed by the mind is had by knowing, and no good is completely known which is not completely loved . . . . And since that which is loved necessarily affects with itself that which loves, it follows that what is eternal, loved in this way, affects the soul with eternity. Wherefore, strictly speaking, it is eternal life which is the happy life. However, what else but God is that eternal object which affects the soul with eternity?[207]

By possessing the eternal good of God through the working of the human person's highest function—the mind—the person can cast off the fear of loss that is incompatible with Augustine's understanding of happiness. To possess God is to know God. To know God, one must love God. To love God most perfectly, and therefore know God most fully, one must be

206. Augustine, *Div. Qu.* 35.1.

207. Ibid., 35.2.

virtuous. Virtue, then, empowers the human person to know God, and in so doing, makes that person happy.[208]

In Augustine's view on the relation between virtue and the knowledge of God, one can discern both Plotinian and Scriptural roots. Plotinus contends that the soul is able to see the One by means of virtue. Virtue purifies the soul of bodily concerns, thus enabling it to ascend to intellect and the One.[209] Here we see three significant elements that have made their way into Augustine's portrait of the moral life. First, for both Plotinus and Augustine, virtue provides a purification (in Augustine's words, a sanctification)[210] of the soul that enables it to see the divine. Secondly, for both thinkers virtue is a means to union with the One or God, rather than an end in itself.[211] Lastly, both Augustine and Plotinus see union with the divine as accomplished by the intellectual function of the mind.[212]

Scripture also offers support for Augustine's understanding of the relation between virtue and knowledge of God. Augustine concludes his discussion of the relation between knowledge and love in Question Thirty-Five of his *Eighty-Three Different Questions* with reference to Scripture's command of love for God and its description of eternal life. Augustine admonishes his reader to carefully consider the importance of the precept to love God with all of one's heart, soul, and mind (Matt 22:37), as well as Christ's summary of eternal life, which is to know God and the one sent by God, Jesus Christ (John 17:3).[213] The juxtaposition of the two verses implies their importance to one another in Augustine's moral thought. It is through

208. Although Augustine shares with Aristotle the idea that virtue produces happiness, the two conceive of the relation between virtue and happiness in significantly different manners. The difference between them lies in the role virtue plays in relation to the human person's end. For Aristotle, virtue is the end of the human person. That person is happy who is able to achieve excellence in his or her operations as a human being. It is the virtuous person that possesses the excellence necessary for an exceptional life and is therefore happy (Aristotle, *Nichomachean Ethics* 1098b21). For Augustine, on the other hand, virtue is only a means to the human person's end, which is the love of God. Virtue, although highly valued by Augustine, is nevertheless relegated to being a mechanism through which the human person achieves his or her end, rather than the end in itself (cf. Babcock "Early Augustine on Love," 53).

209. Plotinus, *Enn.* I.2.4.

210. Augustine, *Mor.* 13.22.

211. Plotinus, *Enn.* I.1.10. Augustine, *Div. Qu.* 35.2. Cf. Babcock, "Early Augustine on Love," 53.

212. Plotinus, *Enn.* I. 2.2, 2.6. Augustine, *Div. Qu.* 35.2.

213. Augustine, *Div. Qu.* 35.2.

loving God with all of one's power—that is through virtue—that one can come to know the true God. This knowledge, although imperfect, is no longer merely the knowledge of faith. It is the wisdom gained through loving Christ, the virtue and wisdom of God (1 Cor 1:24). The happy life, then, is the wisdom bequeathed to the virtuous person through her love for God.

The Humility of Wisdom

Augustine begins his discussion in Book Fourteen of *The Trinity* by describing his view of wisdom. Differing from the Greeks, who define wisdom as knowledge of things human and divine, Augustine asserts that knowledge concerns the intellectual apprehension of things temporal, while wisdom concerns knowledge of the divine.[214] Humility plays an important role for Augustine in relation to both knowledge and wisdom. Knowledge in Augustine's view can leave a person especially susceptible to pride. It plays a positive role, however, as the intellectual aspect of faith that leads to the wisdom constituted by knowledge of God. Humility is especially significant for a person's self-knowledge, which Augustine cites in both *Confessions* and *The Trinity* as the starting point in the search for the wisdom that is knowledge of God.[215] For Augustine, the human person's accurate self-knowledge is established in the humility of Christ's incarnation. God humbled himself in becoming human. The human person must therefore also be humble, but must also remember his dignity as the image and likeness of God. The call to be humble requires that a person remain above the level of an animal but shun the false elevation of pride.[216] It is by shunning false elevation that Augustine sees the height of self-knowledge, even asserting humiliation as the gift of God's mercy that enables a person to see the evil he has done.[217] Humility speaks the truth about each person because it is in humility that one can acknowledge his sins and failures.[218] He makes the point that it

214. Augustine, *Trin.* 14.1.3.

215. Cf. Augustine, *Conf.* book 7 and *Trin.* books 11 and 12 for examples of Augustine's use of the neo-Platonic turn to the interior.

216. Augustine, *Jo. Ev. Tr.* 25.16 (2) (FCNT 79:254). Cf. Augustine, *Trin.* Prologue 4.1. See also Schlabach, "Hermeneutic of Humility," 317 for the importance of humility to authentic self-knowledge.

217. Augustine, *S.* 159B.2 (WSA III/11:147–48).

218. Augustine, *Ep. Jo.* 1.6 (WSA III/14:27).

is humility, particularly the humility of confession, which leads from the knowledge of God provided by faith to the vision of God in wisdom.[219]

Augustine also frequently makes the point that the truth of God shines most brightly through humility. He asserts that the lives of the humble manifest God's grace with a clarity that cannot be replicated in the lives of the rich or the learned. Following the thought of St. Paul (1 Cor 1:27–28), Augustine articulates a developed version of the apostle's argument.

> Our Lord Jesus Christ came not only for the salvation of the poor but also of the rich, not only of commoners, but also of kings. He refused, all the same, to choose kings for his disciples, refused rich people, refused the nobly born, refused the learned; but instead he chose poor, uneducated, low-born fisherman, in whom his grace would shine through more clearly. He came, you see, to give the potion of humility and to cure pride. And if he had first called a king, the king would have said that it was his rank that was chosen; if he had first called a learned man, he would have said it was his teaching that was chosen. Those who were being called to lowliness and humility would have to be called by lowly and humble people. And so it is that Christ did not gain a fisherman through an emperor, but an emperor through a fisherman.[220]

Christ chose humble apostles and followers so that the greatness exhibited by those followers could be clearly seen as the gift of God's grace.[221]

Perhaps the most significant aspect of the relation between wisdom and humility for Augustine is his position that it is through humility that a person is able to see God. Augustine declares time and again that it is the humble that truly know God and should thus be considered truly wise. The mysteries of God, Augustine reminds us, are revealed to the little ones, the humble, but are hidden from the wise and the learned (Matt 11:25, Luke 10:21).[222] The wise and the learned to whom Augustine refers are classical philosophers of all sorts who reject Christ as the mediator between God and humanity.[223] According to Augustine, the fundamental Christian idea they fail to grasp is that all things have been handed over to the humble

---

219. Augustine, *En. Ps.* 146.14 (WSA III/20:437).

220. Augustine, *S.* 360B.24 (WSA III/11:381).

221. Augustine, *Civ. Dei* 18.49.

222. Augustine, *S.* 67.8 (WSA III/3:219); *S.* 68.7 (WSA III/3:227).

223. Augustine, *S.* 68, note 5, (WSA III/3:233). Cf. Schlabach, "Hermeneutic of Humility," 317–18 for a discussion of the Platonist failure to embrace Christ's humility.

Christ by God the Father.[224] Due to their lack of humility, the learned of the world cannot conceive of a God who takes on the flesh of mortality and suffers the disgrace of death on the cross. For Augustine, it is in the philosopher's lack of humility that he fails to understand the nature of God. In Christ, God has provided his definitive self-revelation to humanity. This revelation comes by way of and includes humility as a critical aspect of divine love.[225] By ignoring and even despising humility, philosophers consign themselves to ignorance of Christ who reveals the majesty of God. Stuck in their pride, they understand neither the humble love of God nor the sovereign majesty to which that love leads.[226] Wisdom, then, finds its perfection not in the pride of the philosopher, but in the humility of the lowly. By grasping the humility of God, the lowly grasp authentic knowledge of God. In doing so, the humble not only become wise, but also achieve the sublime happiness only available in the possession of God.

Having examined the role of humility in Augustine's moral thought we can now investigate the importance of humility to Augustine's understanding of the heights of human greatness.

---

224. Augustine, *S.* 68.8 (WSA III/3:228).

225. Studer, *Trinity and Incarnation*, 179.

226. Augustine, *S.* 160.3 (WSA III/5:130).

4

Augustine on Humility and Human Greatness

THE TERMINOLOGICAL ANALYSIS OF the preceding chapter highlighted three issues to which Augustine related the idea of humility most frequently. When discussing humility, Augustine did so most often in reference to the person of Jesus. The second most frequent context in which he raised humility was in relation to the sin of pride. The third, which will be the focus of the ensuing discussion, was the importance of humility to human greatness. In addition to the close relationship between each of these topics and humility, the frequency with which Augustine addresses each in the context of humility betrays a close interrelation among the three issues themselves. Humility's relationship to pride and the light shed on humility in the figure of Christ both have enormous implications for Augustine's paradoxical conception of the relationship between humility and greatness. Pride for Augustine is the greatest impediment to human greatness.[1] As such, its relationship to humility becomes essential to Augustine's view of human excellence. The person of Christ figures prominently in Augustine's discussion of humility and greatness because Christ not only represents both poles of the relationship, but also demonstrates the relationship between the two. Humility is personified in Jesus's incarnation and death, and it is precisely these actions, according to Augustine's interpretation of Scripture, which lead to his exaltation.[2] In light of these considerations, I will begin my examination of humility and greatness with a description of the interaction between pride and humility. Following that discussion, I

1. Augustine, *En. Ps.* 58(2).5 (WSA III/17:171).

2. Augustine, *S.* 142.2 (WSA III/4:413). Cf. Augustine, *S.* 354.9 (WSA III/10:162), *S.*260C.5 (WSA III/7:197).

will depict the manner in which Augustine looks to Jesus as the embodiment of both humility and sublimity. Finally, in the context set by humility's relationship to pride and its manifestation in the humble exaltation of Jesus, I will address Augustine's paradoxical conception of the importance of humility to human greatness.

Humility: God's Therapy for the Sin of Pride

The opposition between humility and pride is fundamental to Augustine's understanding of the moral life and his view of humility and greatness. He frequently employs therapeutic metaphors to depict the relationship. Humility, for Augustine, is the medicine through which the tumor of pride may be healed.[3] The proud are healed by humbly stepping down from their exalted position.[4] Typically, Augustine presents humility as the medicine for pride in the context of Christ's humility. The humility of Christ is the medicine for human pride, which should feel shame in the face of God's humility.[5] Augustine depicts Christ as the doctor who drinks the medicine of humility first to overcome the reluctance of his human patients to embrace such a lowly remedy.[6]

Augustine does more than merely assert humility as the remedy to pride; he also describes the manner in which it acts as a tonic, giving frequent examples of its healing effects. Humility's healing activity affects the many aspects through which pride corrupts a person's soul and will. The reflections to follow will demonstrate how knowledge, the idea of self-purification, the envy that inevitably results from pride, and the soul's orientation away from God are all aspects of pride that the grace of humility is able to overcome.

I have already indicated many of the intellectual aspects of pride to which Augustine gives warning. In addition to those aspects, Augustine asserts that pride of knowledge is the source of heresy and apostasy within the church as seen in the prideful person's desire to draw other people to herself rather than drawing them to Christ.[7] In addressing the intellectual

3. Augustine, *Trin.* 8.3.7. Cf. MacQueen, "*Contemptus Dei*," 283 for a brief discussion of the medicinal effects of humility.

4. Augustine, *S.* 125.6 (WSA III/4:257).

5. Augustine, *S.* 123.1 (WSA III/4:244).

6. Augustine, *S.* 159B.13 (WSA III/11:158–59).

7. Augustine, *S.* 346B.3 (WSA III/10:82). Cf. MacQueen, "*Contemptus Dei*," 274 for discussion of the link between pride and heresy.

pride of the Platonists, he asserted their pride was not only a product of inflated intellectual activity, but was also a rejection of Christ himself. The Platonists were repulsed by the humility of Christ and manifested their pride in their unwillingness to be corrected by Christian doctrine.[8] He even names Porphyry as an example of Platonist pride as he withdrew from the teaching of Christ as a result of his pride of knowledge.[9] In opposition to the pride of the philosophers, Augustine stresses the idea that true knowledge is given to the meek, the humble, and the docile. One who does not humble herself cannot learn the ways of Christ.[10]

Augustine also presents humility as the cure for the social conflict sown by the sin of pride. For Augustine, pride is not only the mother of all heresy, but also gives birth to the discord of envy. Wherever one finds pride, he asserts, there one will also find jealousy and envy.[11] The self-love of pride gives rise to animosity toward others who compete for the temporal goods coveted by the person of pride.[12] The prideful person's dedication to serving himself will inevitably alienate others because selfishness is not an attractive attribute. Augustine maintains that to be free of the child envy, one must strangle the parent, which is pride.[13] Such strangling comes through the agency of humility. A person loves others because love is not puffed up by pride and is therefore not jealous or envious. Humility is the foundational element of such love. To encourage humility is to promote love of others because humility will overcome the envy and alienation generated by pride.[14]

Augustine characterizes the worst form of pride as the human tendency toward self-justification. "There are some people who think that they can purify themselves for contemplating God and cleaving to him by their own power and strength of character, which means in fact that they are thoroughly defiled by pride. No vice is more vehemently opposed by divine law . . . ."[15] He assigns such pride to a variety of groups, one of which yet to be mentioned is the Jews of the New Testament. Having been given the

---

8. Augustine, *Civ. Dei* 10.29. Cf. Schlabach, "Hermeneutic of Humility," 317.

9. Augustine, *Civ. Dei* 10.28.

10. Augustine, *Conf.* 7.9.14.

11. Augustine, *S.* 354.5 (WSA III/10:158).

12. Augustine, *Lib. Arb.* 1.4.10.

13. Augustine, *S.* 399:7 (WSA III/10:462).

14. Augustine, *S.* 142:12 (WSA III/4:421).

15. Augustine, *Trin.* 4.4.20. Cf. *En. Ps.* 58(1).7 (WSA III/17:153).

gift of the Law, the Jews of the Bible believe that they can fulfill the Law's dictates through their own efforts. The exclusion of some Jews from the kingdom even as it is opened to humble Gentiles is based on the pride of their self-justification through the works of the Law.[16] Augustine asserts that this was Saul of Tarsus's spiritual state prior to his humiliation and conversion by Christ.[17] Through humility, Saul the Jew—like any other Jew willing to be humble—could be saved. The view that the human person could fulfill the Law without the aid of grace was a grave error of pride for Augustine. He viewed such notions of self-purification as a great uncleanness of soul[18] that could only be overcome by the humility of Christ.[19]

A last aspect of the opposition between pride and humility that Augustine often emphasized was pride's role as the largest impediment between God and the human person.[20] Augustine draws this conclusion both from his study of Scripture and the experience of his own conversion to Christianity. He cites the *Book of Sirach* often in his characterization of pride as the beginning of sin, which separates the human person from God (Sir 10:13).[21] Irreligious pride is a force that withdraws a person from God.[22] As both the Old and New Testament declare (Prov 3:34, 1 Pet 5:5, Jas 4:6), God resists the proud who in their self-love lack the ability to approach God. Augustine found these scriptural principles confirmed by his own religious experience. Pride prevented him from understanding Scripture, and conceit made him unready to learn.[23] One of the most significant events recalled by Augustine prior to his conversion was the conversion story of the Roman Platonist and aristocrat Victorinus. After having been convinced of Christianity's truth, Victorinus could no longer be ashamed of Christ's humility and bowed his head to the yoke of Christ's cross in his conversion.[24] The humility exhibited by Victorinus would prove instrumental to Augustine's own conversion as he struggled to overcome the

---

16. Augustine, *S.* 77.15 (WSA III/3:325). Dodaro, "Gift of Humility," 87.

17. Augustine, *S.* 169.9 (WSA III/5:227).

18. Augustine, *S.* 198.36 (WSA III/11:208).

19. Augustine, *S.* 169A.1 (WSA III/6:64).

20. Augustine, *Trin.* 13.5.22.

21. Augustine, *S.* 346B.3 (WSA III/10:82).

22. Augustine, *Conf.* 5.3.4.

23. Ibid., 4.15.26. Cf. Schlabach, "Hermeneutic of Humility," 316 on the importance of humility for Augustine's assent to the truth of God.

24. Augustine, *Conf.* 8.2.3–4.

intellectual pride he had developed over the course of his life, which demonstrates one of humility's fundamental roles in Augustine's thought: its power to overcome pride as a barrier between God and the human person. Humility—in particular God's humility—is what brings God and the human person together.

Christ's Humility in Augustine's Thought

A final aspect of Augustine's view of humility is the importance of the figure of Christ as the personification and standard of humility. Christ's incarnation, childhood, lifelong example, and crucifixion all serve to illustrate a view of humility that implies lowliness, love of God, and love for neighbor.[25] In Augustine's view, a humble will provides the means through which a person may draw close to God by emptying the person of self-love and thus making space for the grace of God. Given Augustine's position regarding the priority of grace over the human will, such humility must be seen as the result of God's beneficent grace, which he indicates is a function of God's mercy.[26] For Augustine, the height of that grace is made manifest in the person of Jesus Christ, who is the embodiment of the grace of humility. The Christology of Augustine's approach to humility may be its most consistent and significant characteristic. In the reflections that follow, it becomes evident that for Augustine, Christ's incarnation and death set the highest standard through which humility can be understood. At times he even seems to see Christ's entire mission through the lens of Christ's effort to teach humility.[27] Augustine also emphasizes Christ's humility as "The Way" (John 14:6) for Christians and consistently highlights the link between Christ's humility and his greatness.

Augustine presents the incarnation and Jesus's death on the cross as the standard by which any understanding of humility must be judged.[28] He notes that many of Jesus's actions can be viewed as acts of humility (e.g.,

25. Cf. Augustine, *Conf.*10.42.68 for comments on Christ as example of humility. See also *Conf.* 1.19.30 for Christ's childhood as symbol of humility. Cf. *S.* 68.11 (WSA III/3:230-31) for a discussion of the incarnation and crucifixion in relation to Christ's humility. See also Bacchi, "A Ministry Characterized by and Exercised in Humility," 409.

26. Augustine, *Gr. et Lib. Arb.* 14.28.

27. Cf. Augustine, *S.* 4A.1 (WSA III/1:214) for an example of Augustine characterizing Christ's mission as a mission to teach humility and overturn pride.

28. Augustine, *S.* 68.11 (WSA III/3:230).

his baptism by John in the Jordan River), but none equal the act of humility that constitutes the incarnation.[29] Christ's humility is unequaled[30] because in his person, the perfection and infinity of God took on the limitation of flesh and was thus rendered susceptible to suffering and death.[31] Augustine sees in the incarnation, suffering, and death of Jesus, the freely chosen humbling of the eternal Son of the Father, who saw fit to lower himself to take the form of a mortal creature. Christ's self-emptying in his incarnation and death reveals the true nature of humility and thus becomes the primary example by which Augustine understands the virtue.[32]

Augustine asserts that Christ is not only the preeminent example of humility, but also declares that a chief purpose of Christ's mission is to teach humility.[33] Since human debility finds its source in pride, Augustine sees Christ's humility as the necessary virtue to overturn sinful pride.[34] Augustine observes that Christ teaches by both word and example,[35] and since pride is the primary sin, the primary lesson Jesus communicates is humility.

> What, Lord, are we to learn from you? . . . . How to hang up the sky, fix the earth solid, pour out the sea, spread the air around, fill all the elements with the appropriate animals, arrange the ages, rotate the seasons . . . . Or do you perhaps want us to learn how to do the works you did on earth . . . . So we are to learn from you how to cleanse lepers, how to drive out demons, put fevers to flight, command the sea and the waves, raise the dead? Not things like that either, he says. Tell us, then, what? *Because I am meek and humble of heart.* Let God put you to shame, human pride. The Word of God says it, the Only-begotten says it, the Most High says it: *Learn of me, because I am meek and humble of heart.* Such high majesty came down to humility, and is man going to stretch himself up? Pull in your horns, O man, and reduce yourself to the humble Christ, or you may stretch yourself so far that you burst.[36]

---

29. Augustine, *S.* 292.3 (WSA III/8:139). Cf. Burns, "Origin of Evil," 82.

30. Augustine, *S.* 304.3 (WSA III/8:317).

31. Augustine, *S.* 23A.3 (WSA III/2:69).

32. Augustine, *S.* 68.11 (WSA III/3:230); *S.* 50.11 (WSA III/2:350).

33. Augustine, *S.* 51.4 (WSA III/3:23). Augustine *Jo. Ev. Tr.* 5.3 (2) (FCNT 78:111). Cf. MacQueen, "*Contemptus Dei*," 282.

34. Augustine, *S.* 142.2 (WSA III/4:413–14).

35. Augustine, *S.* 218C.4 (WSA III/6:196).

36. Augustine, *S.* 70A.1 (WSA III/3:243–44).

Augustine also points to the universality of Christ's mission as cause for its emphasis on teaching humility. Had Christ come as a member of the aristocracy with important family connections and other worldly honors, the rich and proud of the world would have seen in Jesus a justification of their roles and perspectives on life. In his concern for all people, rich and poor, Christ came humbly, knowing the poor would be open to his humble message and the rich would be challenged by such a message. For Augustine, the only chance for the rich to learn humility was for them to be saved by a humble God.[37]

The importance of Christ's example of humility can be seen in Augustine's frequent characterization of it as "the Way" all Christians must follow. For Augustine, no one is excused from learning the humility of Christ.[38] It is the unavoidable path to the Christian's destiny of eternal life with God.[39] It is necessary for the rich, who can achieve humility in poverty of spirit,[40] and for the poor, who may not be humble despite their material poverty.[41] This humble way is illustrated for Augustine throughout the life and teaching of Jesus. It is evident in the simplicity of Christ's life as a child, which Augustine considered to be a symbol of humility.[42] For Augustine, Christ's baptism was one of the most important acts of humility in his earthly ministry.[43] Whether it is his interaction with the Canaanite woman (Matt 15:21–28),[44] his use of parables (the Pharisee and Tax Collector being a primary example for Augustine),[45] or his dialogue with the sons of Zebedee (Matt 20:20–23),[46] the humility and lowliness of Christ is the way a Christian must follow, and as a result, becomes the goal to be achieved by a Christian.[47] The humble way takes on such importance that it even compares in significance to that of wisdom. It does not matter, says Augustine, that some people lack the wisdom to see the goal of life. As long

---

37. Augustine, S. 4A.1 (WSA III/1:214).

38. Augustine, S. 164.7 (WSA III/5:191).

39. Augustine, S. 123.3 (WSA III/4:245). Cf. Dodaro, "Gift of Humility," 87.

40. Augustine, S. 14.4–5 (WSA III/1:318–19).

41. Augustine, S. 53A.2 (WSAS III/3:78).

42. Augustine, Conf. 1.19.30.

43. Augustine, Jo. Ev. Tr. 5.5(2), 5.8(3) (FCNT, 111, 112).

44. Augustine, S. 77.1, 11 (WSA III/3:317, 322); S. 60A.3 (WSA III/3:140).

45. Augustine, S. 60A.4 (WSA III/3:140–41); S. 290.6 (WSA III/8:128).

46. Augustine, S. 20A.6 (WSA III/2:24–25); S. 160.5 (WSA III/5:131–32).

47. Augustine, S. 360C.4 (WSA III/11:389).

as one follows the way of humility, he will reach the goal, whether seen or unseen. Those with the wisdom to see the goal can reach it, but only if they do so through humility.[48] Given the penchant of the wise to be puffed up by their knowledge and to tend toward intellectual pride, humility becomes the narrow path to their salvation. A head swollen with pride cannot enter God's narrow gate.[49] The solution Augustine offers to the rich, the aristocrats, the intellectually proud, and even the poor who are conceited is the humble way taught and lived out by Christ.

Augustine's understanding of humility and greatness draws its greatest support from the example of Jesus as portrayed in the passages of Scripture. "Christ the way is the humble Christ; Christ the truth and the life is Christ exalted and God. If you walk along the humble Christ, you will arrive at the exalted Christ; if in your sickly health and debility you do not spurn the humble one, you will abide in perfect health and strength with the exalted one."[50] Humility is not only demonstrated by Christ, it is also necessary for a person to understand Christ as the exalted one. Christ, Augustine asserts, took on the poverty of flesh in order to become the neighbor of the human person. The Platonists in their pride reject a God who has taken on the weakness of the flesh and therefore cannot recognize Christ as the divine Logos precisely because he appears to be a neighbor.[51] One can only recognize Christ as a neighbor if he looks at him through the lens of humility. In doing so, in keeping faith with Christ in his poverty, it is then that one can be lifted up by Christ in his exaltation.[52]

For Augustine, the self-emptying of the eternal Son of the Father in his incarnation and death is not only an example to be emulated by Christ's followers; it is also the grace by which Christ raises up mortal humans to eternal life. Through his humble death and subsequent resurrection, Christ raised "flesh up to heaven, where he is seated as flesh at the right hand of the Father."[53] Those who are measured by Christ's humility in earthly life, the lowly and the poor in spirit, will be honored by Christ,[54] who derives his

48. Augustine, S. 198.61 (WSA III/11:227).

49. Augustine, S. 142.5 (WSA III/4:416).

50. Augustine, S. 142.2 (WSA III/4:413. Cf. MacQueen, "*Contemptus Dei*," 282–83 for a description of Christ as the exemplar of humility.

51. Augustine, *Civ. Dei* 10.29.

52. Augustine, S. 41.7 (WSA III/2:232). Cf. *En. Ps.* 66.10 (WSA III/17:321).

53. Augustine, S. 359.9 (WSA III/10:207).

54. Augustine, S. 68.11 (WSA III/3:230).

nobility from nothing earthly, rather conferring nobility on all who accept his poverty in faith.[55] Christ came humble and lowly, and as he rose, he lifted up anyone who believed in him.[56] In his interpretation of the sons of Zebedee's desire to sit at the right and left of Christ in glory, Augustine asserts that it is Christ's grace that will lift some to such positions of glory. Those people, in Augustine's view, will not necessarily be the apostles. To sit on Christ's right and left hand will be reserved for the humble of heart.

> *Can you drink the cup that I am going to drink?* Then they were so eager for the heights that, ignorant of what they could do, ready to promise what they didn't yet have, they said, *We can.* He answered, "*My cup you shall indeed drink,* because I grant you the power to drink it, because from being weak I will make you strong, because I grant you the grace of endurance so that you may drink the cup of humility; *but to sit on my right hand or my left is not mine to give you, but it has been prepared by my Father for others* (Matt 20:22–23) . . . What does that mean for others? For the humble, not the proud.[57]

For Augustine it is Christ who gives the humble the strength to persevere in his grace, and it is the humble who will sit at Jesus's right and left at the coming of his kingdom. Using Christ's example of humble greatness as his starting point, Augustine becomes the champion of a counterintuitive relationship between human greatness and humility.

Humility and Greatness in Augustine's Thought

Due to the Christological emphasis of Augustine's sermons, the idea of humility and its relationship to greatness is an oft-treated topic.[58] This aspect of Augustine's thought is not confined to his preaching, however. One of the most succinct and powerful presentations of his paradoxical view of humility and greatness can be found in Book Fourteen of *The City of God*. There he asserts,

> In a remarkable way, therefore, there is in humility something which exalts the mind, and something in exaltation which abases

---

55. Augustine, S. 341:4 (WSA III/11:285).

56. Augustine, *Trin.* 4.3.13.

57. Augustine, S. 20A.8 (WSA III/2:25–26).

58. Doyle, "Introduction to Augustine's Preaching," 13.

it. It may indeed seem paradoxical to say that exaltation abases and humility exalts. Godly humility, however, makes the mind subject to what is superior to it. But nothing is superior to God; and that is why humility exalts the mind by making it subject to God. Exaltation, on the other hand, is a vice; and for that very reason it spurns subjection, and so falls away from Him Who has no superior. Thus, it is cast down, and brings to pass what is written: "Thou castedst them down while they were being exalted" (Ps 73:118). It does not say, "When they had been exalted," as if they were first exalted and then cast down. Rather they were cast down even while they were being exalted: their very exaltation was itself a kind of abasement.

This is why humility is most highly praised in the City of God and commended to the City of God during its pilgrimage in this world; and it is especially exemplified in that City's King, Who is Christ. We are also taught by the Holy Scriptures that the vice of exaltation, the opposite of this virtue, holds complete sway over Christ's adversary, the devil. Certainly, this is the great difference that distinguishes the two cities of which we are speaking. The one is a fellowship of godly men, and the other of the ungodly; and each has its own angels belonging to it. In the one city, love of God has been given pride of place, and, in the other, love of self.[59]

Pausing for an examination of this passage reveals many of the elements I have previously identified in Augustine's morality and treatment of humility. Beginning with the function of love in which it subjects a person to the object loved, humility as love for God subjects the person to God.[60] Augustine's description likewise calls to mind his description of the relationship between virtue and its origin in God. A person acquires virtue by adapting himself to the immutable lights of virtue that exist in truth itself.[61] It is through humility that one is able to subject himself to truth and attain virtue, a process Augustine elsewhere describes as following or loving God.[62] The passage also references God as the highest good, which recalls Augustine's formulation of God as the greatest good, surpassing all others as the eternal good that can never be lost,[63] for nothing will separate the

59. Augustine, *Civ. Dei* 14.13.

60. Augustine, *Mor.* 21.39.

61. Augustine, *Lib. Arb.* 2.19.52–53.

62. Augustine, *Mor.* 6.9-10.

63. Augustine, *B. Vita* 2.11.

human person from the love of God (Rom 8:38).[64] In the dynamic aspect of exaltation's abasement of the mind, we can see the power of *cupiditas*,[65] or love for base things. In the exaltation and self-love of the human person, a person is subjected to himself, an object infinitely lower than God, thus representing a degradation compared to the person subjected to the sublimity of God. In addition, we again see Augustine's characteristic emphasis on Christ as the exemplification of humility. Implied in that exemplification is Christ's self-abasement in his incarnation and crucifixion,[66] as well as the glorification to which his self-abasement leads.[67] Augustine also mentions the role of Scripture in the understanding of the vice of exaltation, asserting that Scripture reveals Christ's adversary, the devil, as completely under the sway of the desire for exaltation. Lastly, he mentions the social dimensions of humility and pride as the foundations of the earthly and heavenly cities. The love of self dominates the earthly city bringing to mind the rancor of envy Augustine attributes to pride,[68] while love of God is central to the heavenly city, which is the abode of the godly who have subjected themselves to the infinite goodness of God's love.

Notwithstanding the relevance of the passage to all of these aspects of Augustine's thought, its highlight is Augustine's assertion that humility and greatness, despite an outward appearance of opposition, are inextricably entwined. Augustine proclaims that true exaltation is achieved through humility, and exaltation without humility is a counterfeit soon to be outlived. To demonstrate why and how Augustine feels this to be the case, I will examine his understanding of human greatness or exaltation and how he does not condemn the desire for exaltation, but presupposes it to his elaboration of humility. I will also examine the importance of his frequent admonition to avoid the love of praise and his exhortation to refer all glory to God. Following Augustine's praise for avoiding acclaim, I will conclude the section by drawing out the implications of Augustine's Christological humility in regard to his understanding of human greatness in relation to the human person as the image and likeness of God.

---

64. Augustine, *Mor.* 11.18.

65. Augustine, *Lib. Arb.* 1.11.22. Cf. *En. Ps.* 93:16 (WSA III/18:392) for a similar formulation in which Augustine asserts that the proud are abased in their very act of exaltation.

66. Augustine, *S.* 68.11 (WSA III/3:231).

67. Augustine, *S.* 142.2 (WSA III/4:413).

68. Augustine, *S.* 354.5 (WSA III/10:158).

Augustine's Conception of Human Greatness

Augustine inherits a tradition that views greatness primarily in terms of virtue. Aristotle's magnanimous person holds the virtue of magnanimity as the crown to her possession of all the other virtues.[69] The epitome of a great person in the view of the Stoics is the sage who is able to subdue emotion in relation to goods of indifference in his pursuit of the greatest good, virtue.[70] Likewise, Cicero considers authentic *gloria* to be the approbation given to the person of virtue by others of similar virtue.[71] A modern interpreter of Augustine, Robert Dodaro, provides a similar perspective by defining what he calls the heroic ideal as a person of outstanding virtue who can serve as a prominent and public role model.[72] Augustine's position, aligned most closely with the view of Plotinus in which the highest calling of a person is union with the One, is no doubt influenced by the tradition, but altered based on his understanding of virtue as the perfection of love for God.[73] Virtue is a fundamental element of human greatness for Augustine because of its role in perfecting love for God. Yet just as virtue is not the end of the moral life for Augustine, neither is it the essence of greatness. As we will see shortly, Augustine conceives of human greatness as a person's authentic relationship with God. God, who replaced virtue as the end of the moral life in Augustine's thought, also replaces virtue as the greatest calling of the human person.

Unlike his approach to the idea of humility, Augustine uses many different words to describe human greatness. *Honor verus, melius natura, magna natura, magnum bonum, summae lucis, sapientia, alta, celsus, immortalitas, sursum facere,* and *elatio*[74] are just some of the Latin words and phrases he uses in reference to human greatness. A query of Augustine's entire corpus for synonyms of greatness used in conjunction with the cognates of *humilitas* and *humilis* reveals *excelsus* (fifty-seven uses), *celsitudo*

---

69. Aristotle, *Nicomachean Ethics* 1124a1–2.

70. Schofield, "Stoic Ethics," 247–48.

71. Cicero, *De Republica* 6.23–24.

72. Dodaro, "Augustine's Revision of the Heroic Ideal,"141 (note 1).

73. Augustine, *Mor.* 15.25.

74. Augustine used the terms *honor verus, melius natura, magna natura, magnum bonum, summae lucis,* and *sapientia* in reference to human greatness in Books Twelve and Fourteen of *Trin. Alta, celsitudinem, immortalitatem,* and *sursum faciat* appear in *Serm* 20A.7 to describe human greatness and *elationis* is used in the *Civ. Dei* 14.13 to describe exaltation.

(twenty-one uses), *altitudo* (twenty uses), and *sublimitas* (six uses) as the words Augustine employs most frequently when depicting the relationship between humility and greatness.[75]

Despite the variety of terms to describe the idea, human exaltation for Augustine is definitively understood in relation to one entity, which is God. Augustine categorizes the will, which represents the entirety of the person's status as a moral agent,[76] as only an intermediate good due to the fact that it is not only the mechanism by which a person can live a good life, but it also provides the capability for a person to choose evil.[77] Unlike higher goods (e.g., virtue), which by their nature cannot be misused, the will can be misused. He points out that although human nature is not the greatest good since it can be corrupted through sin, it is capable of sharing in the greatest nature (i.e., God's nature) and therefore must still be considered great despite its vulnerability.[78] That greatness is manifest in the human person's creation in the image and likeness of God, which achieves its highest calling when turned in love toward God.[79] Augustine asserts that the human person can be a created god, so long as that person clings to participation in the life of the true God through humble love and obedience.[80] The image of God in the human person is truly great and wise when sharing in the supreme light of God's eternal existence.[81]

Augustine also describes human greatness in relation to the desire for immortality. That desire is similarly reflected in the portraits of human greatness painted by the likes of Aristotle and Cicero. Aristotle's magnanimous person is concerned with the highest honors, the highest of which rise above the transience of typical human existence.[82] Magnanimity in this sense can be seen as the pursuit of greatness that yields immortality in the memories of succeeding generations.[83] Cicero, too, points to immortality as

75. Library of Latin Texts—Series A, http://clt.brepolis.net.proxycu.wrlc.org/ (accessed April 23, 2012). Cf. Augustine, *S.* 184.1 for examples of Augustine's use of the terms *sublimitas* and *altitudo*. Cf. Augustine, *S.* 206.1 for a typical use of *celsitudo* and *excelsus*.

76. Augustine, *Conf.* 5.10.18. Cf. Schlabach, "Hermeneutic of Humility," 310.

77. Augustine, *Lib. Arb.* 2.19.52–53.

78. Augustine, *Trin.* 14.2.6.

79. Ibid., 12.3.16.

80. Augustine, *Civ. Dei* 14.13.

81. Ibid., 14.4.15.

82. Aristotle, *Nichomachean Ethics* 1125a35.

83. Arnhart, "Statesmanship as Magnanimity," 267.

an intrinsic aspect of *gloria*. True glory for Cicero is not ephemeral but is a real and permanent substance constituted by the acknowledgement of one's virtue by others who are wise and virtuous.[84] Augustine likewise associates greatness with immortality. Immortality for Augustine is not merely the memory of one's excellence in the minds of younger generations, however; it is the eternal life he associates with a person's loving acquisition of God. In Augustine's view, the human longing for immortality grows out of the desire for happiness.

> All people then want to be happy; if they want something true, this necessarily means they want to be immortal . . . . They cannot be happy unless they are alive; therefore they do not want their being alive to cease. So anyone who is truly happy or desires to be, wants to be immortal. But a man does not live happily if he has not got what he wants; so it is altogether impossible for a life to be genuinely happy unless it is immortal.[85]

Immortality for Augustine coincides with his understanding of the human person's *telos* in the intellectual possession of God, for it is in possessing God's eternal goodness that a person achieves his greatest end.[86] Augustine asserts that all desire the heights, which are nothing less than the immortality of possessing and enjoying God's eternal sublimity.[87]

Love of God Rather than Love of Greatness

A final topic to consider before detailing Augustine's view of humility and greatness is the human love or desire for greatness itself. Augustine's many thoughts on the relation between humility and greatness appear to presuppose the idea that the human desire for excellence is a benign or even a good phenomenon. Augustine observes that all people desire to achieve the heights of goodness, yet he does not provide a condemnation of such desire.[88] In his discussions of humility, Augustine takes up the Gospel story regarding the sons of Zebedee who requested seats at Christ's right and left hand once his kingdom is established (Matt 20:20–28; Mark 10:35–45). He

84. Cicero, *De Officiis* 2.43. Cf. Cicero, *Disputationes Tusculanae* 3.2.

85. Augustine, *Trin.* 13.3.11.

86. Augustine, *Div. Qu.* 35.2.

87. Augustine, *S.* 20A.7 (WSA III/2:25).

88. Augustine, *S.* 20A.7 (WSA III/2:25). Dodaro notes psychological literature backing a "universal urge to heroism." Dodaro, "Gift of Humility," 84.

observes that James and John had looked at where they wanted to go (i.e., the heights), but they had not examined the path that led to those heights.[89] In the passage, Christ points to the path of humility as the way to the heights, but neither he nor Augustine rebuke the apostles for having such desires in the first place. At other times, however, Augustine seems to imply that the very desire for greatness is unwelcome. Augustine contends that there is much evil in worldly ambition.[90] His following of St. Paul (Gal 6:14) in the assertion that one should take pride in nothing but the cross of Christ[91] and his admonition to boast in God rather than ourselves express a reluctance to embrace the grandeur humans tend to desire.[92] Similarly, Augustine cites Rome's passion for glory as both the key to its expansion and the ultimate foundation of its demise. Roman desire for glory, although a vice, subjugated all other vices to itself thus providing the foundation for its military and political success. Yet as a vice, it was unable to protect Rome from achieving glory through vicious rather than virtuous means, which led to the corruption of the Roman commonwealth once it had established its dominance.[93] Having provided this analysis of Roman history, Augustine concludes that avoiding love for praise makes a person more like to God. Humans must refer all glory to the agency of God.[94] In addition to these concerns, it is tempting to equate desire for greatness to Augustine's understanding of pride itself. After all, Augustine offers a definition of pride as the love of excelling.[95] Doesn't it follow that since the love of excelling is the foundation of sin as understood by Augustine, the desire for greatness should be likewise condemned by him? The answer to this question lies in the roles played by love and happiness in Augustine's understanding of the moral life.

Augustine's view of the relationship between love and happiness is the foundation for his view on the human desire for greatness, as it is the foundation for his view on any human desire. One of the fundamental aspects of love for Augustine is its faculty of desiring something for its own sake.[96] Love is the principle of motion that directs a person toward the object of his de-

---

89. Augustine, S. 160.5 (WSA III/5:131–32).

90. Augustine, S. 313A.4 (WSA III/9:93).

91. Augustine, S. 160.5 (WSA III/5:132).

92. Augustine, Trin. 13.5.21.

93. Augustine, Civ. Dei 5.12-13.

94. Ibid., 5.14.

95. Augustine, S. 354.6 (WSA III/10:159). Cf. MacQueen, "Contemptus Dei," 241.

96. Augustine, Sol. 1.13.22. See also Babcock, "Early Augustine on Love," 44.

sire.[97] Augustine characterizes a love as good or bad on the basis of the object at which it is directed.[98] A person is happy if he loves what is truly good and has possession of that object.[99] In addition, the object must not only be good, but it must also be permanently available to the person so that it cannot be taken from him against his will. By possessing a good of such permanence, the person can rest in its enjoyment without fear of its loss.[100]

God is the reality that most perfectly fulfills Augustine's criteria as the object whose possession will make a person truly happy. In *On Christian Doctrine*, Augustine further distinguishes what can be considered a good object of love through his distinction between what is to be used and what is to be enjoyed. Exhibiting his Stoic influences, Augustine asserts,

> . . . to enjoy a thing is to rest with satisfaction in it for its own sake. To use, on the other hand, is to employ whatever means are at one's disposal to obtain what one desires . . . . If we wish to return to our Father's home, this world must be used, not enjoyed, so that the invisible things of God may be clearly seen, being understood by the things that are made (Rom 1:20)—that is, by means of what is material and temporary we may lay hold upon that which is spiritual and eternal.[101]

Enjoyment, in Augustine's view, is to use something with delight.[102] Material and temporary objects are to be used as a means to attaining eternal objects, such as virtue or a good will. Eternal objects that are not God (e.g., the soul of another person) can be loved, but that love must be in reference to God, for God ought to be loved above all else. This is true from a philosophical perspective (i.e., God as the greatest good is owed the greatest love) as well as from a scriptural perspective, since such love is the fulfillment of the great commandment to love God with one's entire strength.

Applying Augustine's understanding of love and happiness to the desire for greatness, one can see both a negative manner in which one might desire greatness and a positive approach to the idea. Unsurprising as this may be, the line dividing the bad from the good context is determined by the person's orientation toward love of self (i.e., pride) or love of God. If a person

97. Augustine, *Mor.* 26.48.

98. Babcock, "Early Augustine on Love," 44.

99. Augustine, *Mor.* 3.4.

100. Augustine, *Lib. Arb.* 1.4.10.

101. Augustine, *Doc. Chr.* 1.4.4.

102. Ibid., 1.33.37.

desires greatness for himself without reference to God as a means to achieve self-love, it will (in Augustine's view) inevitably lead to evil. If one were to define greatness in like manner to Cicero's early definition, where *gloria* is widespread popularity, one would be desiring an intrinsically ephemeral good.[103] Such manner of desire for greatness would perfectly fulfill Augustine's understanding of sin. Sin for Augustine is the love of self (*superbia*) that leads a person to satisfy material and bodily desires (*cupiditas*) at the expense of spiritual, eternal goods.[104] If the desire for greatness is chosen or loved for its own sake, it is the manifestation of Augustine's view of *cupiditas*, where some inferior good is loved without reference to God. In the more likely circumstance of a person loving greatness for the sake of her love of self, the desire for greatness could be characterized as the sin of *superbia* in which a form of self-love is preferred to the love of God.[105] In each case, the temporary good of human greatness is desired over eternal goods.

One could counter such an argument on the basis of Cicero's mature conception of *gloria* in which it is viewed as the admiration of the virtuous for a person of great virtue.[106] Would not the pursuit of greatness by way of desire for virtue avoid Augustine's criteria for sin? Virtue, since it is a good that cannot be taken away against a person's will, is an eternal good that is a legitimate object of love both from the perspective of Augustine's Stoic predecessors and of Augustine himself. Such an argument would fulfill the Stoic criteria for a morally licit approach to greatness because in their estimation, virtue is the greatest good, which should be loved above all other realities.[107] The argument, however, falls short of Augustine's view of a morally good love, breaking down along the lines that separate Augustine's moral thought from his Greek predecessors. In Augustine's view, love for virtue without reference to God will lead to evil because it falls into

103. Cicero, *De Inventione* 2.55.166.

104. Cf. Augustine, *Gn. Adv. Man.* 2.15.22 for an account of pride as the root of sin. See *Lib. Arb.* 2.19.53 for Augustine's understanding of the role of *cupiditas* regarding sin. Also, *Civ. Dei* 14.13 for Augustine's position on the link between *superbia* and *cupiditas*. See also MacQueen, "*Contemptus Dei*," 254–55 for a discussion of the relation between *cupiditas* and self-love.

105. As Aristotle observes, most goods are chosen for the end of happiness rather than as ends themselves. Cf. Aristotle, *Nicomachean Ethics* 1097a37–1097b7; 1097b14–18 for his discussion of happiness as the most desirable of all human goods. That such is the case for Augustine is manifest in his many teachings on the nature of pride.

106. Cicero, *De Republica* 6.23–24.

107. Cicero, *De Finibus* 3.22.

the most pernicious aspect of pride's corruption. Pride in virtue leads to *superbia*, which starts the cycle of sin that leads to God's disqualification of a person.[108] The example of the Pharisee is again a powerful support to Augustine's position. The Pharisee's pride leaves the Pharisee unjustified and isolated from the divine love that is the source of his being.[109] The desire for greatness, then, can be properly ordered as long as it is the result of a person's love for God rather than the object of a person's love. The love for virtue or greatness is wholesome if it is a desire through which a person hopes to achieve possession of God.[110]

Humility: The Love of God that Secures Human Greatness

Augustine implicitly links humility to greatness when he defines pride, the principle most intrinsically opposed to humility, as the fundamental cause of moral corruption. Pride is the greatest obstacle to human perfection[111] not only in its function of turning the person away from the light and fire of God's love,[112] but also in its ability to focus a person's love on his own virtues. Augustine declares that it is when a person is acting virtuously that he has the most to fear from pride. Making progress toward virtue is the time in which a person is most sorely tempted by pride, which jeopardizes the very progress in virtue one has made.[113] Given this perspective, one can conclude that humility is the principle most important to human perfection because it is the virtue that keeps a person oriented towards God's grace, the source of goodness and virtue for the human person, while providing the mechanism through which pride of virtue may be overcome.

Augustine's view of pride as the greatest impediment to human greatness indicates the importance of humility to human excellence, but it does not detail how it is that humility, which appears quite literally opposed to exaltation, is in reality its foundation. Augustine turns to Scripture to explain the nature of the relationship. An explicit scriptural foundation for Augustine's view of humility and greatness is his interpretation of St. Paul's personal travails with pride recorded in Paul's *Second Letter to*

---

108. Augustine, *S.* 16B.2–4 (WSA III/1:363–65).

109. Ibid.

110. Augustine, *Doc. Chr.* 1.4.4.

111. Augustine, *En. Ps.* 58 (2).5 (WSA III/17:171).

112. Augustine, *Civ. Dei* 14.13.

113. Augustine, *En. Ps.* 58(2).5 (WSA III/17:171–72).

the Corinthians. Augustine ponders how even the apostle must struggle against pride. It is with dismay and even fear that Augustine recounts Paul's struggles.

> We can't say that God wasn't there with the apostle Paul, who was afraid, while he was engaged in combat, he might get swollen-headed. *In case,* he says, *I should get swollen-headed over the greatness of my revelations.* Notice him engaged in combat and conflict, not yet securely triumphant. *In case I should get swollen-headed over the greatness of my revelations.* Who is saying *In case I should get swollen-headed?* How terrifying, how really frightening! . . . *In case I should get swollen-headed,* he says, *there was given me a goad in my flesh, an angel of Satan . . . I begged the Lord three times to take it from me . . . .* To show you that God was there present, notice what answer he gives to Paul's thrice repeated plea: He said to me, says Paul, *My grace is sufficient for you; for strength is perfected in weakness* (2 Cor 12:8–9).[114]

Thus the foundation for Augustine's view that humility is the key to greatness is the idea that it is only through the humility of one's admission to weakness that a person can be opened up to the infinite grace and power of God.[115] As Dodaro observes, even the apostles and martyrs view themselves as sinners who have been pardoned.[116] It is on this basis that Augustine can assert, "The power of charity (is) brought to perfection in the weakness of humility."[117] When a person is humble or weakened, which Augustine understands as placing no trust in oneself, then he can be made strong, for in placing one's trust in God he is filled with the grace of the almighty.[118]

In addition to the importance of the teaching and experience of Paul to Augustine's understanding of humility and greatness, there are a number of further aspects of the relationship that he consistently emphasizes. Confession of sin, Augustine asserts, is the humble mechanism by which a person is justified and as a result is also exalted.[119] On the basis of Jesus's assertion that the Kingdom of God belongs to ones such as children, he also observes that littleness is proper to great souls; the very souls that will

---

114. Augustine, *S.* 163.8 (WSA III/5:173).

115. Augustine, *En. Ps.* 84.14 (WSA III/18:217).

116. Dodaro, "Heroic Ideal," 144.

117. Augustine, *Trin.* 4.1.2.

118. Ibid.

119. Augustine, *S.* 380.7 (WSA III/10:369).

inherit the kingdom.[120] Augustine also recognizes the fact that the great things in life frequently come by way of minute details. He asserts that one seeking greatness must lay hold of little things, and in so doing she will become great. If one wishes to take possession of God's loftiness, she must embrace God's lowliness.[121] One cannot be worthy of heaven's sublimity without embracing the indignity of Christ's cross.

Perhaps the most powerful link in Augustine's thought between humility and greatness is the idea that when a person voluntarily casts himself down in humility he will be lifted to greatness by God.[122] The paradigmatic example of such humility is Jesus himself. By focusing on the humility and greatness of Jesus's example, Augustine demonstrates the relation between humility, love, and greatness. In Augustine's view, Jesus as the eternal Son of the Father humbled himself by taking on flesh and dwelling among mortal humans.[123] This humbling was an epiphany of God's love for sinful humanity, which though ungodly, was loved by God to such an extent that God was willing to sacrifice his Son for its redemption (Rom 5:6–7).[124] The humiliation of the divine in Christ's mortality and subsequent death was not a humbling without any further end in view, however. Christ's humbling was ordered to his ultimate exaltation and to the exaltation of the human community he had come to save. Christ submitted to the particularly disgraceful death on the cross in order to provide a reward for those who chose not to be ashamed of humility.[125] Those who measure up to Christ's humility will be honored with the highest nobility.[126] The greatest kind of humility, which is seen in the voluntary, self-deprecating, and self-sacrificial love of Jesus, produces the redemption of the human person—the highest exaltation available to those created in God's image and likeness.

---

120. Augustine, *S.* 353.1 (WSA III/10:152). Cf. *En. Ps.* 81.6 (WSA III/18:176–77) for Augustine's similar assertion that Christ makes children of God through humility.

121. Augustine, *S.* 117.17 (WSA III/4:220). This is a significant contrast to Aristotle's magnanimous person who ignores what he considers to be trivial, pursuing only the great deeds worthy of high honor.

122. Augustine, *S.* 354.8 (WSA III/10:161).

123. Augustine, *S.* 23A.3 (WSA III/2:69–70).

124. Augustine, *S.* 23A.2 (WSA III/2:69).

125. Augustine, *S.* 68.11 (WSA III/3:231).

126. Augustine, *S.* 68.11 (WSA III/3:230).

Christ's Image and the Human Image of God

The humility and greatness of the human person preached by Augustine finds its fulfillment in his understanding of that person's dignity as the image and likeness of God. In *The Trinity*, Augustine articulates his understanding of the manner in which Christ images the Father and the manner in which the human person is an image of the Trinity. Although the concept of image is used to represent both relationships, the images are by no means equal. The Son as image of the Father is never by the least "hair's breadth" separated from the Father, since he is of the same substance as that which he images. The Son, born of the Father, is the image, which is the creative light illuminating all other things. Through his illumination of creation, Christ is also the model for all created beings, to include the human person.[127] The human person, on the other hand, is the image of the Trinity[128] but unlike the Son is not of the same substance as the Father.[129] The image of God in the human person is maintained through its orientation toward God's creative light.[130] The human person's orientation toward God's light is his acceptance in faith of the knowledge of God revealed in the person of Jesus Christ.[131] Christ's life and teaching reveals the love of God as a humble love.[132] In imitating the humble love of Christ, the human person is empowered to participate in the divine life of God. "We by pressing on imitate him who abides motionless; we follow him who stands still, and by walking in him we move toward him, because for us he became a road or way in time by his humility, while being for us an eternal abode by his divinity."[133] For Augustine, those who despise Christ's humility will never discover his sublimity,[134] and as a result, will never achieve their greatness as God's image and likeness.

> Do you want to be great? Start from the bottom. Are you thinking of constructing a great skyscraper of a building? First give thought to the foundation of humility. And however much anybody may

127. Augustine, *Trin.* 7.2.5.

128. Ibid., 12.2.6.

129. Ibid., 7.2.5.

130. Ibid., 12.3.16.

131. Ibid., 13.6.24.

132. Studer, *Trinity and Incarnation*, 179.

133. Augustine, *Trin.* 7.2.5.

134. Augustine, *S.* 196A.1 (WSA III/6:64).

wish to spend on piling story upon story in his building, the bigger the building is meant to be, the deeper he digs the foundation. As the building is being constructed, of course, it rises higher and higher, but the one who is digging the foundations is pushed down lower and lower. So the building has to be humbled before it reaches its loftiest height, and its topmost pinnacle can only be erected after it has been humbled to the depths.[135]

Modeling themselves on the example of Christ, humans achieve their greatest calling by humbling themselves, which in turn opens them to the infinite grace of God's love. In turning to God in humility, God's image in the human person is illuminated with the light and fire of God's love.[136] It is in the illumination of the image that the human person reaches her greatest honor[137] and enjoys the happiness available in the intellectual possession of the triune God.[138]

---

135. Augustine, *S.* 69.2 (WSA III/3:235–36).

136. Augustine, *Civ. Dei* 14.13.

137. Augustine, *Trin.* 12.3.16.

138. Augustine, *Div. Qu.* 35.2.

5 ─────────────────────────────

David Hume and Friedrich Nietzsche on Greatness without Humility

ALMOST THIRTEEN CENTURIES SEPARATE the lives of St. Augustine and David Hume, and more than fourteen lie between him and Friedrich Nietzsche. For the Catholic contemporaries of Hume and Nietzsche in the eighteenth and nineteenth centuries, the thought of Augustine would continue to serve as a primary model and inspiration for further intellectual inquiry. Such was not the case, however, for either Hume or Nietzsche. Although the differences between their moral theories are significant, one aspect shared by each was the fact that they both reacted against and offered significant criticism to the Christian intellectual tradition that had been influenced to such a great extent by Augustine's thought.

In the following pages, I will describe the divergent moral theories advanced by both Hume and Nietzsche and the impact of their moral views on the understanding of humility's relation to human greatness. Despite their differences from Augustine, there are still some commonalities between the three authors that pertain to my study. Both Hume and Nietzsche, like their ancient predecessors, offer an account of human excellence on the basis of their moral thought. In addition, both make significant use of virtue in their depictions of human greatness. Notwithstanding these commonalities, which are important as a basis for comparison with Augustine, there is much that distinguishes the moral thought of Hume and Nietzsche from that of Augustine. Augustine's morality is grounded in the rationality of the eudaemonist tradition and finds its center in the love of an omnipotent, yet humble God. Hume rejects rationality as a basis for morality and proposes a moral theory independent of religious thought. We will see that Nietzsche goes further than Hume on both fronts, asserting a relativist account of morality based on the expression of power and positing an adversarial relation to God in which notions of God must be overcome for the human person to claim the greatness that has been wrongfully assigned to a false deity. We will see that the principles upon which Hume and Nietzsche build their moral theories not only differ significantly from those of Augustine, but also yield views that undermine and even repudiate the importance of humility to greatness. I will begin my examination with an account of Hume's moral thought as it bears on the relationship between humility and greatness and will then treat Nietzsche's understanding of the relationship.

Sentiment and Pride as the Foundation for Hume's View of Greatness

The thought of David Hume is important to my study due to the time and attention he devoted to what he called pride and humility, which are better understood in contemporary terms as pride and shame, and due to the fact that he provided a direct and substantive commentary on the relationship between humility and greatness. Hume's thought on the subject is less polemical than that of Nietzsche, but as a result, is a more compelling alternative to Augustine's thought on humility and greatness than is Nietzsche's thought. Having been born in Scotland in the year 1711, Hume was heir to the significant philosophical developments of the seventeenth century. Of particular importance to his thought was the experimental method of Francis Bacon (b. 1561), which Hume endeavored to use in his examination of human nature,[1] and the thought of seventeenth century skeptical philosophers such as Pierre Bayle (b. 1647).[2] Dismissing Christian, Platonic, and Aristotelian doctrine, Hume sought to establish a new science of the human person. In his pursuit of this goal, Hume would abandon teleological and rational approaches to morality, proposing a moral theory based on his view of human nature and his understanding of ethics governed by moral feeling or sentiment. In addition, Hume's moral psychology, constituted on the basis of his notions concerning impressions and ideas in the mind, shaped his view of the virtues in general and also impacted his understanding of humility. The resulting system of morality, combined with his skeptical positions regarding the importance of religion to moral thought, led to

1. Hume, *Treatise of Human Nature*, 10.

2. See Johnson, *Mind of David Hume*, 17, 80 for comments regarding the influence of Bayle on Hume's skepticism.

an understanding of humility and greatness that greatly diverged from the view of Augustine and the Christian tradition.

Elements of Hume's Moral Philosophy: Skepticism and Experimental Method

Hume's approach to human nature has been described as skeptical or even post-skeptical. He gives display to his skepticism succinctly in the conclusion of the *Enquiry Concerning the Principles of Morals*. "I am convinced, that, where men are the most sure and arrogant, they are commonly the most mistaken."[3] In the *Treatise of Human Nature* he goes into greater depth stating,

> When I reflect on the natural fallibility of my judgment, I have less confidence in my opinions, than when I only consider the objects concerning which I reason; and when I proceed still farther, to turn the scrutiny against every successive estimation I make of my faculties, all the rules of logic require a continual diminution, and at last a total extinction of belief and evidence.[4]

Although the skepticism of these statements is clear, David Norton claims that Hume is better understood as a "post-skeptical" thinker because it is not Hume's purpose to support and further the claims of skeptical philosophers of the seventeenth century. He clearly accepts their arguments and acknowledges their victory over the idea that our most fundamental beliefs can be established through mechanisms of reason and sensory knowledge.[5] Despite that fact, Hume asserts that the failure of reason to establish our most basic beliefs is no reason to give up those beliefs. We may not have knowledge of why we believe in external reality or why we believe we have a body, but we must nevertheless continue to believe in such realities because without them "human nature must immediately perish and go to ruin."[6] In light of statements such as this and Hume's goal to establish a new science of human nature, it's evident that his skepticism is not simply aimed at establishing skeptical conclusions. Rather, Hume uses skepticism regarding the limits of philosophical reason to support his recourse to scientific

---

3. Hume, *Enquiry Concerning the Principles of Morals* 9.13.

4. Hume, *Treatise of Human Nature* 1.4.1.

5. Norton, "Introduction to Hume's Thought," 9.

6. Hume, *Treatise of Human Nature* 1.4.4. Cf. Biro "Hume's New Science," 45.

method.[7] For Hume, abstract reasoning cannot uncover the foundational principles of human nature. It is only through the patient observation of human life that the philosopher can establish the science of human nature.[8]

In the introduction of the *Treatise of Human Nature*, Hume notes that even the common man could tell that things were not going well in the philosophical discussions of the times. "There is nothing which is not the subject of debate, and in which men of learning are not of contrary opinions. The most trivial question escapes not our controversy, and in the most momentous we are not able to give any certain decision."[9] A new start was needed, which Hume intended to give by offering his *Treatise*. The subtitle of the treatise, "An Attempt to Introduce the Experimental Method of Reasoning into Moral Subjects," indicates one of the primary ways in which he intended to provide this new foundation. Hume's goal was to apply the experimental method developed and championed by Francis Bacon for inquiry in the natural sciences to the science of the human person.[10] Hume notes that the experimental method in the natural sciences must be adapted in its use for understanding the human person because premeditated and purposeful experimentation is of limited use in the study of human behavior. Nevertheless, he asserts that the cautious observation constitutive of the experimental method is directly applicable to the study of human nature and can serve as the foundation of a new science of the human person superior to any science previously conceived.[11] Armed with this new methodology, Hume intended nothing less than an unprecedented comprehension of the centerpiece and fundamental link of all the sciences: human nature.[12]

Hume's Sentimental Moral Theory

The seventeenth and eighteenth century debate between philosophers who based their understanding of morality on the rational examination of moral principles and those who asserted a foundation of moral distinction derived from an innate moral sense had significant effect on Hume's thought.

7. Biro, "Hume's Science of Mind," 46.

8. Hume, *Treatise of Human Nature*, 10.

9. Ibid., 2. Cf. Norton, "Introduction to Hume's Thought," 9.

10. Norton, "Introduction to Hume's Thought," 4.

11. Hume, *Treatise of Human Nature*, 10.

12. Ibid., 6.

John Locke (b. 1632), in his *Essay Concerning Human Understanding*, gives voice to the rationalist position by arguing that the truths of morality can be demonstrated in like manner to those of mathematics. For Locke, the principles of morality can be understood by examining the terms of moral propositions and specifying the meaning of those terms.[13] Anthony Ashley, the Earl of Shaftesbury (b. 1671), and Francis Hutcheson (b. 1694) are eighteenth-century moralists who contest the rationalistic approach to morality, arguing that moral distinction is based on feeling or sentiment rather than reason. Shaftesbury describes an interior moral eye that is able to distinguish the morally amiable from the morally odious.[14] For Hutcheson, the moral sense is that which perceives properties that arouse moral feelings. One of the distinctions in Hutcheson's moral thought that carries over into Hume's is his position that the moral sense judges properties or character traits and does not judge the moral value of actions. A pleasurable moral feeling is based on the perception of a benevolent character trait, which is manifested through a benevolent action.[15]

Hume sides with Shaftesbury and Hutcheson regarding the rationalist versus sentimentalist debate and even surpasses them in the cogency of his arguments for sentiment as the foundation of morality.[16] Hume lays out his arguments for why morality is not derived from reason in Book Three of the *Treatise of Human Nature*. He begins by asserting that moral judgments are the perceptions of the mind by which people distinguish between good and evil. These perceptions have the function of exciting a person's passions in order to produce or prevent a particular action. Reason, unlike passion, has no such power over a person's action. According to Hume, reason is an inactive principle whose function is to discover truth or falsehood. Since an active principle can never be founded on an inactive one, morality, for Hume, cannot be founded on a rational deduction.[17] In addition, Hume claims that reason relates to ideas or matters of fact and has no direct applicability to our actions. He asserts that actions, like passions or volitions, are realities complete in themselves and therefore cannot correspond to or be contrary to reason. Actions do not derive merit or blame from

---

13. Locke, *Essay Concerning Human Understanding* 4.3.18.

14. Cooper, *Characteristicks of Men, Manners, Opinions, Times,* 2.5.3.1.

15. Hutcheson, *Inquiry into the Original*, Introduction.

16. MacIntyre, *Short History of Ethics,* 169.

17. Hume, *Treatise of Human Nature* 3.1.1.

conformity to reason. They are laudable or blamable but are not reasonable or unreasonable.[18]

Although Hume's opposition to reason as the foundation of morality is clearly evident, he does give reason an indirect role in his moral thought. Reason, for Hume, is the mechanism through which passions are educated. He uses the mathematics employed by a merchant to demonstrate his point. The merchant uses mathematic principles to determine the sum of his debt. The mathematical reason necessary to arrive at this figure plays no role, however, in the merchants desire to pay his debt. It merely directs his judgment to causes and effects, specifying what amount to pay should he decide to make payment.[19] The decision to make payment, however, is caused by sentiments of pleasure or uneasiness. It is on these sentiments that Hume bases his description of the moral sense.

Hume constructs his account of moral sentiment or feeling on his understanding of how the human mind functions. He asserts that all perceptions of the human mind can be divided into two basic categories, which he labels impressions and ideas. The distinction between the two categories lies in the strength of force with which they affect the mind. Impressions strike the mind with greater force than do ideas. Impressions are our sensations, passions, and emotions as they make their first entry into the mind. Ideas, on the other hand, are the fainter images that comprise our thinking and reasoning. The distinction between impressions and ideas is the same as that between feeling and thinking, which Hume assumes to be known by all of his readers.[20] Hume places both pride and humility in the category of impression—the former eliciting good moral feelings, while the latter elicits negative feelings.

Having found that moral distinctions are not based on reason, whose function is to compare ideas, Hume concludes that the difference between moral good and evil finds its basis in impressions and the feelings aroused by moral perceptions. Morality is a matter of feeling rather than a matter of judgment.[21] Hume turns to contemporary science to further describe these perceptions. When a person pronounces a particular act to be praiseworthy or pernicious, he is merely expressing the feeling of approbation or blame provoked in our nature in the presence of the particular action. He

18. Ibid., 3.1.1.
19. Ibid., 2.3.3.
20. Ibid., 1.1.1.
21. Ibid., 3.1.2.

equates this perception of praise or blame with other perceptions of the mind, such as sounds, color, heat, and cold, which modern science had demonstrated to be perceptions of the mind rather than qualities in objects outside of the mind.[22] He concludes that moral sentiments are the perceptions of pleasure or pain human nature associates with the observation of good or evil actions. The pleasure occasioned by good actions manifests in approbation for the person performing the action, and the uneasiness or pain occasioned by a pernicious action manifests in the feeling of blame directed at the person performing the action. Sentiment or feeling is thus the foundation of the difference between moral approval and blame.[23]

Hume's Foundation of Moral Action: Pleasure and Pain

Despite the importance of actions in Hume's analysis, he asserts that it is not in the actions themselves, but in a person's motives and the qualities of mind that give rise to the actions upon which moral distinctions are based.

> 'Tis evident, that when we praise any actions, we regard only the motives that produced them, and consider the actions as signs or indications of certain principles in the mind and temper. The external performance has no merit. We must look within to find the moral quality. This we cannot do directly; and therefore fix our attention on actions, as on external signs. But these actions are still considered as signs; and the ultimate object of our praise and approbation is the motive, that produced them.[24]

As in his sentimentalist approach to morality in general, Hume follows Shaftesbury and Hutcheson in making this assertion.[25] Hume characterizes these motives and qualities that give rise to actions as virtues and vices.

Virtues and vices are the very impressions Hume identifies as the foundation of moral sentiment. At different junctions of his thought, Hume points out different sources that give rise to virtue and vice. In Book Two of the *Treatise*, he states that good and bad actions are the basis of virtue and vice determining the personal character of an individual. He goes on to claim that nothing operates more strongly upon human passions than

22. Ibid., 3.1.1. Hume viewed this equivalence as a discovery of great import, hoping it would advance moral science in the same way it served to advance natural science.

23. Hume, *Enquiry Concerning the Principles of Morals*, Appendix 1.3.

24. Hume, *Treatise of Human Nature* 3.2.1.

25. Norton, "Foundations of Morality," 284.

the character traits that result from good and bad action.[26] This assertion seems to coincide with more traditional Aristotelian conceptions of virtue in which one must exercise an activity in order to acquire a virtue or vice. Yet activity is not the category Hume uses as the foundation of virtue and vice throughout the majority of his work. That distinction belongs to his understanding of pleasure and pain and their relation to virtue and vice.

The fact that human beings seek pleasure and are averse to pain is, for Hume, an ultimate principle. It is a rule so obvious and fundamental that it is absurd to seek a reason for its validity.[27] Given its fundamental nature, Hume asserts that the search for pleasure and the evasion of pain are the chief actuating principles of the human mind. This is so much the case that "when these sensations are remov'd, both from our thought and feeling, we are, in a great measure, incapable of passion or action, of desire or volition."[28] Simply put, pleasure and pain are the primary motives for the actions people chose to pursue. This principle is active in different spheres of human experience. In the aesthetic sphere, beauty and deformity are forms producing pleasure and pain.[29] In the field of morality, moral good and evil give rise to particular pleasures or pains. From Hume's perspective, a person's character is virtuous or vicious because observing that character causes either a moral pleasure or uneasiness in the observer. In feeling that a character is pleasing, we are feeling that it is virtuous. Our approval of the character is the immediate pleasure that it conveys to us.[30]

In his later thought on morality, particularly in his *Enquiry Concerning the Principles of Morals*, Hume expands his notion of the relations between pleasure and virtue and pain and vice, applying it in a social context. He does this by way of the principle of utility, for which he is once again in debt to the thought of Francis Hutcheson.[31] In the *Enquiry*, Hume dedicates an entire chapter on why the principle of utility is pleasing and goes on to use the principle as the criteria that determines the merit of social virtues

26. Hume, *Treatise of Human Nature* 2.1.5.

27. Hume, *Enquiry Concerning the Principles of Morals* Appendix 1.18–19.

28. Hume, *Treatise of Human Nature* 3.3.1.

29. Ibid., 2.1.8.

30. Ibid., 3.1.2.

31. Hutcheson, *Enquiry into the Original of our Ideas of Beauty and Virtue*, 2.3. Cf. MacIntyre, *Short History of Ethics*, 163. Hutcheson provides the starting point for utilitarianism by stating "that nation is best which procures the greatest happiness for the greatest numbers, and that worst which in like manner occasions misery."

and vices.[32] According to Hume, there is no greater eulogy to a person than to display his usefulness to the public.[33] Usefulness plays the same role for morality in the *Enquiry* as pleasure does in the *Treatise*. Usefulness is agreeable and engages the approbation of anyone who observes it. Here Hume renounces an ego-centric morality, like that of Hobbes, because usefulness is a principle that is important to the interests of the moral agent herself and to the interests of those served by the approved action.[34] Since usefulness (or lack thereof) is a source for moral sentiment, and it is not only in reference to the self that usefulness is approved, it follows for Hume that anything useful to society will be an object of approbation. Therefore, usefulness is the principle that accounts for the great part of morality.[35] It is on the basis of humility's apparent lack of utility that Hume will level one of his most significant arguments against its value.

Sympathy as Hume's Criteria for Virtue

Two last elements important to Hume's moral theory and his subsequent thought on humility and greatness are the normative role society plays in determining which qualities are virtues and which are vices, as well as the categories he develops to account for all virtues and vices. Virtue, for Hume, is a quality of mind agreeable to or approved by everyone.[36] It is the intercourse of sentiments in society that form a general standard by which virtue and vice may be judged.[37] Hume observes that no person is indifferent to the happiness or misery of others.[38] The natural sympathy humans display for the happiness or suffering of others is the principle through which one derives the feelings of approbation and blame that constitute our understanding of morality. It is the source of esteem or blame that we pay to virtues and vices.[39] Were humans solitary and unconcerned with the welfare of others, usefulness to society would not be able to provide guidance concerning happiness because the welfare of others would have

32. Hume, *Enquiry Concerning the Principles of Morals* 5.1.4.

33. Ibid., 5.1.1.

34. Ibid., 5.1.15.

35. Ibid., 5.2.17.

36. Ibid., 8, note 50.

37. Ibid., 5.2.42.

38. Ibid., 5, note 19.

39. Hume, *Treatise of Human Nature* 3.3.1.

no impact on the person observing the behavior of others. Hume's study of human behavior, however, notes the operation of sympathy throughout all human intercourse. In this social context of morality where sympathy is the mechanism by which usefulness serves as the norm for morality, Hume devises four categories of qualities that can be considered virtuous. Any qualities useful to ourselves, useful to others, agreeable to ourselves, or agreeable to others are considered virtues.[40] Those qualities that are harmful and disagreeable to ourselves or others are likewise considered vices.

Hume's focus on utility, his conception of virtue, and the categories he develops to recognize various virtues all play significant roles in his treatment of humility and greatness. His view of the two principles diverges from an Augustinian perspective in part because of his different conception of morality. That view also diverges from Augustine's perspective due to Hume's far-reaching religious skepticism. In the context of that skepticism, Hume provides a cogent critique of the relationship between revealed religion and moral thought, which in turn affects his understanding of the relationship between humility and greatness.

Hume's Critique of Religion and Theology's Negative Influence on Morality

Hume wrote about the nature of religious belief in a number of his most important works. The *Treatise of Human Nature, An Enquiry Concerning Human Understanding, The Natural History of Religion*, and *Dialogues Concerning Natural Religion* are all works in which Hume provides significant and controversial commentary on religious thought. Targets of Hume's criticism are the philosophical principles supporting natural religion, as well as those principles supporting the credibility of revealed religion. In his *Enquiry Concerning Human Understanding*, Hume attacks what's considered the *a posteriori* proofs for God's existence, arguments based on the order and beauty of the universe. Hume contends that the typical conception of God is far greater than the meager evidence that an argument from effect to cause (his characterization of the *a posteriori* proofs) can provide and is more the product of human imagination than a logical argument.[41] In part nine of the *Dialogue Concerning Natural Religion*, Hume confronts

---

40. Hume, *Enquiry Concerning the Principles of Morals* 9.1.1.

41. Hume, *Enquiry Concerning Human Understanding*, 480–513.

the *a priori* justification for the existence of God, arguing that a first cause of the universe's existence is not logically necessary. Hume also provides a critique of revealed religion, concluding that the evidence for the truth of human senses is stronger than the evidence for the Christian religion.[42] This is especially true for belief in miracles, for which no human witness can provide stronger evidence than the evidence that exists to support the natural law a miracle supposedly breaks.[43] Given these observations, Hume concludes that no rational person can believe in revealed religion. The real basis for religion, in Hume's view, arose from the human need to cope with the unknown causes of life's events and the uncertainties of the future. These unknown causes are the constant object of our hopes and fears, and we are perpetually anxious in our expectation of future events.[44] In the context of this anxiety, humans turn to a deity that can protect them from the devastating circumstances life may impose. Hume asserts that this deity is nothing more than a fabrication of imagination and the tendency to transfer human attributes to virtually any being, real or imagined.[45] Such an assertion provides a philosophical context radically different from that of Augustine. For the skeptical Hume, the human person has virtually no reliable knowledge of the divine, which prevents a person from making choices on the basis of knowledge concerning God and precludes an intimate relationship between the person and God.

Hume also takes issue with the idea that moral thought is intrinsically linked to religious principle. In the *Treatise* and the *Enquiry Concerning the Principles of Morals*, Hume offers a comprehensive system of morality with no reference to God.[46] Hume devises secular principles within his system that account for the functions traditionally played by religious ideals. Love of neighbor, religious commandments, and the duty owed to God are all replaced by parallel secular principles. Sympathy (rules based on the good of society) and obligation (based on the relative degree of usefulness of a particular action) can not only support morality without reference to God, but in Hume's view, are eminently more effective in that support than the moral principles of religious thought.

42. Ibid., 117.
43. Ibid., 123.
44. Hume, *Hume Selections,* 262.
45. Ibid., 262–63.
46. Gaskin, "Hume on Religion," 505.

Hume not only asserts the independence of morality from religion, but also contends that the application of religious principles to moral thought has been disastrous, and disastrous for a number of reasons.[47] First, he notes that natural inclinations have greater effect on the conduct of humans than do the pompous views devised by theological systems. This is the case because natural inclination works incessantly upon the thoughts of men and women, providing constant motivation to choose particular actions. Religious principles, on the other hand, operate only intermittently and can never become habits of the mind.[48] In addition, religious superstition often places itself in opposition to natural morality, concocting new species of moral merit and developing preposterous assignments of praise and blame. The confusion fostered by these religious distinctions undermines the commitment of many people to the natural principles of morality.[49] Hume asserts,

> . . . As every quality, which is useful or agreeable to ourselves or others is in common life, allowed to be a part of personal merit; so no other will ever be received, where men judge of things by their natural, unprejudiced reason, without the delusive glosses of superstition and false religion. Celibacy, fasting, penance, mortification, self-denial, humility, silence, solitude, and the whole train of monkish virtues; for what reason are they every where rejected by men of sense, but because they serve to no manner of purpose; neither advance a man's fortune in the world, nor render him a more valuable member of society; neither qualify him for the entertainment of company, nor increase his power of self-enjoyment? We observe on the contrary, that they cross all these desirable ends; stupify the understanding and harden the heart, obscure the fancy and sour the temper. We justly, therefore, transfer them to the opposite column, and place them in the catalogue of vices; nor has any superstition force sufficient, among men of the world, to pervert entirely these natural sentiments.[50]

Morality, for Hume, is independent of theological reasoning and will only be properly understood when emancipated from religious thought.

---

47. Ibid.
48. Hume, *Hume Selections*, 392–93.
49. Ibid., 394.
50. Hume, *Enquiry Concerning the Principles of Morals* 9.1.1

Hume on Humility and Greatness

Hume develops his understanding of pride and humility at great length in the *Treatise*, devoting roughly a third of Book Two, "Of the Passions," to the relationship between the two. In his analysis of the passions, he differentiates between impressions that are derived directly from sense experience—for example bodily pains and pleasures—and those that are derived from sense impressions by the interposition of an idea. He calls the first category of impressions original and the second reflective or secondary impressions. Passions such as humility and pride belong to the category of reflective impressions.[51] Hume implicitly distinguishes between passions and virtues through the organization of the *Treatise*, Book Two describing the passions and Book Three describing the virtues. It is evident, however, that the relation between passions and virtues is very close for Hume. He considers virtues (like passions) to be impressions of the mind, and he states in the case of pride and humility that the excesses or just proportions of these passions are what constitute virtue and vice in their regard.[52] In addition, Hume's understanding of pleasure and pain operates in a similar fashion in his description of the passions as it does in that of the virtues. In Hume's view, every cause of pride is always a source of pleasure for a person, and every cause of humility is likewise a cause of pain.[53] It is important to keep in mind that Hume's description of the passion of humility is more akin to a feeling of shame than a Christian understanding of the virtue. As a result, Hume always characterizes humility negatively, although he does recognize a positive role to the closely related virtue of modesty.

In light of the above sentiments and the religious context that had traditionally supported humility as a virtue, one might conclude that Hume would see no positive aspects to any traits associated with humility. Modesty, however, is one trait closely related to humility that Hume understands in a positive light.[54] This is more due to the problems associated with the excess of pride than with any positive value in humility. Hume begins his consideration of greatness of mind in the *Treatise* by noting the universal distaste for excessive pride or overweening conceit.[55] He asserts that exces-

---

51. Hume, *Treatise of Human Nature* 2.1.1.

52. Ibid., 3.3.2.

53. Ibid., 2.1.5.

54. Ibid., 3.3.2.

55. Ibid.

sive pride must be vicious because it causes uneasiness in everyone that observes it in the character of another person.[56] Excessive pride violates Hume's third source of moral distinction in that it is immediately disagreeable to others. Modesty, which Hume defines as diffidence to our own judgment and due attention to the judgment of others, is opposed to impudence and arrogance and therefore provides a correction to excessive pride.[57] Modesty as a just sense of our weakness is virtuous because it is a quality that pleases others, placing it in accord with Hume's dictate that virtues must be agreeable to others. He further argues that modesty is beneficial to society by providing the mechanism through which the young are open to instruction, as well as preserving society from intolerable indulgence in self- praise that would result without such modesty.[58]

It is clear from both the *Treatise* and the *Enquiry Concerning the Principles of Morals* that Hume considers humility in itself a negative phenomenon. When he treats humility as a passion, it is the passion that accounts for any pain associated with self-regard. He asserts that any lack of a proper self-worth, which was often considered the definition of Christian humility, is simply inexcusable.[59] Sincere humility that goes beyond the external façade of modesty is esteemed by no one.[60] Modesty is a virtue for Hume because it adheres to his principle of being agreeable to others. Interior humility, although it is not disagreeable to others, is vicious because it violates another of Hume's moral principles: that which requires qualities agreeable to oneself. Humility, for Hume, is one of the monkish virtues forced upon humanity by religion and is recognized as a vice by any reasonable person.[61]

A well-founded pride, on the other hand, is virtuous. For Hume, there is nothing more laudable than valuing ourselves when we truly have valuable qualities.[62] A certain degree of generous pride is of such fundamental importance that Hume compares its absence to the lack of a nose or an eye on a human face.[63] Despite the difference in his understanding of virtue from that of Aristotle, Hume seems to be in agreement with him when as-

---

56. Hume, *Treatise of Human Nature* 3.3.2.

57. Hume, *Enquiry Concerning the Principles of Morals* 8.8.

58. Ibid., 8.8.

59. Ibid., 7.10.

60. Hume, *Treatise of Human Nature* 3.3.2.

61. Hume, *Enquiry Concerning the Principles of Morals* 9.1.3.

62. Hume, *Treatise of Human Nature* 3.3.2.

63. Hume, *Enquiry Concerning the Principles of Morals* 7.10.

serting the universal approval of magnanimity[64] and declaring it is better to overestimate one's merits than underestimate them.[65] Pride receives Hume's vigorous endorsement because it is supported by two of his moral principles. Since pride is always a source of pleasure, it is in accord with Hume's norm that all virtues are pleasant to the person who is the subject of that virtue. Secondly, Hume notes that pride is not merely pleasurable but is also useful. As a virtue, pride makes one cognizant of her own merit, enabling her to be self-confident. Such confidence capacitates a person for success in business and all human endeavor.[66] Although the excess of pride is of some concern to Hume, he clearly views pride in an almost entirely positive light.

Comparing pride and humility on the basis of Hume's thought, one can see how greatness in his view is built upon pride and is opposed to humility:

> In general we may observe, that whatever we call heroic virtue, and admire under the character of greatness and elevation of mind, is either nothing but a steady and well-establish'd pride and self-esteem, or partakes largely of that passion. Courage, intrepidity, ambition, love of glory, magnanimity, and all other shining virtues of that kind, have plainly a strong mixture of self-esteem in them, and derive a great part of their merit from that origin.[67]

As a historian, Hume remarks that all the great actions admired in history are founded on pride and self-esteem. Fortune favors the bold, and boldness is based on a high opinion of one's own merits. A genuine and hearty pride is essential to the man of honor.[68] In order to act decisively and effectively in the world, one must know one's own strengths and have the ability to employ those strengths without hesitation. For Hume, deploying one's personal strengths would be impossible without an authentic pride that first appreciates a person's character traits as strengths. Since authentic humility for Hume would deemphasize a person's strength, it would depress and impede the human greatness that is founded upon pride and self-esteem. Thus for Hume, humility contributes nothing to greatness and can only serve to undermine its foundation in a person's pride and self-esteem.

---

64. Ibid., 7.4.

65. Hume, *Treatise of Human Nature* 3.3.2.

66. Ibid.

67. Ibid.

68. Ibid.

Nietzsche's Perspective on Humility and Greatness

A little more than a century after Hume published his thoughts concerning virtue and humility, Friedrich Nietzsche began his labors as a relatively obscure philologist in Switzerland. His writing would later become one of the greatest influences on twentieth-century thought and culture in Europe and North America.[69] Nietzsche's philosophy held significant implications for the topic of humility and greatness and was a vehement argument against a positive relation between the two. His thought was marked not only by philosophical elements inimical to a Christian conception of the relationship between humility and greatness, but is also known for its passionate animus against Christian thought in general. Of particular importance for my investigation is the opposition Nietzsche placed between God and human greatness, as well as his disdain for the Jewish and Christian moral perspectives.

The Will to Power as the Basis of Nietzsche's Moral Thought

In order to understand Nietzsche's position regarding humility and greatness, and indeed to understand his moral thought in general, one must examine his understanding of the basic purpose of human life, which he characterizes as the will to power. In his work, *Beyond Good and Evil*, Nietzsche asserts,

> Physiologists should think twice before deciding that an organic being's primary instinct is the instinct for self-preservation. A living being wants above all else to release its strength; life itself is the will to power, and self-preservation is only one of its indirect and most frequent consequences.[70]

The will to power is a theme that appears throughout Nietzsche's philosophy, influencing his understanding of morality and providing one of the foundations for his criticism of Christian thought. In his *On the Genealogy of Morality*, Nietzsche examines the foundations of legal systems, noting

---

69. MacIntyre, *After Virtue*, 113–14. Cf. Bernd Magnus and Kathleen M. Higgins, "Introduction to the Cambridge Companion to Nietzsche," 1–2 for a characterization of Nietzsche's importance from the perspective of twentieth century philosophers and in relation to his impact on western culture in the twentieth century.

70. Nietzsche, *Nietzsche Reader*, 318.

that "they are partial restrictions of the true will of life, which is bent upon power, and are subordinate to its ultimate goal as a single means: namely, as a means of creating *bigger* units of power."[71] Nietzsche explains that every animal, to include the human animal, strives for an optimum condition in which it can fully release its power. Happiness is no longer the fundamental reality pursued by the human person in his or her moral decisions. The optimum for that person is characterized by the path to power and mighty deeds. In many cases, the path to power is not a path to happiness, but a path to misery.[72] Whether the person achieves misery or happiness is not the point of moral striving, however. Only the expression of its power enables an entity to reach its fulfillment.

Nietzsche presents his understanding of the will to power from a number of different perspectives. At times he sees it as a desire to manipulate or control something or someone. In other instances, he poses a less ominous meaning in the principle, viewing it as a need to discharge one's strength—the drive to act spontaneously.[73] It is also, for Nietzsche, the fundamental principle that gives meaning to things in life:

> Anything in existence, having somehow come about, is continually interpreted anew, requisitioned anew, transformed and redirected to a new purpose by a power superior to it; that everything that occurs in the organic world consists of overpowering, dominating, and in their turn, overpowering and dominating consist of re-interpretation, adjustment, in the process of which their former "meaning" [*Sinn*] and "purpose" must necessarily be obscured or completely obliterated . . . . Every purpose and use is just a sign that the will to power has achieved mastery over something less powerful, and has impressed upon it its own idea [*Sinn*] of a use function . . . . The "development" of a thing . . . is a succession of more or less profound, more or less mutually independent processes of subjugation exacted on the thing.[74]

In the above citation, Nietzsche employs the idea of interpretation as a function of the will to power. Interpretation is the process that creates the meaning of something. It is a process in which a more powerful agent imposes meaning on a less powerful subject matter.[75] The idea of interpretation in the

71. Nietzsche, *On the Genealogy of Morality* 1.11.

72. Ibid., 3.7.

73. Hunt, *Origin of Virtue*, 72.

74. Nietzsche, *On the Genealogy of Morality* 2.12.

75. Hunt, *Origin of Virtue*, 73.

context of the will to power is one of the foundations upon which Nietzsche builds his conception of virtue, which in turn is one of the key ideas through which he views morality and the relation between humility and greatness.

Nietzschean Virtue

In *Thus Spake Zarathustra*, Nietzsche discusses the idea of virtue in terms of passions and goals. Nietzsche begins his account with the traditional idea that passions or emotions are things that are undergone, suffered through. There is a passive element in the experience of a passion. Traditionally, the passion is understood to act on the person rather than the person acting on the passion. Nietzsche reverses this relationship in his description of virtue. Passions, he asserts can be undergone passively, but they need not be experienced in such a manner. Passions, when they are aligned with a person's goals, lose their character as something to be passively experienced and become instruments of freedom and power. Passions are transformed into virtues when the passions are directed to a person's highest goals.[76]

Recalling Nietzsche's idea of interpretation as the imposition of meaning by a more powerful agent on a less powerful one (an instance of the will to power), we can see that the process in which passions are changed into virtues is a process of interpretation. In the creation of a virtue, the passion is the subject matter upon which a new meaning is imposed.[77] In this process, a person is able to envision an ideal and make it effective, imposing on the passion a function that is ordered toward a particular goal. Nietzsche describes this effort as overcoming the passion.[78] He further asserts that since passions are elements of a person's very identity, when one changes a passion into a virtue, the person that one once was dies and is changed into something new.[79]

In *Beyond Good and Evil*, Nietzsche asserts that the province of morality concerns people and not actions,[80] which suggests some commonality with a eudaemonist approach to morality that focuses on the development of virtue rather than the moral character of isolated actions. Yet Nietzsche's conception of virtue diverges from that of classical eudaemonism in funda-

76. Nietzsche, *Thus Spake Zarathustra* 1.5. Cf. Hunt, *Origin of Virtue*, 70–71.

77. Nietzsche, *Thus Spake Zarathustra* 1.5.

78. Hunt, *Origin of Virtue*, 74.

79. Nietzsche, *Thus Spake Zarathustra* 1.16. Cf. Hunt, *Origin of Virtue*, 74.

80. Nietzsche, *Beyond Good and Evil*, 265.

mental ways. Unlike classical morality, Nietzsche does not believe in a unity of the virtues. The unity of the virtues proposed by a philosopher such as Aristotle is based on their common source in reason. The integration of reason with a person's character through practical wisdom is the mechanism through which Aristotle asserts the unity of the virtues.[81] Nietzsche, on the other hand, states that reason has little or no role in the formation of virtue. "An earthly virtue is it which I love: little prudence is therein and the least every day wisdom."[82] Based on his understanding of the will to power where one reality always subdues and dominates another, Nietzsche contends that the action of virtue is blind because the operation of a virtue is the manifestation of that virtue's victory over the other virtues with which it was striving.[83] If it has vanquished the other virtue, the victorious virtue cannot take the concerns of the defeated virtue into account. As a result, Nietzsche's concept of virtue rejects both the unity and rationality that are hallmarks of a classical approach to virtue. Rather than the unity of virtue, Nietzsche preaches the enmity of virtue. In place of rational virtues, he proposes ignorant virtues.[84]

An additional area in which Nietzsche diverges in his understanding of virtue from classical moral philosophers lies in his moral relativism. In *Thus Spake Zarathustra*, Nietzsche asserts that virtue is the integration of the human consciousness in which one's passions are directed at achieving that person's highest goals.[85] This definition, however, applies only to an elite minority. Few people actually demonstrate the ability to achieve the integration required by virtue.[86] Such integration requires inner strength and hardness, qualities that are lacking in the large majority of people. For this large majority—a group Nietzsche refers to as the herd—virtue is simply not possible. Morality for the herd is a matter of custom and the adherence to conventional norms that make living in community possible.[87] Since these people of lower rank lack the ability to marshal their

81. Aristotle, *Nicomachean Ethics* 1144b32–1145a2.

82. Nietzsche, *Thus Spake Zarathustra* 1.5.

83. Ibid. Cf. Hunt, *Origin of Virtue*, 81.

84. Nietzsche, *Beyond Good and Evil*, 227, 230. Cf. Hunt, *Origin of Virtue*, 81.

85. Nietzsche, *Thus Spake Zarathustra* 1.5.

86. Cf. Nietzsche, *Thus Spake Zarathustra* 3.3 for a text in which Nietzsche describes the loneliness and hardness of what he calls creators. Cf. 3.12.29 for the discussion of the softness of common charcoal as opposed to the hardness of the rare diamond.

87. Nietzsche, *Beyond Good and Evil*, 201.

passions in support of their highest goals, they will pursue an assortment of goals that produce the things necessary for the upkeep of the community.[88] Nietzsche is thus proposing a relativistic, two-tiered system of morality. For the lower-ranking persons (the herd), custom and convention are the norms for morality. For the elite, virtue is morality's norm. This division not only affects Nietzsche's understanding of virtue, but is also fundamental to his division between master and slave moralities, his criticism of Jewish and Christian morality, and his understanding of humility and greatness.

Master and Slave Morality

In *Beyond Good and Evil*, Nietzsche cites Tacitus' claim that the Jews were ". . . a people born for slavery."[89] Nietzsche maintains that this characteristic of the Jewish people is precisely their contribution to history. It is with the Jews that the slave revolt in morality begins. The Jews inaugurate a complete reversal of values that reaches its pinnacle in the person of Jesus Christ, the "'redeemer' bringing salvation and victory to the poor, the sick, to sinners."[90] In order to understand what Nietzsche means by a slave morality, one must examine his account of how good and bad were initially understood by ancient cultures and how the herd mentality of Judaism and Christianity overcame these earlier notions to establish a moral framework based on good and evil.

Nietzsche asserts that unlike modern conceptions of morality, which equate goodness with utility, the idea of goodness in antiquity was originally derived from the idea of nobility. The definition of good was determined by the nobles, the elite, the mighty and the high placed, who looked upon themselves and their own actions and judged them to be good. It was the prerogative of the great to create values and give those values their names.[91] In contrast to the goodness of the noble was the base, the low, the plebeian. The distance between the noble and good and that which was low and common was the original foundation for the distinction between what was good and what was bad.[92] The distinction between good and evil is a later

---

88. Hunt, *Origin of Virtue*, 141–42.

89. Nietzsche, *Beyond Good and Evil*, 195.

90. Nietzsche, *On the Genealogy of Morality* 1.8.

91. Ibid., 1.2.

92. Ibid.

development arising from the Jewish slave morality, which was ultimately victorious over the original master morality.

Nietzsche's account of master morality has been characterized as an aristocratic morality. Indeed, Nietzsche asserts an aristocratic value equation to describe the mind-set typical of the master morality: good = noble = powerful = beautiful = happy = blessed.[93] Noble moral action is active, as opposed to reactive. It needs no enemy or contrast to establish its goodness.[94] The noble agent is master of himself, as well as the circumstances, nature, and weaker wills that he encounters in life. As a result of this mastery the noble person has the right to make promises and merits the trust, fear, and respect of others. The noble person is marked by a proud state of soul, despises the weak, and is not fearful of telling the truth. Noble morality grows out of the noble tendency to say yes to itself. It is a morality of self-glorification.[95]

The nature of slave morality, on the other hand, is rooted in Nietzsche's principle of *ressentiment*. Those persons who lack the power of action respond to the activity of the powerful through *ressentiment*. *Ressentiment* gives birth to the slave morality in its negative orientation to others.[96] For slave morality to develop, it must first have an external (noble) world to which it may compare itself. In their weakness, the agents of the slave mentality are denied a response of action and must compensate for their failure through an act of imaginary revenge.[97]

> The oppressed, the downtrodden, the violated say to each other with the vindictive cunning of powerlessness: "Let us be different from evil people, let us be good! And a good person is anyone who does not rape, does not harm anyone, who does not attack, does not retaliate, who leaves the taking of revenge to God, who keeps hidden as we do, avoids all evil and asks little from life in general, like us who are patient, humble, and upright"
> —this means, if heard coolly and impartially, nothing more than "We weak people are just weak; it is good to do nothing for which we are not strong enough."[98]

93. Ibid., 1.7.

94. Ibid., 1.10.

95. Nietzsche, *Beyond Good and Evil*, 260.

96. Nietzsche, *On the Genealogy of Morality* 1.10. See also Hicks, *Explaining Post-Modernism*, 193 for a description of Nietzsche's understanding of *ressentiment*.

97. Nietzsche, *On the Genealogy of Morality* 1.10.

98. Ibid., 1.13.

Slave morality, which for Nietzsche is the product of Jewish culture and belief, is the antithesis of master morality on almost every level. Slave moral action is passive and reactive. Slave morality says no to everything outside of itself as opposed to the master morality that says yes to itself.[99] The bad in noble morality is not a primary principle because the noble first define what is good and are only secondarily aware of what is bad. The evil of the slave morality, on the other hand, is a primary principle.[100] The resentment of the slave toward the powerful is the principle that gives birth to the entire structure of the slave morality. The thought of the powerless views anyone with power as evil.[101] Slave morality emphasizes qualities that ease suffering. Pity, a warm heart, a helping hand, patience, diligence, and humility are all prized because they are useful to endure the pressures of life.[102] The good person of the slave morality keeps hidden and avoids all violence. It is a bleak condition that has clad itself in the fine garb of self-sacrificing virtue. It posits the weakness of the weak as a positive achievement.[103]

Slave morality clearly attacks any position that supports a positive relationship between humility and greatness. Despite the cogency of this attack, however, one must also consider Nietzsche's religious philosophy to gather the full force of his argument against a positive view of humility.

Nietzsche's Death of God

Although Nietzsche places the blame for the genesis of slave morality with the Jews, he sees Christianity as the culmination of the slave morality. Indeed, it is not difficult to see in the background of Nietzsche's polemic against slave morality the morality of the New Testament in which Jesus consistently praises the meek and humble of heart. Nietzsche's critique of Christian belief is not merely implicit, however, and though it is intimately related to his moral thought, his critique transcends moral categories attacking the conceptual roots of belief in God.

It is perhaps ironic that the author who proclaimed the death of God was the son of a Lutheran pastor. Although Nietzsche may have believed in God in his youth, in his later autobiographical writings he claimed that

99. Ibid., 1.10.

100. Ibid., 1.11.

101. Nietzsche, *Human, All too Human* 1.45.

102. Nietzsche, *Beyond Good and Evil*, 260.

103. Nietzsche, *On the Genealogy of Morality* 1.13.

atheism was never really a question for him, but was really a matter of instinct, implying he never seriously entertained religious faith.[104] Despite his exposure to Christianity in childhood, Nietzsche in his maturity was profoundly and radically alienated from Christianity. His critique of religion, particularly Christianity, is extensive and highly unfavorable. Due to the breadth of his critique, I will limit my examination to a few significant texts that have bearing on the relationship between humility and greatness.

In *The Will to Power*, a posthumous compilation of Nietzsche's unpublished notes, Nietzsche asserts that the origin of religion lies in the human person's experience of power. The sudden and overwhelming nature of the experience causes an individual to posit a stronger person rather than himself as its source. According to Nietzsche's account, religion is a source of fear of oneself as well as a feeling of extreme happiness. The power of this experience is sufficient to inspire belief in a divine person from whom this power springs.[105] For Nietzsche, the development of religion is a process in which the human person is diminished and belittled. Everything great about human nature is ascribed to a supernatural and divine source. What remains to be claimed by the human person is his impotence and limitation. "Religion has debased the concept of 'man'; its ultimate consequence is that everything good, great, true is superhuman and bestowed only through an act of grace."[106]

Given this state of affairs, Nietzsche asserts his intention to reclaim the beauty and sublimity that have been assigned to an imaginary God as the property and product of humanity alone.[107] This reclamation requires, to put it in Nietzsche's terms, the death of God. The process in which religion originated must be reversed. The great attributes that have been assigned to God must be returned to the human person, and this can only be done by eliminating faith in God.[108] Nietzsche most famously proposes this elimination in his description of the madman in *The Gay Science*. The madman announces to a group of amused atheists that God is dead, and that he and they are his murderers. The madman, however, is distraught by the fact that these unbelievers have yet to grasp the implications of this death and

104. Nietzsche, *Ecce Homo* 2.1.

105. Nietzsche, *Will to Power* 2.135.

106. Ibid., 2.136.

107. Ibid., 2, Preface.

108. Lubac, *Drama of Atheist Humanism*, 46.

concludes that he has come too soon. Later in *The Gay Science*, Nietzsche describes the new horizons opened up by God's death.

> Are we perhaps still not too influenced by the *most immediate consequences* of this event—and these immediate consequences, the consequences for ourselves, are the opposite of what one might expect—not all sad and gloomy, but much amusement, encouragement, dawn . . . . Indeed, at hearing the news that "the old god is dead," we philosophers and "free spirits" feel illuminated by a new dawn; our heart overflows with gratitude, amazement, forebodings, expectation—finally the horizon seems clear again, even if not bright; finally our ships may set out again, set out to face any danger; every daring of the lover of knowledge is allowed again; the sea, our sea, lies open again; maybe there has never been such an "open sea."[109]

God, for Nietzsche, is the great cloud on the horizon of humankind. It is only with God's removal that humanity can begin to reclaim its greatness, the sublimity and beauty that it has erroneously ascribed to a false God.

Humility and Greatness in Nietzsche's Thought

Viewed from one perspective, Nietzsche's thought can be characterized as a prolonged attempt to establish the greatness of humanity. The murder of God is done for the purpose of reclaiming human sublimity and beauty. The will to power, likewise, is a foundation for greatness because power is exercised preeminently by the noble, the aristocrat, the person of great strength.[110] Nietzsche's conception of virtue can also be viewed from the perspective of greatness. Only the great have the inner strength and hardness to align their passions with their greatest goals, thus achieving virtue.[111] It is only to the great few that the idea of virtue can be applied; the rest of mankind—the herd—is relegated to a life of adherence to custom and convention deprived of true virtue. Possibly the most direct construct in Nietzsche's thought relating to greatness is his structure of master and slave morality. In his conception of master morality, great persons—the noble—provide the very foundation of morality. "The judgment 'good'

---

109. Nietzsche, *Gay Science* 5.343.

110. The power of the noble and the aristocracy is manifest in their ability to create the values that constitute goodness. Cf. Nietzsche, *On the Genealogy of Morality* 1.2.

111. Nietzsche, *Thus Spake Zarathustra* 3.3, 3.12.29.

does *not* emanate from those to whom goodness is shown! Instead it has been 'the good' themselves, meaning the noble, the mighty, the high-placed and the high-minded, who saw and judged themselves and their actions as good."[112] For Nietzsche, human existence is simply the realm in which the great seek to exercise their power. Master and slave morality, virtue, the will to power, and even the existence of God are all subject to the greatness of humanity striving to express itself.

Turning to humility, it is in the context of the slave morality that Nietzsche mentions the idea of humility. The slave morality, as was discussed earlier, is the conspiracy of the sickly, the lowest of those who suffer against the successful and victorious. The sick impose their misery on the healthy so that the healthy feel guilt about their happiness. In their hatred of the healthy, the sick people attempt to monopolize virtue, saying that only the weak are truly just. In their attack against the strong, the weak give testimony to a noble lie that traits such as a "sugared, slimy, humble humility" are really strengths of character.[113] For Nietzsche, these lies stand reality on its head, making weakness virtuous. Perhaps no one but Nietzsche can describe such a turn of events.

> This grim state of affairs . . . has, thanks to the counterfeiting and self-deceptions of powerlessness, clothed itself in the finery of self-denying, quiet, patient virtue, as though the weakness of the weak were itself—I mean its *essence*, its effect, its whole unique, unavoidable, irredeemable reality—a voluntary achievement, something wanted, chosen, a *deed*, an *accomplishment*.[114]

Humility is precisely one of these sham virtues foisted upon the strong by the slave morality. It is nothing other than timid baseness turned into a virtue by the lying rhetoric of the slave mentality.[115] To link such timid baseness with the greatness Nietzsche associates with strength and power is manifestly absurd. And he says as much asserting, "It is . . . absurd to ask strength not to express itself as strength, not to be a desire to overthrow, crush, become master, to be a thirst for enemies, resistance and triumphs as it is to ask weakness to express itself as strength."[116] Greatness for Nietzsche is an exercise of power. It is the ineradicable drive of the powerful

---

112. Nietzsche, *On the Genealogy of Morality* 1.2.

113. Ibid., 3.14.

114. Ibid., 1.13.

115. Ibid.

116. Ibid., 1.13.

for domination over all other things. Thus from Nietzsche's perspective, humility and greatness are as profoundly opposed as are the master and slave moralities he describes. Humility can only be taken as strength in the context of the fiction that slave morality attempts to assert. In Nietzsche's world, humility is an aspect of sickliness and must be shunned by the great lest their power be corrupted by the sickness of the slave.

Ancient Challenges to Modern Morality

My study of Hume's and Nietzsche's positions regarding humility and greatness reveal wide disparities between their views and those of Augustine. The benefit of these contrasts comes from the questions those differences raise and the answers I hope to provide for them. There are aspects to Hume's thought that seem eminently reasonable. Reasonable may not be a term easily applied to Nietzsche's morality, but there is something of his thought that is attractive to his reader. Augustine notes that all persons are drawn to or desire greatness,[117] and Nietzsche's notion of the will to power and the human longing to express one's power is a cogent expression of a manner in which that desire may be fulfilled. Could we characterize Hume's and Nietzsche's perspectives as long-needed corrections to the one-sided Augustinian and Christian tradition that held humility and its relation to greatness in an inexplicably high regard? Or are there aspects of Augustine's thought that shed light on that of Hume and Nietzsche through which one can correct their repudiation of humility as inimical to greatness? It is to the answers of these questions that I will now turn.

117. Augustine, S. 20A.7 (WSA III/2:25).

6

The Greatness of Humility

THE IMPORTANT DIFFERENCES IN thought between the authors of my study present significant challenges when attempting to compare the content of that thought. The writing of these authors was composed in four different languages, and more than two thousand years separate the work of the earliest, Aristotle, from that of the latest, Nietzsche. Each author developed his thought in historical circumstances significantly or even gravely different from those of the others. Given such disparate historical circumstances for the composition of each author's work, it is important to recognize the barriers to superficial comparisons so as not to distort either the original intent of the authors or the meaning of the concepts subject to comparison. In my effort to avoid facile comparisons, I will rely on the approach of Alasdair MacIntyre, who addressed the challenges to comparing authors of different intellectual traditions in his works *Whose Justice? Which Rationality?* and *Three Rival Versions of Moral Enquiry.*

MacIntyre's Method for Comparing Rival Moral Traditions

In the former work, MacIntyre asserts that rational enquiry is a historical endeavor. He argues for an understanding of rational enquiry ". . . as embodied in a tradition, a conception according to which the standards of rational justification themselves emerge from and are part of a history in which they are vindicated by the way in which they transcend the limitations of and provide remedies for the defects of their predecessors within the history of that same tradition."[1] Such enquiry is a product of the historical circumstances and social setting in which it is undertaken.

---

1. MacIntyre, *Whose Justice?*, 7.

Failure to recognize this, in MacIntyre's view, will inevitably lead to the misunderstanding of the thought in question.[2]

A consequence of MacIntyre's historical approach to rational enquiry is the necessity of positing many traditions of rational enquiry based on the ever-changing historical context in which rational enquiry is pursued. Considering the different historical settings in which the authors of my study wrote—which presupposes (among others things) significant cultural and linguistic dissimilarity—is to observe the substantive differences in the way each particular tradition approached morality. MacIntyre confronts his reader with a diversity of traditions concerning rational enquiry, each of which employ their own modes of rational justification, which often are at odds with rival traditions.[3] Such discrepancies in method and content exist between the authors of my study, which must be accounted for in a comparison of their rival positions.

This brings us back to the challenge of comparing the authors of my study whose conclusions are based on the differing and even conflicting moral principles of rival traditions. Given that my methodology has been to identify and explain the importance of such differences, it would be somewhat contradictory to attempt to downplay those differences in an effort to compare each author's thought. MacIntyre, too, emphasizes the importance of such dissimilarities, reflecting on examples in which linguistic and cultural dissimilarities provide insuperable boundaries to translation from one tradition to another.[4] He notes that some authors understand such comparisons as impossible. They argue that in cases where large-scale systems of thought (examples of which can be seen in Aristotelian ethics or the moral enquiry founded on enlightenment views of rationality) are in disagreement, there can be no independent measure by which the systems may be compared. Since each system is comprised by internal standards of judgment that differ one from the other, such systems are incommensurable because their terms of judgment cannot be translated into the rival tradition without distorting those terms in the process of translation.[5] MacIntyre, however, does not hold that view. He believes that comparisons between such systems of thought are possible, although he is careful to keep

2. Ibid., 8.

3. Ibid., 9.

4. Cf. MacIntyre, *Whose Justice?*, 370–88 for his discussion concerning traditions and their ability to be translated in coherent terms into other languages or traditions.

5. MacIntyre, *Three Rival Versions*, 4–5.

in mind the above mentioned concerns regarding translatability and the importance of differences in principles of judgment unique to each tradition of enquiry. He makes the point that even to recognize the fact that rival traditions of enquiry contradict each other concerning a particular belief or practice requires some level of translatability between the two systems. Such a difference can only be observed in the context of some common norms of intelligibility and evaluation shared by each system.[6] Without some common reference, it would be impossible to detect difference or contradiction between two systems.

MacIntyre goes further in his assertion of the importance of such commonality, claiming that not only can disparate systems be compared on this basis, but that it is in the context of such comparisons that rival systems can challenge one another and provide a measure to determine the relative superiority of one tradition over another.[7] Systems that differ fundamentally on some topics may actually share texts and beliefs regarding other issues. In such situations, a tradition that ignores the opposing viewpoints of its rival is ignoring a resource through which it could evaluate its beliefs on the basis of its own standards.[8] Put more positively, the interaction of two traditions can raise new questions and open up opportunities in which established beliefs and practices can be reappraised. Such reappraisal, based upon the tradition's intellectual assets and the ingenuity of its members, will either reveal a lack of resources with which to address the new concerns or an ability to reform and strengthen the beliefs and practices called into question.[9] A key to this process, which will be particularly relevant to my analysis, is recognizing that each tradition must be evaluated on the basis of its own standards of judgment.[10] For MacIntyre, there are no independent standards of enquiry by which rival traditions may be evaluated or compared.[11] To compare rival systems, one can confront one system with questions raised by another, but the answers provided must be on the terms of the system questioned if one is to offer an appraisal of that system's ability to support its own conclusions.

6. Ibid., 5.

7. Ibid.

8. MacIntyre, *Whose Justice?*, 350.

9. Ibid., 350, 355.

10. MacIntyre, *Three Rival Versions*, 5.

11. MacIntyre, *Whose Justice?*, 351.

Given the wide differences in the history and principles separating the authors examined by this study, there is little doubt they represent rival traditions of moral enquiry. In light of this circumstance, I will offer my comparison between them on the basis of the principles MacIntyre articulates regarding the evaluation of differing traditions of enquiry. I will begin the comparison with a discussion on how belief or lack of belief in God affects each author's view of humility and greatness. This aspect of the comparison will demonstrate the importance of the differences in each system's standards of judgment and how the differences regarding the belief in God have a profound effect on each author's subsequent view of humility and greatness. Following the discussion of atheistic and theistic approaches to the issue, I will examine the differences and commonalities between Aristotle's understanding of magnanimity and Augustine's view of greatness based on humility. Lastly, I will examine the strengths and weaknesses of Hume's, Nietzsche's, and Augustine's views concerning greatness on the basis of principles internal to their discussion and through questions that can be raised from rival perspectives.

Theistic and Atheistic Approaches to Humility and Greatness

Among the authors of my study, Augustine is the one who views God and the relationship of God to the human person in the most intimate and positive terms. He is also the one thinker to put significant emphasis on the importance of humility to greatness. Given the separation between Augustine and the other authors on this issue, I will begin with his view of God and its effect on his understanding of humility and greatness. I will then examine the positions of the other writers.

Augustine's Understanding of God and Humility

The attention Augustine devoted to understanding God throughout his writing career makes any attempt to provide a succinct characterization of that view a difficult task. The extremely narrow presentation of Augustine's understanding of God I will offer will be limited to its relationship to his view of humility and greatness.[12] Five aspects of Augustine's view of God

12. Cf. Holte, *Beatitude et Sagesse* as a representative of the many works on Augustine's

and his relation to the human person have appeared particularly important in my study concerning his view of humility and greatness. The first of
these concerns the human ability to know God. It is important to initially
point out that Augustine sees God's nature as inexpressibly superior to that
of created beings.[13] This, however, does not preclude discussion of God,
and Augustine clearly acknowledges the ability of the human mind to grasp
in both faith and wisdom something of God's nature.[14] The human person's
ability to know God is not only a feature of her greatness, but also provides
her an understanding of that in which her greatness consists. Second, and
related to the idea that the knowledge of God yields a particular conception of human greatness, is Augustine's view of the person as created in
the image and likeness of the triune God.[15] The human person's capacity
to image God yields a view of humility and greatness in which the person
is called to the fullness of his existence through the love and knowledge of
God. Third, Augustine's view of God's nature as love (1 John 4:8)[16] is of fundamental importance to the human person's ability to know and love God.
By reflecting on the human experience of love, a person can come to know
God's very nature.[17] By embracing God's love, the human person is able to
transcend love of self and embrace the humility of love for God. Fourth, in
his work *On the Nature of the Good* Augustine asserts that God is the highest good, and that God is therefore immutable and eternal.[18] The mystery
of God's all-encompassing perfection is the source of awe and chastening
from which a person's humility grows.[19] Fifth and finally, the love of God
revealed by the incarnation of Jesus is a humble love.[20] The perfection of
God did not preclude God from humbling himself to take the form of a
human. In his strength and greatness, God lowers himself in order to lift up
a fallen humanity.[21] The divine model of humble strength sacrificing itself

understanding of God. See also Studer, *Trinity and Incarnation* for a treatment of Augustine's view of God in relation to humility.

13. Augustine, *S.* 117.15 (WSA III/4:219).

14. See also Augustine, *Trin.* 8.3.6 for his discussion of the importance knowledge
of God plays in the human person's ability to love God.

15. Augustine, *Trin.* 12.2.6.

16. Augustine, *Trin.* 8.5.12.

17. Ibid.

18. Augustine, *Nat. B.* 1.

19. Dodaro, "Gift of Humility," 90.

20. Studer, *Trinity and Incarnation*, 179.

21. Augustine, *S.* 68.11 (WSA III/3:230–31).

for the good of others becomes, for Augustine, the foundation of human strength and greatness as well.[22]

Classical Views of the Divine in Relation to Human Greatness

God, for the other classical authors of my study, is neither humble nor intimate nor loving. In the thought of Aristotle, God is seen as the unmoved mover, which is the end that causes the movement observed throughout the universe.[23] Since the unmoved mover can only be contemplated through the intellectual virtues[24] and is not an end that can be achieved by any action of the human person, it has little bearing on Aristotle's view of magnanimity.[25] In addition, since Aristotle recognizes only the natural cosmos as a context in which to understand the human person, magnanimity becomes the only mechanism through which an individual may overcome the obscurity of death. For Aristotle, it is through the honor and glory of magnanimity that a person can pursue immortality.[26] The Stoic conception of God as a material body immanent in the operations of the universe is significantly different from that of Aristotle and holds greater importance for their understanding of human greatness.[27] The greatness of the Stoic sage is based on the Stoic valuing of virtue beyond all other goods[28] and the sage's ability to integrate reason, which finds its source in the Stoic notion of God, with her emotions concerning the good of virtue and the indifferent value of all temporary objects.[29] Similar to Augustine, the Stoic view of God—in particular the reason of God—shapes their moral thought. In contrast to Augustine, however, the Stoic focus on the divine through

22. Augustine, *En. Ps.* 92.3 (WSA III/18:364).

23. Aristotle, *Metaphysics* 1072b4–29.

24. Aristotle, *Nicomachean Ethics* 1177a11–18.

25. Ibid., 1096b30–34.

26. Arnhart, "Statesmanship as Magnanimity," 267.

27. Cf. Diogenes, *Lives of Eminent Philosophers* 2.7.137 for the Stoic description of God as the being whose whole is made of all substances and from whom all substances are drawn. See also Cicero, *De Natura Deorum* 2.13.36–37 for a description of the divinity of the world, which embraces wisdom, virtue, and even perfection. In addition, Cicero asserts the Stoic positions that the world is God and is of a spherical shape in *De Natura Deorum* 2.17.46–47.

28. Cicero, *De Finibus* 3.11.

29. Ibid., 3.22.

their notion of fate leads not to humility and love, but to resignation in a fate little concerned with the travails of the individual person. Turning to Cicero's conception of *gloria*, we see a depiction of greatness that draws heavily on Stoic notions of virtue but has little to do with an understanding of the divine. Cicero, unlike Aristotle or the Stoics, does make room for humility in his account of *gloria*, which provides a parallel with Augustine's focus on humility. Cicero's role for humility, however, finds its source in the importance of modesty in the experience of the wise person rather than a relationship to a divinity.[30] Given the significant parallels in the thought of Plotinus with that of Augustine, one might expect to see a parallel role for humility in his thought as well. Plotinus's understanding of the soul's desire for independence as the source of its fall[31] and his focus on the intellectual union of the soul with the One as the greatest end to which the person is ordered[32] provides a hypothetical basis on which Plotinus could have developed a role for humility similar to that of Augustine. Despite these affinities, Plotinus's account of the relationship between the soul and the One neglects any role for humility, focusing instead on the soul's self-sufficiency to reach the One[33] and its subsequent absorption into the One.[34] As a result, Plotinus's conception of the One plays no role in fostering a focus on humility.

The above investigation demonstrates, in contrast to Augustine's thought, that classical notions of God do not support the importance of humility to greatness. That lack of support is based both on an absence of intimacy between classical understandings of God and the individual person and the nonexistence of a Christian or Augustinian view of creation in which the human person is radically dependent upon God for his very existence. The gods of classical philosophy are for the most part aloof from temporal human existence, and in that separation from mere mortals, provide no context in which love or awe can give rise to the importance of humility.

---

30. Cicero, *De Officiis* 1.90.

31. Plotinus, *Enn.* V.1.1. Cf. Torchia, "St. Augustine's Treatment of *Superbia*," 67 for a discussion of Plotinian *tolma* and its correspondence to Augustine's notion of *superbia*.

32. Plotinus, *Enn.* I.2.1.

33. Plotinus, *Enn.* VI. 9.11.

34. Ibid., 9.10.

Modern Views of God and Human Greatness

The positive role Augustine assigns to humility in its relationship to human greatness reflects the positive relationship he construes between God and the human person. The absence of any significant role for humility to greatness in classical thought is likewise based on the aloof and neutral interaction between the divine and individual human persons in that tradition. The modern thought of Hume and Nietzsche continues the pattern in which the presence or absence of God has a significant effect on an author's view of humility. The role of God in the moral thought of both Hume and Nietzsche takes on very negative connotations, which supports their negative view of humility's relation to human greatness.

Given Hume's consistent skepticism, it is unlikely that he came to the conclusion that God certainly does not exist.[35] Despite what may have been an inability to completely repudiate the possibility of God's existence, Hume lays the dominant conceptions of God at the doorstep of human imagination rather than any rational basis for belief in an all-powerful, all-loving deity.[36] Hume's agnosticism, however, did not lead him to a neutral characterization of religion's influence in moral discussion. For Hume, the historical relationship between religion and morality had been a catastrophe. Hume asserts that the role of religion in morality had undermined the natural understanding of morality. The opposition between religious morality and natural morality gave rise to confusion over the source and nature of ethics. Adding to this confusion were the preposterous virtues and assignments of praise and blame proposed by religious morality.[37] The virtue of humility was, for Hume, one of those absurd virtues championed by religious morality. In the context of his skepticism, Hume's notion of God is unlikely to have had significant effect on his view of humility, but the negative role he assigns to religious moral thought surely did have an effect on that view.

Approaching Nietzsche's position on the issue is to confront one of the most consistent and significant aspects of his thought: its anti-theism. Since God is the entity to which Nietzsche assigns all the powerful and great aspects of human nature,[38] God becomes the principle that must be elimi-

35. Gaskin, "Hume on Religion," 488–89.

36. Hume, *Hume Selections,* 262–63.

37. Ibid., 394.

38. Nietzsche, *Will to Power* 2.135.

nated for humanity to achieve its true greatness.[39] Combining Nietzsche's antagonism toward God with his notion of greatness as the expression of the will to power resulted in a view of humility as the antithesis of human greatness.[40] In Nietzsche's view, human greatness supplants the greatness of the Christian God and is manifest in the assertion of will by the powerful. Humility can only have a negative role in such a context. Thus, Nietzsche's antipathy toward God is a significant basis for his antipathy toward humility and his repudiation of it as having any positive value in regard to the great person.

In comparing the views of God in relation to the human person articulated by each of the study's authors, we see a demonstration of what MacIntyre would consider rival standards of judgment and evaluation. The thought of each author on the issue of God and his subsequent treatment of human greatness with or without humility manifests what would be considered incommensurable values. As a result, despite the consistent pattern that arises regarding the relationship between notions of God and the subsequent portrayal of humility and greatness, the differences in the principles supporting each author's perspective inhibit comparison between the strengths and weaknesses of such approaches. Those differences leave us only with the ability to note the many significant distinctions between the approaches of the various authors. I will turn now to areas in which comparison and evaluation between these rival conceptions of humility and greatness are possible and where such comparison helps to shed light on the strengths and weaknesses each system holds in relation to the issue.

Aristotelian Magnanimity and Augustine's Humble Greatness

Two authors have addressed the relationship between Aristotle's view of magnanimity and the Christian view of humility in relation to statesmanship in recent philosophical literature. Larry Arnhart argues that outside the generation of statesmen who established the United States, great statesmen are generally lacking in American history due to the influence of Christian humility, which precludes an understanding of ambition and

---

39. Ibid., 2, Preface. Cf. Lackey, "Killing God, Liberating the 'Subject,'" 737–54 for a discussion of Nietzsche's view that it is only in killing God and doing away with faith that a person can be free to create herself.

40. Nietzsche, *On the Genealogy of Morality* 1.13.

greatness that could serve as the foundation from which individuals pursue great statesmanship.[41] Taking his understanding of Christian humility from the thought of Augustine and Thomas Aquinas and citing the analysis of Alexis de Tocqueville, Arnhart claims that humility in the context of creation overtook classical views of magnanimity and glory grounded in the nature of the cosmos. He asserts, "If nature is purely contingent, then all pride is vanity, and the only appropriate moral and intellectual stance for human beings is humble submission to the creative principle that transcends natural understanding."[42] Augustine, he points out, by directing all virtue toward God as the source of creation rather than the temporal sphere, denies the possibility of establishing true justice in the earthly realm. The only goal of politics in such a context is the establishment and maintenance of domestic peace.[43] The result is a culture in which people of great potential shrink their ambition, ordering it toward material comfort and the administration of the established state.[44]

In response to Arnhart, Carson Holloway posits an understanding of Christian humility and charity compatible with and even perfective of Aristotelian magnanimity. Relying on the presentation of humility in Scripture and the thought of St. Augustine and St. Thomas, Holloway asserts that humility did not prevent Christ from demonstrating the virtue of magnanimity, and that it is only the closely related virtue of charity that will inspire the great person to take on the responsibility and travails of a life dedicated to statesmanship in the service of the state.[45] While opposition between two philosophers on a particular issue is hardly surprising, it does raise the question of who actually got it right. Is Aristotelian magnanimity compatible with Christian humility, and if so, how? Using Macintyre's criteria for comparing rival systems of enquiry, I will offer an answer through a comparison of Aristotle's and Augustine's thought.

In examining the moral principles guiding the thought of Aristotle and Augustine, one sees both significant commonalities and important contrasts. Both Aristotle and Augustine approached morality from the perspective of classical eudaemonism in which the *telos* of the human person is achieved in the acquisition of the greatest good. Although Aristotle and

41. Arnhart, "Statesmanship as Magnanimity," 263–64.

42. Ibid., 271.

43. Ibid., 272.

44. Ibid., 264.

45. Holloway, "Christianity, Magnanimity, and Statesmanship," 581–604.

Augustine conceive of the greatest good in significantly different manners, the eudaemonistic structure is common to both thinkers.[46] Another aspect shared in the thought of each is their focus on the role of virtue in securing the human person's greatest good. Again, despite the differences in the way each understands the importance of virtue to happiness,[47] their focus on virtue provides a common ground in which their thought might be compared. Two further similarities can be seen in the central role played by practical wisdom or prudence in each authors' moral thought[48] and the role of *eros* for Aristotle and grace for Augustine as the source of inspiration for the good choices constitutive of virtue.[49]

Despite these significant similarities, there are also important differences in each thinker's morality that make reconciliation between Aristotelian magnanimity and the humble greatness proposed by Augustine difficult to achieve. I discussed one of the most significant differences between the two in the previous section concerning the relationship of God to the world of human experience. Growing out of these contrasting divine contexts is a difference of fundamental importance to each author's morality. In the natural order of the cosmos, Aristotle (like the Stoics and Platonists) never questioned the moral self-sufficiency of the human person. For Aristotle, self-sufficiency is a mark of greatness exhibited by a magnanimous person.[50] Augustine's view of the moral self-sufficiency of the human person could hardly be more different. For Augustine, no one is morally self-sufficient. All have sinned (Rom 5:12), and as a result of that sin, all are in need of God's grace to choose anything good.[51] A third difference separating the moral thought of each and significant to their pre-

46. For Aristotle, the end of moral striving is happiness. Cf. *Nicomachean Ethics* 1097b20. For Augustine, the end of the human person is the happiness achieved through the intellectual possession of God. Cf. Augustine, *Div. Qu.* 5.2 for a typical formulation concerning God as the human person's greatest good. Cf. Augustine, *B. Vita* 2.11.

47. Cf. Aristotle, *Nicomachean Ethics* 1098b29–30 for his account of the relation between virtue and happiness. Cf. Augustine, *Div. Qu.* 35.2 for Augustine's characterization of the relation of love to happiness. This view combined with his description of virtue as the perfection of love (*Mor.* 15.25) yields an understanding of Augustine's conception of the relationship between happiness and virtue. Cf. Babcock, "Early Augustine on Love," 53.

48. Cf. Aristotle, Nicomachean Ethics 1144b16–20 for his description of the central role played by practical wisdom. See also Augustine, *Mor.* 24.45 for his view on the importance of prudence.

49. Rist, *Augustine*, 180–81.

50. Aristotle, *Nicomachean Ethics* 1125a10–11.

51. Augustine, *Gr. et Lib. Arb.* 4.7. Cf. *En. Ps.* 70(1).19 (WSA III/17:433), 93.15 (WSA III/18:392).

sentations of magnanimity and humble greatness is Augustine's concept of the will. Although scholars have described Aristotle's notions of voluntary action, deliberation, and wish as precursors to Augustine's understanding of the will, Augustine's development of the concept provides a significant distinction from Aristotle's morality.[52] For Aristotle, the choice of actions leading to vice or virtue stem from the deliberation that is the hallmark of choice.[53] For Augustine, the person's ability to choose good or evil resides in the freedom of the will.[54]

Magnanimity and Humble Greatness Compared

The primary similarity between the magnanimity of Aristotle and the greatness achieved through humility in Augustine's thought lies in the relationship between each conception of greatness and that thinker's understanding of virtue. The fullness of virtue does not exist for Aristotle without the presence of magnanimity, which is likewise the case for Augustine's conception of humility. Aristotle's description of the relationship between magnanimity and the other virtues states that "[m]agnanimity thus is the crown, as it were, of the virtues: it magnifies them and it cannot exist without them. Therefore it is hard to be truly magnanimous and, in fact, impossible without goodness and nobility."[55] The magnanimous person, for Aristotle, is truly virtuous, and it is in holding the other virtues that the value of magnanimity displays itself. For the role of magnanimity in relationship to the other virtues is one in which it brings the other virtues to perfection and completion. The ability of the magnanimous person to understand himself accurately as deserving of great honor will drive that person to undertake great actions, which will in turn lead to the development of greater virtue.[56] The magnanimous person's concern for honor will also reinforce the other virtues because it will drive that person to do only the great things worthy of honor, thus choosing virtuous activity, which is a particularly important source of honor for Aristotle.[57] The high-minded person will also look to

52. Cf. van Riel, "Augustine's Will," 255–79 for a discussion of the relationship between Augustine's view of the will and Aristotle's moral psychology.

53. Aristotle, *Nicomachean Ethics* 1113a3–11. Cf. ibid., 1113b3–5.

54. Augustine, *Civ. Dei* 14.13.

55. Aristotle, *Nicomachean Ethics* 1124a1–4.

56. Ibid., 1123b1–1124b25.

57. Ibid., 1124a8. Cf. 1106b24–30.

do good to others as a mark of his superior character, which again fosters the development of the virtues necessary for such good works.[58]

In Augustine's thought, one sees an even greater emphasis on the importance of humility to the flourishing of the other virtues. Augustine's account of the relationship between humility and virtue details three ways in which humility aids in the development and maintenance of the other virtues. First, humility is the mechanism through which virtue is established in a person. Virtues, for Augustine, originate in the unchanging rules and lights of God's truth.[59] Since love for God subjects the person to God as the object of that love, humility as the initial love a person has for God enables the human person to come into contact with the forms of the virtues present in God's own existence. Here we find a more significant role for humility in relation to virtue than Aristotle's view of magnanimity's effect on the virtues, for it is through humility that virtue finds its source in God. The contact with God established by humility is critical to the second manner in which humility fosters virtue as well. Augustine's conception of humility, like magnanimity, is an important mechanism through which the other virtues are able to grow. Humility, by turning a person's will toward the fire of God's love,[60] enables the person's virtue to grow because God's grace and love not only establish virtue, but also continue to nourish a person's virtue so long as that person remains turned toward God in humility.[61] The third aspect in which humility promotes virtue is its function to protect virtue from the encroachments of pride. For Augustine, even the virtuous must be ready to defend against the evil of pride.[62] This is done through humility, which prevents pride of virtue from growing by focusing a person's attention on her characteristics in need of improvement rather than the self-congratulation that can come as the result of holding authentic virtue.[63] Augustine's assertion of humility's protection of virtue is absent in Aristotle's account of magnanimity. Yet despite the greater importance of humility's sustenance of virtue in Augustine's thought, the similarity in

58. Ibid., 1124b9–12.

59. Augustine, *Lib. Arb.* 2.19.52–53.

60. Augustine, *Civ. Dei* 14.13.

61. Augustine, *Trin.* 12.3.16.

62. Cf. Augustine, *Conf.* 10.38.63 for his account of how pride can undermine virtue in his description of the contempt of vainglory leading to further vainglory.

63. Augustine, *S.* 16B.3 (WSA III/1:364). Cf. Augustine, *S.* 159B.15 (WSA III/11:160).

which humility and magnanimity support and further a person's possession of the other virtues remains a commonality between the two systems.

Another manner in which Aristotelian magnanimity and Augustinian humility function similarly is the accurate self-understanding provided by each virtue. For Aristotle, the reason magnanimity can be considered a mean between extremes and thus be seen as a virtue is the fact that the magnanimous person has an accurate view of herself. The magnanimous person believes she is worthy of great things and is accurate in that self-estimation.[64] The magnanimous person's accurate self-vision places her in the mean between the vain person, who foolishly overestimates her self-worth, and the small-minded person who deprives herself of things that she deserves.[65] Augustine's understanding of humility, although more inclined to recognize a person's imperfection rather than the greatness seen by the magnanimous person, is also marked by accurate self-vision. For Augustine, humility speaks the truth about a person because it is in humility that a person can acknowledge sin and failure.[66] Augustine sees this aspect of humility especially manifest in the greatest of Christian heroes: the martyrs, who despite their greatness are still cognizant of their weakness.[67] Thus, both Christian humility and Aristotelian magnanimity are virtues that exhibit a person's ability to accurately assess herself.

Despite these parallels between the two virtues, the number of differences between them is greater and more substantive. I will begin my description of these differences with one of the more unattractive features of Aristotelian magnanimity, which is characterized by some as its tendency toward pretension or snobbishness.[68] According to Aristotle, the magnanimous person has a right to look down on others because in his greatness, the magnanimous person is superior to others.[69] This is also the result of the magnanimous person's commitment to truth and his lack of timidity. The magnanimous person cares more for the truth than for the opinion of others and as a result of his fortitude speaks openly. The combination of his openness, his commitment to truth, and his low estimation of most

---

64. Aristotle, *Nicomachean Ethics* 1123b1–2.

65. Ibid., 1125a16–35.

66. Augustine, *Ep. Jo.* 1.6 (WSA III/14:27).

67. Dodaro, "Heroic Ideal," 144.

68. Cf. Curzer, "Maligned Megalopsychos," 135–37 for a discussion of the pretentious aspect of magnanimity.

69. Aristotle, *Nichomachean Ethics* 1124b5–6.

people in reference to himself would likely make the magnanimous person somewhat obnoxious in his relations to others. This differs distinctly from Augustine's view of humility. Augustine uses the parable of the Pharisee and the tax collector to drive home the point that the person of humility, no matter how virtuous, cannot legitimately look down upon others. Augustine notes that the Pharisee of the parable lives his life in what would be considered by most to be an upright fashion. One of the outcomes of the Pharisee's lack of humility, however, which is condemned by Augustine, is the fact that he looks down upon others. In his pride, the Pharisee looks with disdain upon the tax collector, which Augustine views as contrary to the love of humility.[70] This is a point missed by Carson Holloway in his treatment of humility and magnanimity. Holloway takes the position that a Christian can legitimately look down upon others so long as that contempt holds no animosity for another person. He makes his claim on the basis of a passage in the *Summa Theologica* of Thomas Aquinas where Thomas maintains that humility is primarily concerned with a person's relationship to God rather than with other men and women.[71] Holloway's interpretation of Thomas on the point is questionable as it neglects the next sentence of the *Summa* where Thomas notes that the humility required for one's relationship with God is achieved by subjecting oneself to one's neighbor.[72] Holloway's view is contrary to Augustine's thought from three perspectives. Augustine asserts that in its function of placing a person in contact with the love of God, humility cultivates authentic concern for others. Humility developed on the foundation of God's love is simply incapable of wishing another person ill, and one can affirm that contempt for another is a particularly potent form of thinking ill of another.[73] Augustine also sees a primary expression of the humble love for God in a person's love of others. Love of neighbor is the cradle in which the love of God is nurtured and is thus at odds with looking at another contemptuously.[74] Lastly, if a person of virtue follows Augustine's advice regarding a focus on one's weaknesses rather than her accomplishments, it is difficult to develop a perspective that focuses on the inferiority of others.[75] Clearly, then, the manner in which a

70. Augustine, *En. Ps.* 31(2):11 (WSA III/15:374).

71. Holloway, "Christianity and Statesmanship," 589.

72. Thomas Aquinas, *Summa Theologica* II–II, q. 161, a.1.

73. Augustine, S. 353.1 (WSA III/10:153).

74. Augustine, *Mor.* 26.48.

75. Augustine, S. 16B.3 (WSA III/1:364). Cf. S. 159B.15 (WSA III/11:160).

magnanimous person and a humble great person view others offers a significant distinction between the perspectives of Aristotle and Augustine.

A second aspect in which Augustine's view of humble greatness offers a significant contrast to Aristotle's view of magnanimity is based on what might be described as the interiority of the former as opposed to the exterior focus of the latter. As I noted earlier, Augustine's notion of an interior spiritual life, which he developed on the basis of neo-Platonic thought, is both a significant intellectual innovation and an important structural theme in both the *Confessions* and *The Trinity*.[76] Augustine, like Plotinus, turned to the interior of his soul in his search for God. The difference between the two lies in Plotinus's advocacy for the divinity of the soul on the basis of its contact with the forms of intellect, while Augustine asserts that once a person gazes inward upon his soul, he must then look above the soul to find the source of God's light.[77] Humility for Augustine is the key to discovering the interiority of the soul and also expresses the aspect of that interiority in which God's grace fills the spiritual space made available by humility. Returning to his exegesis of the parable of the Pharisee and the tax collector, Augustine describes the tax collector as spiritually empty, which he equates with humility. It is through humility that one understands his inner emptiness and is then able to seek God's grace as the reality capable of filling that emptiness.[78] Augustine perceives of the greatness achieved by receiving God's grace in one's spiritual emptiness primarily as an interior greatness. "You mustn't suppose that this exaltation . . . will occur in the sight of men by means of any terrestrial promotions or elevations . . . . So where has he arranged ascents? In the heart . . . . Ascent, after all signifies exaltation, so the valley indicates humility . . . ."[79] In Augustine's view, the greatness achieved in humility finds its source and orientation in the interior relationship between the soul and God.

76. Cf. Augustine, *Conf.* Book 7 and *Trin.* Book 12 for Augustine's use of the turn to the interior.

77. Cary, *Invention of Inner Self*, 39.

78. Augustine, *S.* 36.11 (WSA III/2:181).

79. Augustine, *S.* 351.1 (WSA III/10:119). There is some controversy over whether this sermon was actually written by Augustine. The Maurists believe that it was, but Erasmus and the translator of the WSA sermons, Edmund Hill, disagree. Without trying to settle the dispute, I would merely claim that even if penned by another person, the text represents an authentic aspect of Augustine's view regarding humility, interiority and greatness. The greatness humility leads to is, for Augustine, always oriented toward the interior heights of God and the heavenly city rather than the exterior concerns of humans in the earthly city.

The exteriority of Aristotle's treatment of magnanimity provides a contrast to the interiority of Augustine's humility. The stage for the magnanimous person is the exterior world of human interaction. This aspect of his treatment is most manifest in the magnanimous person's concern for honor. Here we see another context in which commentators have been critical of Aristotle's portrait of the high-minded person, asserting it conveys a picture of a conceited person concerned primarily with accruing the praise of others.[80] Despite the many references Aristotle makes with respect to the focus of the magnanimous person on honor, one can make a defense of his position on the basis of the relative importance of external goods compared to goods of virtue. Despite Aristotle's emphasis on the greater value of the interior good of virtue compared to an external good such as honor, his presentation of magnanimity has a pronounced exteriority in its emphasis on the honors that should accrue to the high-minded person.[81] As the person of the highest character, the magnanimous individual is deserving of the greatest things. Honor, in its typical attribution to the gods, strikes Aristotle as being greater than all other external goods and is therefore the good that the magnanimous person deserves and strives after.[82] In addition, it is not merely honor that the magnanimous person desires, but the right type of honor. Honor offered to a magnanimous person by an ordinary person or on the basis of a trivial matter will be despised by the high-minded person.[83] It is only honor bestowed by the noble for the accomplishment of great deeds that is worthy of the magnanimous person's desire.[84] While Aristotle's understanding of magnanimity is grounded in the internal value of virtue, its desires and expressions are oriented toward an exterior view of greatness that is significantly different from the view of Augustine.

A third difference between Aristotle and Augustine related to Aristotle's formulation of the honor a magnanimous person deserves is the issue of desert. For Augustine, even the greatest person is undeserving of reward in a strict sense. His perspective is grounded in his notions of creation, sin, and the gratuity of God's grace. The context for the relation between the deeds of a person and the rewards merited by those deeds is set for Augustine by the Christian understanding of creation. The human person, in

---

80. Curzer, "Maligned Megalopsychos," 134–35.

81. Aristotle, *Nicomachean Ethics* 1124a8.

82. Ibid., 1123b17–23.

83. Ibid., 1124a9–10.

84. Ibid., 1123b17–20.

Augustine's view, is dependent upon God for his very existence. Augustine's understanding of the human person's creation in the image and likeness of God also makes the manner of a person's existence directly dependent upon God's creative act.[85] It is in the context of creation that Augustine can assert that a person is in debt to God not only for his existence and manner of existence, but also for any good that he may have achieved or received throughout his life (1 Cor 4:7).[86] In addition, Augustine's position that all have sinned (Rom 5:12) has two further implications for the relation between deeds and desert.[87] First, as a result of the damage done by sin to the will, no one is able to choose the good without the help of God's grace.[88] Reward for good action, then, is nothing more than a reward given on top of the grace already received that made the good work possible in the first place.[89] In Augustine's view, then, reward finds its source in the grace of God that makes the good work possible. Second, since all people have sinned, all deserve punishment rather than reward. It is only the gift of God's love that merits a person reward over the just punishment of sin.[90] Despite his heavy emphasis on how all people are undeserving of reward, however, Augustine does not sever the relation between deeds and deserts completely. He maintains the link in the context of his understanding of the will. Although grace is the source of a person's ability to do the good, it is only in cooperation with the will that grace can serve as that source. The will is free to refuse the promptings of grace, and it is on this autonomy that Augustine asserts a person truly deserves God's reward for her cooperation with grace.[91]

Unlike Augustine's notion of creation in which humility finds a secure foundation, Aristotle proposes his understanding of virtue and magnanimity within the natural order of the cosmos. The constant change and danger to human happiness manifest in that order causes Aristotle to seek for a stable foundation of happiness in the excellence procured by virtue. His view of magnanimity is the highpoint of moral virtue and becomes

85. Augustine, *Trin.* 12.2.6.

86. Augustine, *Gr. et Lib. Arb.* 6.15.

87. Augustine, *Nat. et Gr.* 41.48. Cf. *Trin.* 13.4.16.

88. Augustine, *Gr. et Lib. Arb.* 4.7. Cf. *En. Ps.* 70(1).19 (WSA III/17:433), 93.15 (WSA III/18:392).

89. Augustine, *Gr. et Lib. Arb.* 8.20.

90. Augustine, *Trin.* 4.3.15.

91. Augustine, *Gr. et Lib. Arb.* 2.4.

a foundation in which he seeks to tether human happiness.[92] Within the context set by the contingency of nature, Aristotle develops a notion of morality that presupposes moral self-sufficiency. It is through the development of virtue that a person can be happy and maintain some semblance of happiness should severe misfortune strike.[93] Happiness, for Aristotle, is the consequence of virtue, which provides the link between desert and great deeds readily apparent in his depiction of magnanimity.[94] In choosing good actions, a person becomes morally good.[95] It follows, then, that the magnanimous person—a person in possession of all the virtues and capable of the greatest actions—will accrue the goods consequent to the greatest actions. It is on this basis that Aristotle describes the magnanimous person as deserving great things. To do great things is to deserve great rewards, the greatest of which is the reward of honor.[96] The idea of desert is also manifest in the magnanimous person's ability to accurately assess her own greatness. The high-minded person recognizes that she is worthy of great things, and in this recognition, discerns her greatness. Desert distinguishes Aristotelian magnanimity from Augustinian humility as the link between a person's great deeds and the great rewards she deserves as well as in its service of providing the evidence upon which a person can recognize her grandeur.

A last important contrast between Aristotle and Augustine is Aristotle's focus on the magnanimous person's tendency to give gifts and Augustine's focus on the humble person's ability to receive grace. One might think that it would be the Christian who would emphasize greatness as an ability to give of oneself, and certainly Augustine's presentation on humility captures that aspect;[97] but Aristotle, too, describes how the magnanimous person would rather give gifts then receive them. For Aristotle the magnanimous person is

> . . . the type of man who will do good, but is ashamed to accept a good turn, because the former marks a man as superior, the latter as inferior. Moreover, he will requite good with a greater good, for

92. Cf. Arnhart, "Statesmanship as Magnanimity," 265 for an account of the relationship between nature, happiness, and virtue in Aristotle's thought.

93. Aristotle, *Nicomachean Ethics* 1100b22–33. Cf. Arnhart, "Statesmanship as Magnanimity," 265.

94. Aristotle, *Nicomachean Ethics* 1098a7–18.

95. Ibid., 1103b30.

96. Ibid., 1124a19–20.

97. Augustine, *S.* 28A.4 (WSA III/11:51).

in this way he will not only repay the original benefactor but put him in his debt at the same time by making him the recipient of an added benefit. The high minded also seem to remember the good turns they have done, but not those they have received. For the recipient is inferior to the benefactor, whereas a high-minded man wishes to be superior. They listen with pleasure to what good they have done, but with displeasure to what good they have received.[98]

As can be seen in the above text, the magnanimous person's inclination to give rather than receive is not born out of love for others, but really manifests a prudence to maintain his superiority in reference to others. While giving gifts typically reflects well on a person, giving gifts to maintain one's superiority relative to a recipient is unlikely to win admiration. It seems to reflect an unwarranted concern for one's self-esteem achieved through the manipulation of the magnanimous person's relationship to others. It also manifests what might be described as a fear of inferiority. Aristotle's magnanimous person is so anxious about appearing subordinate to one who might show him generosity that it causes him to respond in a way that attempts to suppress the superiority of the other through generosity. Such fear appears contrary to the fortitude a magnanimous person would supposedly possess as a person in possession of all the virtues.

Augustine paints a different picture regarding humility and its relationship to greatness. Augustine does link the height of self-giving—the sacrifice of oneself for the good of another—to humility, representing it as the end toward which humble love is ordered.[99] At the foundation of Augustine's notion of humility, however, is gratitude for gifts received. Here we again see his notion of grace at work. It is in humility that a person can receive God's grace, which then becomes the source of her greatness. Augustine encourages the believer to give thanks to God for all the gifts of his grace.[100] It is in the receipt of God's gifts that Augustine posits a strength that runs counter to the fear that seems to drive the Aristotelian high-minded person's desire to give gifts. Augustine follows the teaching of St. Paul (2 Cor 12:10) on the issue by asserting, "The power of charity (is) brought to perfection in the weakness of humility."[101] The effect of humility's turn to God as the source of strength is a confidence built upon the perfection of

98. Aristotle, *Nichomachean Ethics* 1124b9–15.

99. Augustine, *S.* 28A.4 (WSA III/11:51).

100. Augustine, *S.* 30:7 (WSA III/2:127).

101. Augustine, *Trin.* 4.1.2.

God rather than the fear one might feel in relying on human power alone. Augustine contends that

> Whatever is strong finds its home in humility, for all pride is fragile . . . the Lord (is) girded with strength, a strength that, as always, expresses itself in humility . . . . If strength expresses itself in humility, do not be intimidated by the proud. Humble people are like rock. Rock is something you look down on, but is solid. What about the proud? They are like smoke: they may be rising high, but they vanish as they rise.[102]

Despite the difference in context, one is tempted to see Aristotle's portrait of magnanimity in Augustine's description of the proud. The proud are concerned about their standing among others, and in their neglect for the interior strength provided by humility, they are vulnerable to becoming inferior. Augustine's view of humility, on the other hand, connotes the strength and confidence expressed in Paul's exclamation, ". . . For when I am weak, then I am strong" (2 Cor 12:10). For Augustine, the strength of greatness is established in the perfection of humility.

To conclude my comparison of Aristotle's view of magnanimity and Augustine's understanding of humble greatness I will borrow from MacIntyre's methodology making brief observations on each tradition and offering each questions from the perspective of the other tradition. I will begin by raising questions on Aristotle's view of magnanimity from an Augustinian perspective. One of the strengths of Aristotle's moral theory is its distinction between virtuous, continent, and incontinent moral agents. It is by means of this distinction that Aristotle provides a sophisticated explanation of the ability of some people to know and choose the good, while others with this knowledge fail to choose the good.[103] The aspect of this discussion pertinent to his description of magnanimity is virtue's ability to correct for human weakness. The value of virtue is its ability to correct human imperfection. It is through the development of virtue that a person is able to confront and overcome moral weakness and the greatest challenges offered by life. Within this discussion, Aristotle also takes note of what he calls a god-like character. This is a person of such great virtue that he is more like to a god than a human. Such persons are rare, but do

---

102. Augustine, *En. Ps.* 92.3 (WSA III/18:364).

103. Cf. Aristotle, *Nichomachean Ethics* Book 7, Chapters 1 through 10 for his discussion of moral strength and weakness.

seem to exist from Aristotle's perspective.[104] Aristotle's superhuman virtue would seem to be akin to his earlier depiction of the magnanimous person who not only holds all the virtues, but magnifies them through magnanimity. It is at this pinnacle of virtue that Aristotle's account seems weak and vulnerable to questions from Augustine's perspective. Is it possible for a person to achieve the heights of virtue without the humility necessary for self-correction and improvement? Aristotle seems to posit the possibility of a perfect moral agent, which begs the question, "Has anyone actually encountered a perfect moral agent?" No matter how virtuous a person appears in real life, doesn't the character of all people manifest some weakness? It seems that the addition of Augustinian humility to Aristotle's portrait of the magnanimous person would not only make the portrait more realistic, but would also make a magnanimous person better than what they appear to be without it.

Taking up Augustine's thought from the perspective of Aristotle, one can make the argument that Augustine's emphasis on humility is so pronounced that it could lead to the pusillanimous character Aristotle posits as the primary vice opposed to magnanimity.[105] In being always concerned with the lowness of humility, a person might withdraw from the heights of their true potential. An Augustinian answer to such a charge would likely be two-fold. First, although there is no doubt that Augustine places a heavy emphasis on humility, the context of humility is always understood in relation to the greatness to which God calls a person as his image and likeness. Humility is not an end in itself but is rather "the way" in which the person must trod to reach his true greatness. Second, given Augustine's belief in a loving God who is the source of one's strength, a heavy emphasis on humility is nothing other than an argument for making great use of the source of a person's strength, which is the infinite love of God. A weakness in Augustine's argument for humble greatness, however, can be seen in its dependence on the relationship between God and the human person presupposed by Augustine. Shorn of this relationship, the importance of humility to greatness becomes more difficult, although not impossible, to discern.

104. Aristotle, *Nicomachean Ethics* 1145a18–30.
105. Ibid., 1125a17–26.

Hume, Nietzsche, and Augustine:
Competing Accounts of Greatness

The disparity between Hume's, Nietzsche's, and Augustine's accounts of human greatness is indeed immense. Although caused in part by each author's view of the relationship between God and morality, the disparity also results from the manner in which each conceives of morality.

Hume's Greatness

Turning first to an examination of Hume's moral principles yields insight into his view of human greatness, revealing characteristics produced both by his methodology and the principles on which his moral thought is based. Although Hume carried forward some of the prevailing theories of seventeenth century moral philosophy, his approach to morality via the cautious observation of Bacon's experimental method was a significant innovation. The philosophical system Hume devised with the help of his scientific method was one of the most compelling presentations produced by modern philosophy, moving Kant out of his "dogmatic slumber,"[106] and as MacIntyre notes, affecting generations of Scottish philosophers as well as the western moral tradition as a whole.[107] Yet despite this influence, his methodology by its nature does not depict spiritual aspects of human morality well, and as a result, lacks depth when Hume articulates his view of human greatness. An examination of Hume's moral principles reveals the sources of what I describe as a superficial approach to morality, which is the result of his methodology, his focus on sentiment or moral feeling, his marginalization of reason, and the absence of a *telos* for the moral life. These aspects of Hume's thought conspire to paint a picture of human greatness that lacks authenticity.

Applying Bacon's scientific method to morality, Hume asserts that one must study the behavior of individuals to understand moral phenomena.[108] On the basis of his observations, Hume states that pleasure and pain are the primary motives for human action. Hume proposes his methodology and position on pleasure and pain within the context of the sentimentalist

---

106. Kant, *Prolegomena and Metaphysical Foundations of Natural Science* 4.260.10.

107. MacIntyre, *Whose Justice? Which Rationality?* 322.

108. Hume, *Treatise of Human Nature*, 10.

morality he took over from his predecessors, Shaftesbury and Hutcheson.[109] Morality, for Hume, is based on the positive or negative feelings particular actions may elicit from those observing the person undertaking the action. Yet it is not the action that actually gives rise to such feelings, but the character of the person who chooses the actions. Actions for Hume are signs of the virtues or vices a person has that motivate her specific choices. A virtue is a quality of mind agreeable to all observers, and vice causes anxiety to those who observe it.[110] The positive or negative feelings that a person's behavior arouses in others is a reaction to the motives and temper of the mind driving the person's choice rather than the action itself.[111] As a result, Hume's ultimate norm for morality lies in the nature of the feelings of the observers of the action rather than in the actor or the act.[112] Hume later broadens this criterion to include the idea of utility, asserting that useful actions are precisely the actions that give rise to positive moral feelings.[113] A last important feature of Hume's moral system for my discussion is the minor role played by reason. Reason is an educator of passions, but in itself, is impotent to cause moral activity.[114] Passions, in their effort to seek pleasure and avoid pain, are the sole cause of moral action.

The observational or external approach Hume takes to understanding morality seems to leave him on the outside of the moral phenomena he is trying to describe. With the exception of his account concerning virtue and vice, which attempts to highlight the moral relevance of interior motives rather than external actions, each of Hume's moral principles has a focus on exterior or public behavior. The experimental method relies on the observance of behavior, but even Hume admits that visible choices are frequently driven by interior motives. In similarly external fashion, Hume asserts that the morality of a person's actions is characterized by the feelings of others external to the actions. Although those feelings begin as what Hume calls internal impressions or emotions, they are only known once they have been expressed or externalized by the observers. Such expression can and frequently would change the nature of the feeling. This is especially true because people would be inclined to change or form their moral feelings on the basis of society's

109. MacIntyre, *Short History of Ethics*, 169.

110. Hume, *Concerning the Principles of Morals*, *Appendix* 1.10; 8, note 50.

111. Hume, *Treatise of Human Nature* 3.2.1.

112. Ibid., 3.1.2.

113. Hume, *Concerning the Principles of Morals* 5.2.17.

114. Hume, *Treatise of Human Nature* 2.3.3.

consensus concerning utility, which is yet another public or external phenomenon claimed by Hume to be fundamental to morality.

Applying Hume's moral principles to his understanding of human greatness we find a description that only scratches the surface of the moral phenomenon he attempts to describe. It fails to recognize the strength of character and recourse to reason necessary for a human person to be morally great. Hume asserts that pride, which is a virtue because of the positive moral feelings it elicits, is the foundation of human greatness. Relying on his observational skills, he declares that greatness and elevation are ". . . nothing but a steady and well establish'd pride and self-esteem, or partake largely of that passion."[115] Hume does caution that excessive pride can cause negative moral feelings and thus recognizes a role for an external modesty that softens the edges of an overweening pride.[116] He limits the extent of such modesty, however, claiming that no one admires a sincere humility that goes beyond the façade of modesty.[117] Such an account of human greatness seems inadequate to the excellence typically associated with greatness and the formidable challenges posed by human life in the pursuit of moral excellence. Beginning with his description of an external modesty, one might ask if it is possible to demonstrate such an external behavior consistently or under difficult circumstances without some interior foundation in a person's character. Given the human tendency to value self over others, it seems reasonable to assert that an inauthentic modesty will have difficulty holding back a well-founded self-esteem in situations that called for modesty. Similar concerns arise when considering the human tendency to avoid self-criticism and pursue service to self. If people always seek pleasure and avoid pain, how does a person become great without the pain of self criticism and the humility that makes such criticism possible and effective? In the search for the pleasure provided by pride, would not a person be more likely to avoid the pain that comes through confronting one's weaknesses or failings? In addition, great people are often admired for putting the needs of others before themselves. Is that possible or likely in a moral context where seeking pleasure and avoiding pain are the paramount principles? Does the principle of utility provide the power necessary to overcome the instinct to serve oneself before others? Combining the two

115. Ibid., 3.3.2.

116. Hume, *Enquiry Concerning the Principles of Morals* 8.8.

117. Hume, *Treatise of Human Nature* 3.3.2.

concerns one might ask, "Can a self-serving person with little ability for self-criticism become great?"

Further concerns regarding Hume's account of greatness can be raised in the context of his focus on pleasure and pain, his marginalization of reason and the absence of a teleological framework, and the manner in which he characterizes the nature of a virtue. Can a person without significant input from reason put off short-term pleasures and endure pain in order to achieve a remote goal? History is marked by great people who overcome unimaginable hardship to achieve a purpose. Would people endure such suffering and pain if the Humean moral context was accurate? With little aid from reason, could they ascertain what great good could be accomplished through perseverance and suffering? Without reason and an end to which the human person is ordered, is that person even capable of determining a good worth suffering for? One can also question if Hume's characterization of virtue as a quality of mind, impression, or emotion provides a notion of virtue that holds the power and stability necessary to achieve greatness. Does an impression in the mind give one the ability, the power to achieve greatness? Aristotle conceived of virtue as the establishment of a good habit, a *hexis*,[118] which was a power of the mind. Given the real obstacles to greatness provided by the challenges of life, it seems that a conception of virtue as a stable power better describes virtue's ability to overcome adversity than does an understanding characterizing it as a quality of the mind deemed good by the feelings it arouses in others. Greatness requires the power to overcome adversity. Does virtue described as an impression or an emotion provide that stability and power?

Such questioning gives one pause when considering the strength (or viability) of Hume's account regarding greatness. I will offer three reasons that suggest the inadequacies of his account. First, the dependence of his method on the observation of human behavior yields a moral system incapable of adequately uncovering the interior, spiritual resources necessary to support human greatness. Hume's analysis obscures a notion of virtue in which a power of the soul is capable of overcoming the allure of ephemeral pleasures and the discouragement of pain.[119] Second, his emotional rather

118. Cf. Aristotle, *Nicomachean Ethics* 1103a14–26 and 1105b19–1106a12 for Aristotle's description of the relationship between virtue, habit, and character.

119. Cf. Mcintyre, "Strength of Mind," 393–401 for an account of Hume's view concerning the virtue strength of mind. Strength of mind is Hume's characterization of the virtue in which the calm passions that calculate what's best for a person over the course of her life take precedent over the concerns of short term, violent passions. J. Mcintyre

than rational approach to morality and the absence of an end in terms of which human greatness can be defined yields a moral agent unqualified to develop the rational virtue necessary for greatness. To be great, a person needs not only strength of virtue, but also an intelligence of virtue that can see beyond the immediate concerns of pleasure and pain to the achievement of a goal that would make the person great.[120] Third, Hume's neglect of humility as an integral component of greatness produces a moral agent who would have difficulty rising above service to self and would be poorly equipped to undertake significant self-criticism. There are many adjectives to describe a self-serving person who is blind to his failings, but great is not typically one of them.

Nietzschean Greatness

The substance of Nietzsche's philosophy and moral thought presents challenges in attempts to compare his thinking with that of other philosophers, particularly those of antiquity. One reason for this is the lack of systematization in Nietzsche's thought, a fact which makes drawing general conclusions from his writings more difficult than most authors.[121] In addition, his

asserts that while elements in Hume's thought are present to develop the idea of strength of mind, Hume lacks a systematic presentation of the virtue (395). She also notes that holding such a virtue would likely be rare in Hume's view and is even contradicted in his own writing. In the *Treatise of Human Nature*, Hume asserts humans ". . . are always much inclin'd to prefer present interest to distant and remote; nor is it easy for them to resist the temptation of any advantage, that they may immediately enjoy." (*A Treatise of Human Nature* 2.3.8). Alasdair MacIntyre notes that Hume's view on the genesis of government arises from the need to keep such self-interest in check, which serves to deemphasize the role strength of mind might play in taming the violent passions. Cf. MacIntyre, *Whose Justice?*, 312.

120. Cf. MacIntyre, *After Virtue*, 54–55 for a discussion concerning the enlightenment rejection of teleology in morality. According to MacIntyre, Hume (along with other enlightenment philosophers) is engaged in the task of defining what's good on the basis of a human nature that isn't always good. Without a goal, end, or good to which the person can be measured it becomes difficult to define what is good. Human greatness likewise becomes difficult to define if there is no ultimate good against which to measure it. The lack of an ultimate end combined with the human tendency toward short term pleasure and avoidance of pain would likely impair the ability to see and adhere to a path toward greatness.

121. Cf. Danto, *Nietzsche as Philosopher*, 19–28 for a discussion concerning the absence of system in Nietzsche's writing. Canto offers to impose a system of his own design upon those writings in an attempt to interpret Nietzsche's thought, but asserts that no such system actually exists in Nietzsche's work.

relativistic and perspectival approach to morality, which posits that virtue applies only to the elite few and consigns the rest of humanity to a morality of convention, is dramatically different than a eudaemonistic account that can offer a system of morality applicable to all moral agents; thus, comparison with such systems is problematic.[122] Still another significant difference lies in his emphasis on the will to power that yields an understanding of morality omitting the eudaemonistic pursuit of happiness. Indeed, Nietzsche's view of morality for his "higher men"[123] rejects happiness as the motive for moral activity. In expressing his power, the higher person is more likely to cause misery, his own misery included, than he is to cause happiness.[124]

A last aspect of Nietzsche's thought that makes comparisons specific to the study of greatness challenging is the solitary and isolated manner in which he views human greatness. Nietzsche's characterization of great people focuses on creativity and the relentless pursuit of their work or art-form. In his creative genius, drive to excel, and ability to even create his own standards of excellence, figures such as Beethoven or Goethe fit Nietzsche's paradigm of the higher person.[125] In addition, Nietzsche paints a picture of the higher person as almost adversarial in nature. For Nietzsche the great person ". . . knows how to make enemies everywhere, ... [He] constantly contradicts the great majority not through words but through deeds."[126] The goal of moral striving is only the expression of power, no matter what the consequence, no matter the pain that might be inflicted. This trajectory toward conflict and confrontation can be similarly observed in Nietzsche's conception of virtue in which the virtues are adversaries to one another, only becoming part of one's character through discord and the defeat of other virtues.[127] The indifference or animosity the higher person has toward others is also a result of her dedication to her craft. Other persons are viewed as either instruments to the end of the higher person's

122. Hunt, *Origin of Virtue*, 141–42.

123. Cf. Nietzsche, *Beyond Good and Evil*, 212 for a description of great or higher people. See also Nietzsche, *Will to Power*, 957 for additional commentary regarding human greatness.

124. Nietzsche, *On the Genealogy of Morality* 3.7.

125. Cf. Nietzsche, *Will to Power*, 842 for his characterization of great artists and how Beethoven is the first great romantic composer. Cf. Nietzsche, *The Will to Power*, 1051 for Nietzsche's grouping of Beethoven with Goethe, Shakespeare, and Raphael as the great figures of latter-day culture.

126. Nietzsche, *Will to Power*, 944.

127. Hunt, *Origin of Virtue*, 81.

objective or a hindrance to that objective.[128] For Nietzsche, the great are not concerned with society or community. They are great in the prosecution of their individual art form, and their ability to transcend the concerns of a mundane community is a mark of that greatness.

I would offer that Nietzsche's individualist and isolationist approach to greatness is contrary to the classical formulations of human greatness. Aristotle, as I've described, saw the magnanimous person as highly concerned with honor, a notion naturally bound to an individual's relation to the wider community.[129] Cicero, too, saw the social aspect of *gloria* as intrinsic to its nature. *Gloria*, for Cicero, was achieved through the display of great virtue in public venues, the greatest of which he considered to be political forums.[130] An additional social aspect was *gloria's* relation to the appraisals of other people. To achieve *gloria*, in Cicero's view, one not only had to be virtuous, but she must also be praised as virtuous by other people of virtue.[131] Augustine's notion of humble greatness likewise has a significant social aspect in its emphasis on humility's ability to nurture love of neighbor.[132] Nietzsche's view of greatness, on the other hand, is contemptuous of social considerations. Like the virtues that consume one another in their interior conflict, Nietzsche's higher people would likely also devour one another. For Nietzsche, strength expresses itself in opposition and confrontation. "It is . . . absurd to ask strength not to express itself as strength, not to be a desire to overthrow, crush, become master, to be a thirst for enemies . . ."[133] Nietzsche's understanding of greatness is at best indifferent to the views of society and can equally be described as combative toward the beliefs of others.

Does it matter that Nietzsche's view of greatness lacks the social setting evident in the ancient context? One can certainly make the argument that in proposing such a conception Nietzsche is merely drawing out the implications of his own principles. Nietzsche conceives of power, the will to power, as the domination of a more powerful entity over a less powerful one.[134] Thus, strength's desire to express itself by becoming master over

---

128. Nietzsche, *Beyond Good and Evil,* 273.

129. Aristotle, *Nicomachean Ethics* 1123b23.

130. Cicero, *De Officiis* 2.46.

131. Ibid., 2.36–37.

132. Augustine, *Mor.* 26.48.

133. Nietzsche, *On the Genealogy of Morality,* 1.13.

134. Ibid., 2.12.

others is merely a result of the dynamism his view of power implies. In addition, in his commitment to his project or art form, the higher person is consumed by passion for his work. Part of the great person's virtue is to overcome the distraction that society or other people may pose in fulfilling his mission. Society—and indeed all other human relationships—are subjugated to the passion for the higher person's project and thus are of little importance relative to the achievements the great person has as his goal.[135]

Despite this consistency, however, Nietzsche's thought on greatness suffers from two weaknesses, one of which stems from the principles he uses to advance his view; the other is based on the narrowness of the view itself. Nietzsche asserts in his formulation of master and slave moralities that the idea of the good originated in antiquity from the nobles who had the power to look upon themselves and define the good on the basis of their own good actions and their own attributes.[136] An important aspect of Nietzsche's evaluation is that the goodness of those who are noble is not asserted in reference to any other entity. Unlike persons of the slave mentality who define their goodness by reference to the powerful people they see as evil, people of the master morality need no enemy to establish their virtue. Noble moral action is active rather than reactive and needs no contrast to demonstrate its goodness.[137] It is a morality of self-glorification without reference to other people or groups.[138] Yet despite Nietzsche's assertion that such is the case, imbedded in the terminology he uses to describe the goodness of the noble are notions of relationship to others. To be noble, to be high and mighty, to be beautiful, all imply relationship. One is only noble in relation to or in reference to something that is not noble. If there is nothing that is base or less distinguished than the noble, then the idea of nobility loses its meaning. To be high is defined in reference to what is lower than that which is high. If nothing is lower than the high, it is not high; it just is. Thus, even in the solitude of genius that Nietzsche defines as greatness lies an implied relation. Were all of Beethoven's audiences also deaf, the beauty of his genius could not be recognized. The greatness of the individual can only be recognized within a social setting. This reality is present in the

---

135. Nietzsche, *Beyond Good and Evil*, 273. Cf. Nietzsche *Ecce Homo* 2.9 for Nietzsche's view concerning the absolute priority of the task.

136. Nietzsche, *On the Genealogy of Morality* 1.2.

137. Ibid., 1.10.

138. Nietzsche, *Beyond Good and Evil*, 260.

principles Nietzsche uses to articulate his view of human greatness, but it also undermines the isolationist picture he attempts to paint.

Where the above critique employs the standards of evaluation used by Nietzsche to criticize Nietzsche's own conclusion, the following critique concerning the narrowness of Nietzsche's view of greatness will proceed according to his moral principles. But it will also look to rival conceptions of greatness as a means to question the validity of Nietzsche's conclusions. In confining his conception of greatness to lone individuals of genius, Nietzsche narrows the idea of human greatness, reducing greatness to only one of its important characteristics. One aspect of greatness completely omitted from his viewpoint is the aspect in which a person is considered great in his ability to make other people or a group of other people great. Effective leadership of a group requires the type of comprehensive virtue recognized in Aristotle's account of magnanimity and Cicero's view of *gloria*. Leadership not only requires the cardinal virtues as the foundation of trust between the leader and the group he hopes to inspire to greatness, but it also requires virtues that enhance interpersonal relations in a way that encourages a member of the group to follow the direction of the leader. Cicero details such virtues in his account of *gloria* when he asserts that the good will of others is aroused by the reputation of kindly service. Others will admire a person who is known to be beneficent, just, gentle, and faithful in his commitments.[139] It is through such admiration that a leader can influence the behavior of the group's members. Augustine's formulations of humility and greatness further the point. Envy, Augustine points out, is always a by-product of an individual's pride in relation to other people.[140] To encourage humility, however, is to advocate for love of others because humility, in its inability to feel ill will toward its neighbor, will overcome the envy and alienation generated by pride.[141] Such an attribute would contribute significantly to the good will of the group, thus enhancing the ability of members to work well together or follow the instruction of the group's leader. The primary example of such leadership can be seen in Augustine's proposal of Jesus as the personification of humble greatness. In his Christological presentation, Augustine proposes a model of humble, self-sacrificial love that has consistently drawn followers in large numbers over the course of two millennia.

139. Cicero, *De Officiis* 2.32.
140. Augustine, *S.* 354.5 (WSA III/10:158).
141. Augustine, *S.* 142.12 (WSA III/4:421).

Certainly an argument for greatness based on the large number of people drawn to its character would have little effect on Nietzsche's position, which would counter that the herd is in need of the slave morality offered by Christianity. In Nietzsche's view, large numbers of followers merely confirms the mediocrity of the herd for which he argues so vehemently. Yet in his neglect of or blindness to the social aspect of greatness, Nietzsche is making a significant omission. By ignoring this aspect of greatness Nietzsche ignores a feature that was emphasized by Aristotle, Cicero, and Augustine alike. He also ignores social aspects of greatness that are evident in the cultural values of contemporary western society. In athletics, with almost universal consistency, champions are valued and revered far above individuals of outstanding talent. Although outstanding musicians may at times attract the spotlight of attention, the conductor of an orchestra, as its leader, is typically the person considered to be most important to the performance of the group as a whole and is thus its most prominent or greatest member. In military units, operational commanders are always more important than individual warriors.

It is no accident that Nietzsche's account of greatness overlooks the social aspects of greatness taken for granted in the examples just cited. It is an omission caused by the nature of his moral principles. The very virtues Nietzsche extolls as constitutive of the great person—the desire to overthrow, crush, and become master—would render leading a group difficult, if not impossible. The adversarial and self-serving attributes that constitute Nietzsche's great person would lead to the quick and utter demise of any group such a person attempted to lead. Nietzsche's higher person would be more likely to alienate or even dispose of the other members of a group than inspire them to greatness. Nietzsche also asserts it is an absurdity that strength would not express itself in a manner of crushing or overthrowing an adversary. Yet such a description cannot account for universal phenomena, such as parents placing their strength at the service of their children's welfare or teachers using the strength of their learning to guide a younger generation of students. Nietzsche's moral principles yield an impoverished view of human greatness that cannot account for its intrinsically social nature and is, as a result, not equal to the task of articulating a comprehensive account of that greatness.

Augustine's Humble Greatness

Turning finally to Augustine, the question remains how his understanding of greatness may be evaluated and what resources it offers to those examining the issue. One weakness of Augustine's position can be seen in its intrinsic link to God, and specifically, the person of Jesus Christ. Of course Augustine would consider this aspect one of the greatest, if not the greatest, strengths of his position. Yet if one is not a believing Christian or is an atheist, Augustine's position regarding the importance of humility to greatness is shorn of one of its fundamental assets: the access to God's unlimited power provided by humility. This absence leads to the other most significant weaknesses of his position, which is a conception of humility that views a person negatively in relation to others.[142] Without reference to God, humility's focus on lowliness and comparison to others can indeed lead to the useless and negative outlook Hume ascribes to it.[143]

Despite the possible detachment of humility's function as the mechanism through which a person becomes close to God, humility still poses significant resources for the achievement of true human greatness in three significant and related ways. First, humility is valuable both for Nietzsche's lone genius and the leader of a group in its facilitation of self-criticism. The ability to rise above the tendency to overlook one's own weaknesses and failings is critical to a person's ability to adjust her behavior and character to achieve greatness. Augustine's humility offers not only the clarity of self-vision necessary to correct one's faults, but it also provides the willingness to address them.[144] Second, humility is able to overcome the discord of pride, which is a primary inhibition of greatness in social settings. Assuming a leader holds the basic competencies necessary for a particular position of leadership, the humble leader will outstrip a prideful or arrogant leader's ability to influence and inspire others to follow her in the accomplishment of a particular mission. Thirdly, Augustine's assertions regarding humility's role in preventing the pride of virtue or the pride of success is often critical to the great person's ability to maintain her own level of excellence.[145] Recent literature in business ethics has coined the term "The Bathsheba

---

142. Augustine, *S.* 68.10 (WSA III/3:230). Augustine argues that humility only in reference to others and not in reference to God is really an instance of pride. Such comparisons, Augustine asserts, foment arrogant competition.

143. Hume, *An Enquiry Concerning the Principles of Morals* 9.1.1.

144. Augustine, *En. Ps.* 84:14 (WSA/18:216–17).

145. Augustine, *S.* 16B:2–4 (WSA III/1:363–65).

Syndrome" in reference to King David's ethical failings after having established himself as king. David's failings are not an isolated phenomenon, as contemporary research in the ethics of business points out that many highly successful professionals succumb to the temptations of power in a manner quite similar to King David.[146] The contemporary literature takes up the issue in a manner similar to that of Cicero. Cicero contends that a person who has become overconfident through repeated success must be educated concerning the frailty and variability of human affairs. Such education for Cicero comes by way of a humility that acknowledges the fortuitous aspects of a person's success.[147] Augustine likewise asserts that the practice of humility requires one to emphasize how she can still improve rather than enjoying virtue already achieved.[148] Practiced in this manner, humility is an authentic and effective method through which a person can avoid the temptations to self-service that grow from an ever inflating self-esteem developed on the basis of sustained success.

Of course, Augustine's most cogent arguments for the importance of humility to greatness come in the context of belief in God and the humble greatness displayed by Jesus Christ. It is in this context that Augustine can account for the authentic aspects of greatness championed by Hume and Nietzsche. Hume asserts that a worthy self-esteem is the foundation of human greatness, and while I am critical of such an assertion in the context of Hume's other moral principles, there is no doubt that confidence and belief in one's capacities are important to great accomplishments.[149] Augustine's depiction of humility accounts for this aspect of greatness in its assertion that the human person discerns his intrinsic value in observing the lengths Jesus goes to, as the eternal Son of the Father, in his effort to redeem sinful humanity. The incarnation and crucifixion are remarkable acts of humility that God undertakes solely for the sake of saving humans from their sin. Only a being of extraordinary value would cause God to take such extraordinary measures.[150] In addition, Augustine's presentation of humility nearly always expresses or implies its relation to greatness. Humility is not advocated for its own sake by Augustine. It is advocated as a means to a closer relationship with God,[151] which is the foundation of the person's greatness

---

146. Ludwig and Longenecker, "The Bathsheba Syndrome," 265–73.

147. Cicero, *De Officiis* 1.90.

148. Augustine, *S.* 159B.15 (WSA III/11:160).

149. Hume, *Treatise of Human Nature*, 3.3.2.

150. Augustine, *S.* 371.3 (WSA III/10:314).

151. Cf. Augustine, *S.* 270.6 (WSA III/7:294) and *S.* 335J.4 (WSA III/9:253) as just

as God's image and likeness.[152] The self-esteem and self-confidence advocated by Hume as the foundation of greatness can be derived from Augustine's account of a humility that provides access to the greatness of God. For the believer, such self-confidence finds a two-fold strength in humility. First, it is based not on the finite and imperfect resources of the individual person, but on the infinite perfection of God to which the humble believer has access. Secondly, humility's ability to acknowledge one's imperfections allows the confidence enabled by dependence on God to be grounded in a realistic assessment of one's own strengths and weaknesses.

Augustine's Christological interpretation of humility and greatness is a last aspect of his thought that supports an understanding of humility that lends to strength in confidence. The humility of Christ reveals humility as an aspect of God's sublimity. The incarnation demonstrates that the omnipotence of an all-powerful God is willing to take on the weakness of his creation.[153] By embracing the incarnation and crucifixion, the strength of Christ is willing to undergo humiliation and death.[154] The power of God is so secure it is prepared to experience the contempt of its creatures in pursuit of its mission. Christ presents a model of humility in which strength of character is demonstrated in its willingness to endure the disdain of superficial misunderstanding. In Augustine's view of Christ's mission, the fact that many (if not most) humans would not recognize Jesus as God nor understand his purpose was no deterrent. True greatness possesses the humility to shrug off the misperceptions of those who don't understand the nature of that greatness.

Turning to Nietzsche's account of greatness, we see a view of the great person as one who does not incline to the whims of the crowd. Nietzsche's higher person is independent from others, especially in his ability to set norms and standards of excellence. The noble person is able to stand alone, independent from the larger community; in that independence, he is able to distinguish himself as great.[155] While my earlier analysis questioned Nietzsche's tendency to emphasize this aspect of greatness to the exclusion of

two of many examples in which Augustine posits the importance of humility for a person's relationship to God. These citations focus on the importance of humility as the mechanism through which a person receives the Holy Spirit.

152. Augustine, *Trin.* 14.1.4.

153. Cf. Augustine, *En. Ps.* 92.3 (WSA III/18:364) for a description of the manner in which Christ's strength expresses itself in humility.

154. Augustine, *S.* 68:11 (WSA III/3:230–31).

155. Nietzsche, *Beyond Good and Evil*, 212.

all else, there is certainly truth to the idea that a great person is able to see what is truly good where others cannot and when others try to convince him otherwise. The interiority of Augustine's understanding of humility is also a support to this aspect of greatness. Humility is an important aspect to the turn to the interior Augustine posits in the search for God. Through humility, a person becomes interiorly capacious and is able to receive God's grace.[156] In that capaciousness, a person is able to join his will to the truth and light of God in which the principles of goodness and virtue dwell.[157] In this manner, the person is conformed to the eternal goodness of God rather than the ephemeral whims of the surrounding environment. Augustine's humble, great person recognizes the superior value of eternal goods relative to the temporary goods coveted by the earthly city.[158] Thus, the humble greatness proposed by Augustine accounts for the concern in Nietzsche's depiction of greatness in which the great can stand apart from, and if need be, in contradiction to the prevailing norms of a society.

A last aspect of Augustine's conception of humble greatness distinguishing it from all the other authors of my study is what might be described as its universal availability. For each of the philosophers investigated in my study, greatness is a function of what a person is capable of accomplishing. Aristotle's magnanimous person does few things, but the few she does are indeed great.[159] The Stoic sage is able to integrate reason with emotion in his pursuit of virtue through a lifetime of intense thought, consistency, and exemplary strength.[160] The person who achieves Ciceronian *gloria* is a person of eloquence who has striven on the public stage through the great conflicts of his time.[161] For Hume, the great are people who are able to perform great actions on the basis of their pride and self-esteem.[162] Lastly, in the case of Nietzsche, greatness is manifest in individuals of great creativity who are driven to express their power through that creativity.[163] Common to each of these conceptions of greatness is the superlative natural aptitudes a person must have in order to achieve greatness. Superlative natural capac-

156. Augustine, *S.* 270.6 (WSA III/7:294).

157. Augustine, *Lib. Arb.* 2.19.52–53.

158. Ibid., 1.4.10.

159. Aristotle, *Nicomachean Ethics* 1124b25–26.

160. Cicero, *De Finibus* 3.50.

161. Cicero, *De Officiis* 1.85.

162. Hume, *Treatise of Human Nature*, 3.3.2.

163. Nietzsche *Will to Power*, 957.

ity is not constitutive of Augustine's view of greatness, however. Greatness for Augustine is following the humble example of Jesus Christ. A person who learns from Christ, who is meek and humble of heart, will be great in Augustine's view.[164] It is a vision of greatness grounded in the spiritual aspect of human existence. As spiritual creatures, all humans have the ability to humble themselves if they so choose, and in doing so, they can become great. It is an appalling notion of greatness for someone such as Nietzsche, but for those in the herd it is "Christ the power of God and the wisdom of God" (1 Cor 1:24).

Concluding Reflections

The modern authors of my study present notions of human greatness clearly at odds with humility. The lowliness and passivity of humility are the antithesis of power for Nietzsche and serve no purpose that Hume can discern to be beneficial to the individual or human society. While the representatives of classical thought in the study do not repudiate humility as do the moderns, there is little recognition for its importance in their work. Aristotle has little use for *micropsychia*, the smallness of mind that opposes his understanding of magnanimity.[165] Humility likewise finds little or no emphasis in the thought of the Stoics and Plotinus. In Cicero, one can see the clearest non-Christian endorsement of a relation between humility and greatness in his allowance for humility's role in which the person of great accomplishment can counter the ignorance born from lack of failure.[166]

Such approaches to greatness are a far cry from that of Augustine. As we've seen throughout the course of this study, it is difficult to underestimate the importance of humility to Augustine's thought. In a letter to Dioscorus, he again describes that importance:

> Him, my Dioscorus, I desire you to submit yourself with unreserved piety, and I wish you to prepare for yourself no other way of seizing and holding the truth than that which has been prepared by Him who, as God, saw the weakness of our goings. In that way the first part is humility; the second, humility; the third, humility: and this I would continue to repeat as often as you might ask direction, not that there are no other instructions which may be

164. Augustine, *S.* 117.17 (WSA III/4:220).
165. Aristotle, *Nicomachean Ethics* 1125a33.
166. Cicero, *De Officiis* 1.90.

given, but because, unless humility precede, accompany, and follow every good action which we perform, being at once the object which we keep before our eyes, the support to which we cling, and the monitor by which we are restrained, pride wrests wholly from our hand any good work on which we are congratulating ourselves . . . so if you were to ask me, however often you might repeat the question, what are the instructions of the Christian religion, I would be disposed to answer always and only, Humility, although, perchance, necessity might constrain me to speak also of other things.[167]

Augustine posits humility at the center of the Christian religion because he sees humility as the primary lesson Christ came to teach a humanity suffering from the effects of pride. In drawing his understanding of humility from the person of Christ, Augustine hits upon still another aspect of humility and greatness that is missing from the other authors. Excellence attracts the attention and admiration of other people. The truly great person who has cause to be haughty but chooses to be humble cannot fail to attract others to herself. This is the case because the beauty of that excellence will attract others, while humility—with its orientation away from self and concern for others—will serve to augment that attraction. The epitome of this powerful combination is Jesus. Christ's humble greatness can be seen in his origin as the eternal Son of the Father, who did not think divinity something to be grasped, but emptied himself by taking the form of the human slave (Phil 2:5). It can be seen in the earthly ministry of Christ, in which he always shunned the adulation of the crowds, claiming only for himself the title of Son of Man (Matt 16:27, Mark 14:62, Luke 22:69, John 12:23). It is seen in the lowliness of his criminal's death on the cross. Yet Jesus's humility is always oriented toward his ultimate exaltation, which is again reflected in Paul's Letter to the Philippians.

> He humbled himself, becoming obedient to death, even death on a cross. Because of this God greatly exalted him and bestowed on him the name that is above every name, that at the name of Jesus every knee should bend of those in heaven and on earth and under the earth, and every tongue confess that Jesus Christ is Lord, to the Glory of God the Father (Phil 2:8–11).

167. Augustine, *Ep.* 118.3.22.

It was the beauty of Christ's humility that attracted Augustine to the church and was what finally enabled him to overcome his own pride.[168] The beauty of humility, however, was not a cause for Augustine to lower his estimate of the glory reserved for the human person. Rather it opened new vistas of glory that Augustine had never before thought possible. And it was to this vision of humble greatness that he would bear witness throughout his career as writer, preacher, and bishop.

168. Augustine, *Conf.* 6.4.6.

Bibliography

Aquinas, Thomas. *Summa Theologica*. 4 vols. Translated by Fathers of the English Dominican Province. New York: Benziger, 1948.

Aristotle. "Metaphysics." In *The Complete Works of Aristotle*, vol. 2, edited by Jonathan Barnes. Princeton: Princeton University Press, 1984.

———. *Nicomachean Ethics*. Translated by Martin Oswald. New York: Macmillan, 1962.

Armstrong, A. Hilary. *St. Augustine and Christian Platonism*. Philadelphia: Villanova University Press, 1967.

Arnhart, Larry. "Statesmanship as Magnanimity: Classical, Christian, and Modern." *Polity* 16 (1983) 263–83.

Augustine. *Answer to Adimantus, A Disciple of Mani*. Translated by Roland Teske. In *The Manichean Debate*, The Works of St. Augustine: A Translation for the 21st Century, edited by Boniface Ramsey, I.19:176–226. Hyde Park, NY: New City, 2006. *Contra Adimantum Manichei Discipulum*. CSEL 25.1.

———. *Answer to Felix, a Manichean*. Translated by Roland Teske. In *The Manichean Debate*, The Works of St. Augustine: A Translation for the 21st Century, edited by Boniface Ramsey, I.19:271–98. Hyde Park, NY: New City, 2006. *Contra Felicem Manicheum*. CSEL 25.2.

———. *Augustine's Commentary on Galatians*. Translated by Eric Plumer. Oxford: Oxford University Press, 2003. *Expositio Epistuale ad Galatas*. CSEL 84.

———. *The Catholic Way of Life and The Manichean Way of Life*. Translated by Roland Teske. In *The Manichean Debate*, The Works of St. Augustine: A Translation for the 21st Century, edited by Boniface Ramsey, I.19:17–106. Hyde Park, NY: New City, 2006. *De Moribus Ecclesiae Catholicae et de Moribus Manichaeorum*. CSEL 90.

———. *On Christian Doctrine*. Translated by J. F. Shaw. Mineola, NY: Dover, 2009. *De Doctrina Christiana*. CCL 32.

———. *The City of God Against the Pagans*. Translated by R. W. Dyson. Cambridge: Cambridge University Press, 1998. *De Civitate Dei*. CCL 47–48.

———. *Confessions*. Translated by Henry Chadwick. Oxford: Oxford University Press, 1991. *Confessiones*. CCL 27.

———. *Eighty-Three Different Questions*. Translated by David L. Mosher. The Fathers of the Church: A New Translation 70. Washington, DC: The Catholic University of America Press, 1982. *De Diversis Quaestionibus Octoginta Tribus*. CCL 44A.

————. *Expositions of the Psalms*. 6 vols. Translated by Maria Boulding. The Works of St. Augustine: A Translation for the 21st Century, edited by John E. Rotelle, III.15–20. Hyde Park, NY: New City, 2001. *Enarrationes in Psalmos*. CCL 38–40.

————. *Faith, Hope and Charity*. Translated by Bernard M. Peebles. New York: Cima, 1947. *Enchiridion ad Laurentium de Fide Spe et Caritate*. CCL 46.

————. *The First Catechetical Instruction*. Translated by Joseph P. Christopher. Baltimore: J. H. Furst, 1946. *De Catechizandis Rudibus*. CCL 46.

————. *On Free Choice of the Will*. Translated Anna S. Benjamin and L. H. Hackstaff. New York: Macmillan, 1964. *De Libero Arbitrio*. CCL 29.

————. *On Genesis*. Translated by Roland J. Teske. The Fathers of the Church: A New Translation 6. Washington, DC: The Catholic University of America Press, 1991. *De Genesi ad Litteram Imperfectus Liber*. CSEL 28.1. *De Genesi Adversus Manicheos*. CSEL 91.

————. *Grace and Free Will*. Translated by Robert P. Russell. The Fathers of the Church: A New Translation 59. Washington, DC: The Catholic University of America Press, 1968. *De Gratia et Libero Arbitrio*. PL 44.

————. *The Happy Life*. Translated by Ludwig Schopp. Writings of St. Augustine 5. New York: Cima, 1948. *De Beata Vita*. CCL 29.

————. *Homilies on the First Epistle of John*. Translated by Boniface Ramsey. The Works of St. Augustine: A Translation for the 21st Century, edited by Boniface Ramsey, III.14. Hyde Park, NY: New City, 2008. *In Epistulam Joannis ad ParthosTractatus*. PL 35.

————. *Letters*. Translated by Wilfrid Parsons. The Fathers of the Church: A New Translation 18. New York: Fathers of the Church, 1953. *Epistulae*. CSEL 34, 44, 57, 58, 88.

————. *The Nature of the Good*. Translated by Roland Teske. The Works of Saint Augustine: A Translation for the 21st Century, edited by Boniface Ramsey, I.19. Hyde Park, NY: New City, 2006. *De Natura Boni*. CSEL 25.2.

————. *On Nature and Grace*. Translated by Peter Holmes and Robert Ernest Wallis. In *Augustine: Anti-Pelagian Writings*, The Nicene and Post-Nicene Fathers, edited by Philip Schaff, 5. Peabody, MA: Hendrickson, 1994. *De Natura et Gratia*. CSEL 60.

————. *Sermons*. Translated by Edmund Hill. The Works of St. Augustine: A Translation for the 21st Century, edited by John E. Rotelle, III.1–11. Brooklyn, NY: New City, 1990. *Sermones*. CCL 41; PL 38, 39; PLS 2.

————. *Soliloquies*. Translated by Thomas F. Gilligan. The Fathers of the Church: A New Translation 1. New York: Cima, 1948. *Soliloquia*. CSEL 89.

————. *Tractates on the Gospel of John*. Translated by John W. Rettig. The Fathers of the Church: A New Translation 78–79. Washington, DC: Catholic University of America Press, 1988. *In Johannis Evangelium Tractatus*. CCL 36.

————. *The Trinity*. Translated by Edmund Hill. The Works of Saint Augustine: A Translation for the 21st Century, edited by John E. Rotelle, I.5. Hyde Park, NY: New City, 1991. *De Trinitate*. CCL 50, 50A.

————. *The Two Souls*. Translated by Roland Teske. The Works of St. Augustine: A Translation for the 21st Century, edited by Boniface Ramsey, I.19. Hyde Park, NY: New City, 2006. *De Duabus Animabus*. CSEL 25.

Babcock, William. "Augustine on Sin and Moral Agency." In *The Ethics of St. Augustine*, edited by William Babcock, 87–114. Atlanta: Scholars, 1991.

Babcock, William S. "Cupiditas and Caritas: The Early Augustine on Love and Human Fulfillment." In *The Ethics of St. Augustine*, edited by William S. Babcock, 39–66. Atlanta: Scholars, 1991.

Bacchi, Lee F. "A Ministry Characterized by and Exercised in Humility: The Theology of Ordained Ministry in the Letters of Augustine of Hippo." In *Augustine: Presbyter Factus Sum*, edited by Joseph T. Lienhard, Earl C. Muller, and Roland J. Teske, 405–16. New York: Peter Lang, 1993.

Berkowitz, Peter. *Virtue and the Making of Modern Liberalism*. Princeton, NJ: Princeton University Press, 1999.

Biro, John. "Hume's New Science of the Mind." In *The Cambridge Companion to Hume*, 2nd edition, edited by David Fate Norton and Jacqueline Taylor, 40–69. New York: Cambridge University Press, 2009.

Bobb, David Jonathan. "Competing Crowns: An Augustinian Inquiry into Humility, Magnanimity, and Political Pride." PhD diss., Boston College, 2006.

Bonner, Gerald. "Augustine as Biblical Scholar." In *The Cambridge History of the Bible Volume One: From the Beginnings to Jerome*, edited by P. R. Ackroyd and C. F. Evans, 541–63. Cambridge: Cambridge University Press, 1970.

Brennan, Tad. "Stoic Moral Psychology." In *The Cambridge Companion to the Stoics*, edited by Brad Inwood, 257–94. Cambridge: Cambridge University Press, 2003.

Brown, Peter. *Augustine of Hippo: A Biography*. Berkeley: University of California Press, 1967.

Burnaby, John. *Amor Dei: A Study of the Religion of St. Augustine*. London: Hodder and Stoughton, 1938.

————. "Amor in St. Augustine." In *The Philosophy and Theology of Anders Nygren*, edited by Charles W. Klegley, 174–86. Carbondale and Edwardsville, IL: Southern Illinois University Press, 1970.

Burns, J. Patout. "Augustine on the Origin and Progress of Evil." In *The Ethics of St. Augustine*, edited by William S. Babcock, 67–86. Atlanta: Scholars, 1991.

Carney, Frederick S. "The Structure of Augustine's Ethic." In *The Ethics of St. Augustine*, edited by William S. Babcock, 11–38. Atlanta: Scholars, 1991.

Cary, Phillip. *Augustine's Invention of the Inner Self: The Legacy of a Christian Platonist*. Oxford: Oxford University Press, 2000.

Cessario, Romanus. *The Moral Virtues and Theological Ethics*. Notre Dame, IN: University of Notre Dame Press, 2008.

Cicero. *Disputationes Tusculanae*. Translated by J. E. King as *Tusculan Disputations*. Loeb Classical Library 141. Cambridge: Harvard University Press, 1971.

————. *De Finibus Bonorum et Malorum*. Translated by H. Rackham as *On Ends*. Loeb Classical Library 40. Cambridge: Harvard University Press, 1971.

————. *De Inventione*. Translated by H. M. Hubbell as *On Invention*. Loeb Classical Library 386. Cambridge: Harvard University Press, 1976.

————. *De Natura Deorum*. Translated by H. Rackham as *The Nature of the Gods*. Loeb Classical Library 268. Cambridge: Harvard University Press, 1979.

————. *De Officiis*. Translated by Walter Miller as *On Duties*. Loeb Classical Library 30. Cambridge: Harvard University Press, 1938.

————. *De Republica*. Translated by Clinton Walker Keyes as *On The Republic*. Loeb Classical Library 213. Cambridge: Harvard University Press, 1977.

Cooper, Anthony Ashley, Earl of Shaftesbury. *Characteristicks of Men, Manners, Opinions, Times*, edited by Douglas Den Uyl. Indianapolis: Liberty Fund, 2001.

Crouse, Robert. "*Paucis Mutatis Verbis*: St. Augustine's Platonism." In *Augustine and his Critics*, edited by Robert Dodaro and George Lawless, 37–50. London: Routledge, 2000.

Curzer, Howard J. "Aristotle's Much Maligned Megalopsychos." *Australasian Journal of Philosophy* 69 (1991) 131–51.

Danto, Arthur C. *Nietzsche as Philosopher*. New York: Columbia University Press, 1965.

Dideberg, Dany. *Saint Augustin et La Premiere Epitre De Saint Jean: Une Theologie De L'Agape*. Paris: Editions Beauchesne, 1975.

Dillon, John M. "An Ethic for the Late Antique Sage." In *The Cambridge Companion to Plotinus*, edited by Lloyd P. Gerson, 315–35. Cambridge: Cambridge University Press, 1996.

Diogenes Laertius. *Lives of Eminent Philosophers*. Translated by R. D. Hicks. Cambridge, MA: Harvard University Press, 1979.

Dodaro, Robert. "Augustine's Revision of the Heroic Ideal." *Augustinian Studies* 36 (2005) 141–57.

———. "The Secret Justice of God and the Gift of Humility." *Augustinian Studies* 34 (2003) 83–96.

Doyle, Daniel E. "Introduction to Augustine's Preaching." In *Essential Sermons* by Saint Augustine, translated by Edmund Hill, 9–22. Hyde Park, NY: New City, 2007.

Drobner, Hubertus R. "Studying Augustine: An Overview of Recent Research." In *Augustine and His Critics*, edited by Robert Dodaro and George Lawler, 18–34. London: Routledge, 2000.

Freeman, Curtis W. "Figure and History: A Contemporary Reassessment of Augustine's Hermeneutic." In *Augustine: Presbyter Factus Sum*, edited by Joseph T. Lienhard, Earl C. Muller, Roland J. Teske, 319–30. New York: Peter Lang, 1993.

Fullam, Lisa. *The Virtue of Humility: A Thomistic Apologetic*. Lewiston, NY: Mellen, 2009.

Gaskin, J. C. A. "Hume on Religion." In *The Cambridge Companion to Hume,* 2nd ed., edited by David Fate Norton and Jacqueline Taylor, 480–514. New York: Cambridge University Press, 2009.

Gerson, Lloyd P. *Plotinus*. London: Routledge, 1994.

———. "Plotinus and the Rejection of Aristotelian Metaphysics." In *Aristotle in Late Antiquity*, edited by Lawrence P. Schrenk. Washington, DC: The Catholic University of America Press, 1994.

Hagendahl, Harald. *Augustine and the Latin Classics*. Goteborg, Sweden: Elanders Boktryckeri Aktiebolag, 1967.

Hicks, Stephen R. C. *Explaining Post-Modernism: Skepticism and Socialism Rousseau to Foucault*. Tempe, AZ: Scholargy, 2004.

Hill, Edmund. "Introductory Essay on Book IV." Translated by Edmund Hill. In *The Trinity*, The Works of St. Augustine: A Translation for the 21st Century, edited by John E. Rotelle, I.5:147–51. Hyde Park, NY: New City, 1991.

Holloway, Carson. "Christianity, Magnanimity, and Statesmanship." *The Review of Politics* 61 (1999) 581–604.

Holte, Ragnar. *Beatitude et Sagesse: Saint Augustin et le Probleme de la Fin de l'Homme dans la Philosophie Ancienne*. Paris: Etudes Augustiniennes, 1962.

Hume, David. *An Enquiry Concerning Human Understanding*. New York: Liberal Arts, 1955.

———. *An Enquiry Concerning the Principles of Morals*. Edited by Tom L. Beauchamp. Oxford: Oxford University Press, 1998.

————. *Hume Selections*. Edited by Charles W. Hendel. New York: Charles Scribner's Sons, 1955.

————. *A Treatise of Human Nature*. Oxford: Clarendon, 1967.

Hunt, Lester. *Nietzsche and the Origin of Virtue*. New York: Routledge, 2001.

Hutcheson, Frances. *An Inquiry into the Original of Our Ideas of Beauty and Virtue*. Edited by Wolfgang Leidhold. Indianapolis: Liberty Fund, 2004.

Hutchinson, D. S. "Ethics." In *The Cambridge Companion to Aristotle*, edited by Jonathan Barnes, 195–232. Cambridge: Cambridge University Press, 1995.

Johnson, Oliver A. *The Mind of David Hume*. Urbana and Chicago: University of Illinois Press, 1995.

Kant, Immanuel. *Prolegomena and Metaphysical Foundations of Natural Science*. Translated by Ernest Belfort Bax. London: George Bell and Sons, 1891.

Keating, Daniel. "The Ethical Project of Alasdair MacIntyre: 'A Disquieting Suggestion.'" *Lyceum* 4 (Spring 1992) 101–16.

Kenney, John Peter. *The Mysticism of Saint Augustine: Rereading the Confessions*. New York: Routledge, 2005.

Kidd, I. G. "Moral Actions and Rules in Stoic Ethics." In *The Stoics*, edited by John M. Rist, 247–58. Berkeley: University of California Press, 1978.

Kolbet, Paul R. *Augustine and the Cure of Souls*. Notre Dame, IN: University of Notre Dame Press, 2010.

Lackey, Michael. "Killing God, Liberating the "Subject": Nietzsche and Post-God Freedom." *Journal of the History of Ideas* 60 (1999) 737–54.

Leo XIII. *The Practice of Humility*. Translated by Joseph Jerome Vaughan. New York: Benziger, 1898.

Library of Latin Texts—Series A. Brepols. http://www.brepols.net/Pages/BrowseBySeries.aspx?TreeSeries=LLT-O.

Locke, John. *An Essay Concerning Human Understanding*. Edited by Peter H. Nidditch. Oxford: Clarendon, 1975.

Lubac, Henri de. *The Drama of Atheist Humanism*. Translated by Edith M. Riley, Anne Englund Nash, Mark Sebanc. San Francisco: Ignatius, 1995.

Ludwig, Dean C., and Clinton O. Longenecker. "The Bathsheba Syndrome: The Ethical Failure of Successful Leaders." *Journal of Business Ethics* 12 (April 1993) 265–73.

MacIntyre, Alasdair. *After Virtue: A Study in Moral Theory*. Notre Dame, IN: University of Notre Dame Press, 1984.

————. *A Short History of Ethics: A History of Moral Philosophy from the Homeric Age to the Twentieth Century*. Notre Dame, IN: University of Notre Dame Press, 1998.

————. *Three Rival Versions of Moral Enquiry: Encyclopaedia, Genealogy, and Tradition: Being Gifford Lectures Delivered in the University of Edinburgh in 1988*. Notre Dame, IN: University of Notre Dame Press, 1990.

————. *Whose Justice? Which Rationality?* Notre Dame, IN: University of Notre Dame Press, 1988.

MacQueen, D. J. "Contemptus Dei: St. Augustine on the Disorder of Pride in Society, and its Remedies." *Recherches Augustiniennes* 9 (1973) 227–93.

Magnus, Bernd, and Kathleen M. Higgins. "Introduction to the Cambridge Companion to Nietzsche." In *The Cambridge Companion to Nietzsche*, edited by Bernd Magnus and Kathleen M. Higgins, 1–17. Cambridge: Cambridge University Press, 1996.

Margerie, Bertrand de. *An Introduction to the History of Exegesis, Volume III: Saint Augustine*. Translated by Pierre de Fontnouvelle. Petersham, MA: Saint Bede's, 1991.

Marx, Karl, and Friedrich Engels. "Excerpt From The Communism of the Paper Rheinischer Beobachter." In *The Basic Writings on Politics and Philosophy*, edited by Lewis S. Feuer. Garden City, NY: Anchor, 1959.

Mayer, Cornelius, ed. *Augustinus-Lexikon*. Vol. 1. Basel: Schwabe, 1986.

Mcintyre, Jane L. "Strength of Mind: Prospects and Problems for a Humean Account." *Synthese* 152 (2006) 393–401.

Nietzsche, Friedrich. *Beyond Good and Evil*. Translated by Helen Zimmern. Amherst, NY: Prometheus, 1989.

———. *Ecce Homo*. Translated by Walter Kaufmann. New York: Vintage, 1989.

———. *The Gay Science*. Translated by Josefine Nauckhoff and Adrian Del Caro. Edited by Bernard Williams. Cambridge: Cambridge University Press, 2001.

———. *Human, All too Human*. Translated by Helen Zimmern. New York: The Macmillan Company, 1924.

———. *The Nietzsche Reader*. Edited by Keith Ansell Pearson and Duncan Large. Malden, MA: Blackwell, 2006.

———. *On the Genealogy of Morality*. Translated by Carol Diethe. Edited by Keith Ansell-Pearson. Cambridge: Cambridge University Press, 1994.

———. *Thus Spake Zarathustra*. Translated by Thomas Common. New York: The Macmillan Company, 1930.

———. *The Will to Power*. Translated by Walter Kaufmann and R. J. Hollingdale. Edited by Walter Kaufmann. New York: Vintage, 1968.

Norton, David Fate. "The Foundations of Morality in Hume's Treatise." In *The Cambridge Companion to Hume*, 2nd ed., edited by David Fate Norton and Jacqueline Taylor, 270–310. New York: Cambridge University Press, 2009.

———. "An Introduction to Hume's Thought." In *The Cambridge Companion to Hume*, 2nd ed., edited by David Fate Norton and Jacqueline Taylor, 1–39. New York: Cambridge University Press, 2009.

Nygren, Anders. *Agape and Eros*. Translated by Philip S. Watson. London: SPCK, 1953.

O'Brien, Denis. "Plotinus on Matter and Evil." In *The Cambridge Companion to Plotinus*, edited by Lloyd P. Gerson, 171–95. Cambridge: Cambridge University Press, 1996.

O'Donovan, Oliver. *The Problem of Self-Love in St. Augustine*. 1980. Reprint, Eugene, OR: Wipf & Stock, 2006.

Powell, J. G. F. "Introduction: Cicero's Philosophical Works and their Background." In *Cicero the Philosopher*, edited by J. G. F. Powell, 1–36. Oxford: Clarendon, 1995.

Plotinus. *Ennead I*. Translated by A. H. Armstrong. Loeb Classical Library 440. Cambridge: Harvard University Press, 1966.

———. *Ennead V*. Translated by A. H. Armstrong. Loeb Classical Library 444. Cambridge: Harvard University Press, 1984.

———. *Ennead VII*. Translated by A. H. Armstrong. Loeb Classical Library 468. Cambridge: Harvard University Press, 1988.

Riel, Gerd Van. "Augustine's Will, an Aristotelian Notion? On the Antecedents of Augustine's Doctrine of the Will." *Augustinian Studies* 38 (2007) 255–79.

Rist, John. *Augustine: Ancient Thought Baptized*. Cambridge: Cambridge University Press, 1994.

Ruddy, Deborah Wallace. "A Christological Approach to Virtue: Augustine and Humility." PhD diss., Boston College, 2001.

Schlabach, Gerald. "Augustine's Hermeneutic of Humility: An Alternative to Moral Imperialism and Moral Relativisim." *Journal of Religious Ethics* 22 (Fall, 1994) 299–330.

Schofield, Malcolm. "Stoic Ethics." In *The Cambridge Companion to the Stoics*, edited by Brad Inwood, 233–56. Cambridge: Cambridge University Press, 2003.

Sedley, David. "The School, from Zeno to Arius Didymus." In *The Cambridge Companion to the Stoics*, edited by Brad Inwood, 7–32. Cambridge: Cambridge University Press, 2003.

Sharples, R. W. *Stoics, Epicureans, and Sceptics: An Introduction to Hellenistic Philosophy.* New York: Routledge, 1996.

Studer, Basil. *Trinity and Incarnation: The Faith of the Early Church.* Edinburgh: T. & T. Clark, 1993.

Sullivan, Francis A. "Cicero and Gloria." *Transactions and Proceedings of the American Philological Association* 72 (1941) 382–91.

Tessitore, Aristide. *Reading Aristotle's Ethics: Virtue Rhetoric, and Political Philosophy.* Albany: State University of New York Press, 1996.

Testard, Maurice. *St. Augustin et Ciceron.* Paris: Etudes Augustiniennes, 1958.

Thorsteinsson, Runar M. *Roman Christianity and Roman Stoicism: A Comparative Study of Ancient Morality.* Oxford: Oxford University Press, 2010.

Torchia, N. Joseph. "St. Augustine's Treatment of Superbia and its Plotinian Affinities." *Augustinian Studies* (1987) 66–80.

Wetzel, James. *Augustine and the Limits of Virtue.* Cambridge: Cambridge University Press, 1992.

Whittaker, Thomas. *The Neo-Platonists: A Study in the History of Hellenism.* Freeport, NY: Libraries, 1970.